ALL THE
PARTS OF ME

ALL THE
PARTS OF ME

One woman's detour into fear and her trip back to love

JEN FIORE

inspired girl BOOKS

ALL THE PARTS OF ME by Jen Fiore
Published by Inspired Girl Books
www.inspiredgirlbooks.com

Inspired Girl Books is honored to bring forth books with heart and stories that matter. We are proud to offer this book to our readers; the story, the experiences, and the words are the author's alone.

The events are portrayed to the best of the author's memory. While all the stories in this book are true, some names and identifying details have been changed to protect the privacy of the people involved.

The author has tried to recreate events, locales, and conversations from her memories of them. In order to maintain their anonymity in some instances she has changed the names of individuals and places, she may have changed some identifying characteristics and details such as physical properties, occupations, and places of residence.

The conversations in the book all come from the author's recollections, though they are not written to represent word-for-word transcripts. Rather, the author has retold them in a way that evokes the feeling and meaning of what was said. In all instances, the essence of the dialogue is accurate.

The author and publisher do not assume and hereby disclaim any liability in connection with the use of the information contained in this book.

This book is written as a source of information only. The information contained in this book should by no means be considered a substitute for the advice of a qualified medical professional, who should always be con- sulted before beginning any new diet, exercise, or other health program and before taking any dietary supplements or other medications.

Products, books, trademarks, and trademark names are used throughout this book to describe and inform the reader about various proprietary products that are owned by third parties. No endorsement of the information contained in this book is given by the owners of such products and trademarks, and no endorsement is implied by the inclusion of products, books, or trademarks in this book.

ISBN: 978-1-7350944-8-9
Cover design and typesetting by Roseanna White Designs

Author photograph by Fred Shimalla

CONTENTS

My husband, Fred, who was given to me through a prayer I asked of God and my angels a long time ago. You're my teacher, my partner, my supporter, and the love of my life.

A Note from the Author

At first, I thought I was writing a book about the wild things that happened on this journey of my life. I made attempts to write what seemed impossible to express, but something was off. I realized that I wasn't supposed to write a book only about the crazy things that I survived, but rather to show how the healing of the mind and body was facilitated by my understanding of what we were all created to be. The focus of this book shifted much like I did when I realized my opinion of myself and of my life needed to change: It became a passion of mine to share with people what changed my life-and how.

If someone were to be bold enough to ask, "Jen, are you saying that you have no more ailments in your body? That you cured yourself of degenerative arthritis!?" My answer would be, "I am unsure if I have completely removed arthritis from my body, but I can tell you that arthritis, pain, or any other ailment that pops up in this body I am using, no longer rules my life. I give it no more attention and energy to it than it requires. I am free."

I wish that each reader of this book finds what they need between these pages and within their heart. I pray that you know that you are infinitely loved and have a place here on this earth and with God and his divine team. And lastly, my wish is that each of you find the happiness and inner peace, that will set you free to enjoy this life here as a spiritual being having this human experience.

Share your unique gift and light with the world!

With Love,

Jen

FOREWORD

by Alex Shimalla

I'm a writer. It's what I do. By education, career choice, and creative pursuit, I write for a living. Yet the one topic that I've never been able to properly distill into words, the one person who has always eluded my writing is my mother.

I've tried for years to capture her essence in words and have consistently failed. I once wrote an essay on my mom's countless surgeries and medical mishaps just to show that this kind of stuff doesn't normally happen to people, and the feedback I received in workshop was all basically, "But, tell us about the kind of person your mom is. What is she really like despite all these crazy things that have happened to her?"

I'd stare blankly at the page, waiting for inspiration to strike, hoping that I'd be able to explain the importance of our Thursday night rituals when I was in high school, when we'd stay up late watching the newest episode of "Bones," both of us sprawled out on my parents' bed. How she always remembers the things that my siblings and I like, even the most minute details, years after the fact, so I'll find a box of my favorite chicken nuggets in the freezer, permanently stocked—just in case I want them. How she'd send me random letters while I was away at college and then graduate school; they were little notes, but meant the world to me to see that she took the time to write me a "Happy Halloween" card and would even attach a small care package of homemade pumpkin seeds (because they're my favorite). How she's just my mom and how do I distill my entire lifetime of loving memories of this amazing woman into a few words on a page? It seems like an injustice to the impact she's had on my life and the memories that I carry with me daily that remind me how much I am loved.

Growing up, my mom was never sick. Even when we were all ravaged by Celiac disease but didn't know it yet, Mom was never sick. She still baked us cookies and made dinner every night. She still drove us to school if we missed the bus. She still made our lunches every morning until we started middle school. She still took us to the pool and park and mall and movies and friends' houses. She still let us throw sleepovers and cooked us Sprite pancakes with extra chocolate chips in the morning.

Mom was never sick.

Even when she had surgery after surgery after surgery, Mom was still Mom. She made sure we did our homework, studied for tests, and cleaned our rooms. She kept the fridge and pantry stocked with our favorite desserts and snacks. She even threw a surprise birthday party for me.

I took over during those times she was recovering from another surgery by becoming Mommy's Little Helper, fulfilling my rightful duty as second mom to my two younger siblings. I made bread, watered the plants, did the laundry, and was generally the boss (or so I thought). Mom wasn't sick, but I got to help and then watch TV with her in bed.

It's funny that when we're children, we never see our parents as anything other than merely parents. Mom wasn't Jen; she was Mom. Mom didn't get sick. Mom was never a kid; she's always been an adult. Mom was just Mom. It's not until you're living on your own, away from the safety net of home, and have the flu in college when there's no parent around to take care of you that you begin to think (and appreciate). What's it like to be a parent and not feel well one day? Mom was never sick. I wonder how she managed that.

I always hated going to the grocery store with my mom. I hated it. Although I wasn't aware of my own issues with time and scheduling, there was never a "quick" grocery run. Even if there were mere two things to grab at the store, it would still take a solid 30 minutes for Mom to get in and get out. It wasn't just because we lived in the same small town for years and knew everyone; my mom seemed to have this innate ability, this magnetism, that would draw complete strangers into her orbit.

It drove me crazy.

Do we really need to tell everyone our entire life history in exchange for theirs?

But again, when you're older and interacting with the world without the lens of your parents, you begin to see childhood and your parents for the reality and not what your young mind conjured up to make sense of the world. Not so ironically given who my mother is, I'm quite the chatterbox, yet ironically to my younger self, I've grown to love being around people. I make a point of learning the names of the people I see frequently, whether that's at the gym or the physical therapy office. I make small talk with the cashiers at the grocery store, the librarians, the waiters and waitresses, my Uber drivers, the bank tellers. I'd rather make the person smile or laugh, to remind everyone that I see and value them, than keep the exchange silent and stilted until it's over.

I may not talk to a stranger for 20 minutes while picking out avocados at Publix, but I'm grateful for the role model my mother was in helping me see everyone through the love and light that we all bring to this life. As I listen more closely to the stories of the people she meets, I see all the ways in which she helps those strangers by telling them about Celiac disease, this surgery or that medical complication, or how she was going to cook an eggplant. There never was (and never is) an exchange between two people that doesn't impact one or both parties in some way. Mom was making an impact in every conversation she had while standing in line at the grocery store. I was too young, too impatient, too self-conscious to understand the gravity of all that my mom truly is.

The stories that follow showcase my mom's life through her eyes and will do a far better job than I at trying to explain her dedication to love and life and family, even during immense pain and suffering. The phrase "This only happens to Mom" was a common refrain in our family, but that doesn't even begin to scratch the surface of the kind of woman my mother is. Not only did she acknowledge her physical "limitations," but she persevered like a motherfucker to make sure my siblings and I had the best, most loving lives possible.

I'll never be able to say thank you enough for the woman I've become because of the role model I had, the one who taught me laughter, kindness, and the importance of nightly family dinners. I hope you'll remember my words, my naivety to the tragedies and struggles of my mother, as you read her stories.

Life is all about how we perceive and react to the big and little situations that make up each day. These happy or sad, exciting or scary moments are our lives. The collection of these responses are how we choose to live.

My mother was never sick.

She was (and is) simply my amazing mom.

PART ONE

My Humanness

humanness [ˈ(h)yōōmənəs]

adjective

a form of human; relating to or characteristic of people or human beings.

Humanness: that part of you that forgets it was created in unlimited love, forgiveness, and magnificence.

Humanness: that part of us that lives and reacts to the stimulus of life from the perspective of only the body. Humanness is the part that listens to the ego-mind (a part of ourself) that tells us we are a body that is limited and can be attacked.

happiness [ˈhapēnəs]
noun

    the state of being happy.

    Happiness is skipping minnows at the bay, playing in the sand by myself, floating in the water, cruising in Dad's car just the two of us, going to Abe's candy store on my bike for a piece of candy, laughing until my face hurts, jumping out of bed excited to start the day, spending time with friends, sleepovers, pining over how beautiful Sean Cassidy was, eating dinner with family . . .

CHAPTER 1

Being Happy

"Home should be an anchor, a port in a storm, a refuge,
a happy place in which to dwell, a place where we are loved,
and where we can love."
- Marvin J. Ashton

"Jen, stop screaming! We can't tell if it's an emergency!"

Yeah, that's me, Jen, and I was screaming because I was being chased in an awesome game of tag. If that is not a reason to scream with joy, I have no idea what is. That was how I thought of my youth, being outside, playing and having fun. The moment homework was done, it was game on until I was called in for dinner. If I was in the house at any other time, it was because of bad weather or getting ready for bed. You might've caught a peek of me singing into my brush in front of the mirror while looking at my Scott Baio poster, swaying to the music flowing from my record player.

I enjoyed pretty much all of it: playing, singing, eating, and being with my family, too. I loved to have attention, so singing and dancing to entertain my family was fun, probably in part to being the middle child. I had an older brother and younger sister. But I also loved to have attention because that was just me.

SUNDAY DINNERS, DOLLAR BILLS, AND FAMILY GALORE

I have the greatest memory of cooking for my dad. This story was told many times over in my life and just stuck with me in my heart. We were living in the basement apartment of a house in Queens, New York. I learned many years later that my parents owned the house, and to help pay for the mortgage, we lived in the basement and they had tenants on the top floor. I remember there was a door off the kitchen that led out to the backyard.

It was on this evening in particular that I recall this basement apartment and its kitchen as vividly as my three-year-old self could take in. I was standing on a chair in the small kitchen at a counter. My mother was busy cooking next to me, but she set me up with a patterned apron—just my size—a bowl, two pieces of bread, some milk, sugar, salt, and a variety of spices. It was there that I made my first "cooking" masterpiece.

Oh, I remember how excited I was for my dad to try this dish that I created for him. I loved him so very much, and I wanted to please him. By the look on his face, I truly believed I did. Even though I was just a little girl, there was something that told me that combination of spices and bread and milk didn't look so great. I'm pretty sure that it didn't taste that good either. But Dad made it seem like it was one of the best things he had ever eaten. I know this was the moment I formed a belief that I could make people happy through my cooking. This was the moment I learned I could pour my love for people into food.

My family life was that of a typical Catholic Italian-American. If you don't know what that means, it is family, extended family, and food. Lots of family gatherings marked by FOOD! Every evening we would wait for Dad to walk in the door—dinner would magically be ready at that exact time. Mom was a great cook and always cooked to please Dad. All types of meats and a variety of vegetables were present. We did go through the 1980's stage of American meals, like mac and cheese and meatloaf with a seasoning packet, but the Italian special dishes—escarole and beans, baked ziti, or stuffed peppers— won out every time.

This was my life, and I guess I assumed it was "the norm." I just thought everyone gathered with grandparents, aunts, and uncles on the weekends. We would gather in Queens on Sunday, after church, for a big Italian meal. Now these meals were legendary—with a meat, pasta dish, variety of vegetables, a salad, and fresh sauce bubbling from early morning until dinner time. Sometimes my grandmother would start the sauce the night before. As a young girl, I would marvel at her dedication, thinking of her standing before the stove, stirring her delicious sauce through the wee hours of the morning.

My maternal grandparents (where my strongest memories lie because of our frequency to their house and the meals we shared) had a house that sat on a double lot in Queens. The property in this neighborhood was narrow, shaped like a strip, and plants stood like soldiers protecting the house beyond. My grandfather took full advantage of this long double lot and had an extensive vegetable garden as well as my ultimate favorite, fig trees.

After a Sunday afternoon spent running around the yard or

sneaking into the neighborhood to follow my brother and cousin, we would all return to the house before dinner, which was early, partly so we could get back home and partly so the adults could chat and share more time together. We would tiptoe into the kitchen to covertly grab a hot meatball off the dish near the stove. This was a big no-no in Grandma's book, yet we still did this each weekend. Sneak, grab, stuff. All while she is yelling at us in Italian to stop. The word she would say sounded a lot like "ashpet" (osh-bet). It's slang for the Italian word *aspettare*. I had no clue what word she was saying back then, but I did know she was telling us to hold off. She was probably hoping we would wait for dinner. I always found it curious that even though Grandma would shoo us and tell us "ashpet," she always had a line of toothpicks right near the meatballs.

Oh, the good times we had—so many memories. That was happiness, for sure. At some point in the day, we would receive a very coveted dollar bill. The only kids were me, my brother, and our two first cousins (unless our five first cousins who were now living in Vermont came to visit, which wasn't too often). Our burly, hazel-eyed Grandfather, who could be seen most weekends in a white t-shirt (complete with a pack of cigarettes rolled up in the sleeve!) and jeans, was so proud to hand out those dollar bills, and we reacted with surprise and "thank you's" each and every time. He would tell us to have fun as he doled out his hard-earned dollars. Each time it was like we won the lottery, and we felt so lucky. When our cousins would come to New York to visit, Grandpa would give them more than a dollar because of all the weekends he missed them. Such a kind man.

And this was *every* Sunday.

Now, you can just imagine a special occasion. We always had a lot of family around for celebrations and holidays. It was Sunday dinner on steroids. Lots of my grandparent's siblings and cousins coming over to say hi with a platter of cannolis, cake, or some other Italian pastry. There were lots of conversations going on at once, lots of eating, and all-in-all, lots of love, even when the occasional argument broke out.

My paternal grandparents were in Queens as well. My dad's father passed away when I was very young, too young to remember much about him. But his mom (my grandmother) was a very important person in my life until I was eight, when she too passed. I loved my grandmother with all my heart, and I knew she loved me. She talked to me like I was important, she showed me so much in the short time I had with her, and we both valued the time we spent together. She was an amazing seamstress, and she showed me her work and all the tools she used. She made my First Holy Communion gown; it was like a wedding dress with little pearls and button details, and I felt so special that day. I always felt so special when I was with Grandma.

Food was important on my dad's side, too. Grandma taught me how to clip the end off of green beans and how to tend to a sauce. I loved to just watch her cook. She took cooking seriously, and eating her meals made with love was a symbol of loving her back. I vividly remember Grandma crying one night at the dinner table, telling my parents that she worried so much that I was so skinny. She thought I was ill and that they were missing something. That particular night, she was crying about this because I didn't want to eat the meal of pasta, sauce, and chicken. I asked for a raw onion instead. That was too much for my beloved grandmother to handle. I was just a young girl and not very hungry, but Grandma, oh how she worried about us all.

My love of food was not only because I liked the taste and the variety of all the different meals we had, but it was also a way to be close to those I adored, like my paternal grandmother, Corina. Food meant family, friends, and celebration. And yes, as I said before, food meant happiness.

MOVING OUT OF THE CITY
AND LIVING ON THE WATER

I peered out the window of our car as we pulled up to our new house. I was jumping up and down in my seat. "Jennifer Marie, I know you are excited. Just wait to open that door. I haven't stopped the car yet. Please calm down!" How is that possible, I thought to myself. The second the car stopped, I ran to the front yard and watched in utter amazement as the birds swooped down into the water and boats moseyed by in the slow no-wake zone. I couldn't help it. I know I am going to get in trouble . . . I let out a scream of joy!

Before I turned five, my father moved us out to Long Island. Queens was great to me, but he wanted us to have a different life. Long Island was a little slower, a little calmer. Dad owned a stair manufacturing business in Queens, so he would wake up early Monday through Friday to beat traffic and commute 45 minutes to work—all so we could enjoy life on the coast of Long Island. Dad saw how busy and populated the areas around Manhattan were becoming, and he wanted a bigger house, land, and water. Pretty sweet gig.

The first house Dad built sat right on the bay, across the street from the Long Island Sound. On a clear day you could see straight across to Connecticut. Our boat *"Up the Creek"* sat on a mooring right outside our kitchen window. I would spend time by the bay watching tadpoles and tiny minnows swim around. Our town was only four miles long and had streets off one main road. We were able to ride bikes up and down these roads safely.

Several of my close friends' fathers owned their own businesses, and we all had stay-at-home moms. Even though I thought my family life was "the norm," something deep down inside me knew, even when I was younger, how very lucky we all were to live in this great small town on the north shore of Long Island and have the close-knit family lives we all had. I loved the comfort I felt in our town and with my family. When dad walked in and gave out a hug before sitting down to eat, I knew I was blessed and lucky to have this life. I was so happy all of the time, and the happiness was such an important part of me.

My father really loved being near the water. To Dad, coming home to Long Island was like living life on vacation whenever he wasn't working. He loved where we lived, and he knew just about everyone. Dad could've definitely been the mayor: There was no such thing as a stranger as far as my dad was concerned. "Tommy Inspector, how's your daughter's business comin' along?" The ease he had about him was a comfort for others. He never met a stranger.

He found value in sharing a moment with people and loved hearing their stories. A smile, a strong pat on the back, and a handshake for the men and a peck on the cheek for the ladies. That was what it was like with Dad. I often think that my siblings and I are a lot like our dad in that respect. Enjoying people and life are traits we learned from the master. I don't think my personality is by chance. No, it is not 100% like Dad's, but very similar in many respects.

Life on the north shore of Long Island provided a lot of amazing seafood, which provided me with fond memories from family meals to festivals. In our small town, everyone knew everyone. Dad would go to a friend's seafood market and get steamers, and we would chow down. They were also called "piss clams" for more than one reason, which wasn't at all proper. I thought it was hysterical, so we always called them by their funnier name.

Quick side note: when I was pregnant with our first child (a time before there were tons of warnings about a variety of clams, shellfish, and fish), my dad surprised me with steamed littles necks and piss clams. When I walked into the kitchen and he told me what he was preparing for me, I cried! Call it hormones if you want, but Dad knowing that those clams would make me laugh after months of all-day morning sickness warmed my heart and made me so incredibly happy. He always knew just what I needed, and not just with food. He knew me inside and out, and he cheered me on, no matter what. I think having him in my corner gave me so much confidence, when it came to many things.

I had dreams! (To be an Academy Award-winning actress.)

I wanted to be rich and famous. (Heck yeah, because I could sing, so I thought, and I would envision all the people clapping for me.)

I wanted to fall in love. (When I was really young, I thought if I was lucky and famous, Sean Cassidy would definitely fall in love with me.)

I wanted to always have fun and be happy. (Laughing, playing, joking around, and always having a good time was where it was at for me.)

My list of desires seemed simple enough.

Oh wait, one more . . . I wanted to have a different body.

CHA-CHA-CHANGES
AND A GOOD LOOK IN THE MIRROR

High school started off bumpy because I was still "putting the polish on the diamond" so to speak. It had its awkward growing-up moments like when Tim S. from the 9th grade, a year above me, passed me in the hallway and said, "Wow, that girl has a bigger mustache than me!" Blessed with the Italian genes, I knew he had to be talking about me, and even if he wasn't, I stopped bleaching that day and began using Nair instead.

Despite the blatant honesty and random comment from a passing person, there was just too much around me not to get involved. I just couldn't resist it all. From prom committee to honors club, I achieved a pretty good balance and still was able to sign up for just about anything that was happening. Organizing events and hard work were part of it, but spending time with friends and socializing were the bigger picture. Being on the athletic council, manning the snack stand at football games, and cheering loudly could have contributed to me earning the most class spirit my senior year.

The things I avoided were science and math. Totally not my thing, unless you consider the day I went up against Mr. Lambrech to disapprove a theory in science class.

"There is no machine that is a perpetual motion machine. Zero." *Oh, this guy was so stiff and unmoving. Surely, he has never laughed.* These were the thoughts flowing through my mind when I turned to my lab partner and whispered, "I know of a perpetual motion machine . . . my thighs!" An involuntary laugh erupted from him as he shushed me through gritted teeth with mixed emotions of laughter and fear in his eyes. "Is there something you would like to share, Jennifer? Please stand and tell the class."

I stood, pinching the sides of my jeans and praying silently that I wouldn't die right there on the spot. I reached down deep and mustered the courage with the thought that I would not be taken down. "I know of a perpetual motion machine." I looked into that stark face that had one eyebrow raised. How do people raise only one eyebrow? Is that a heredity trait, I wonder? "Go on," he said.

I placed both my hands on the outside of my right thigh and wiggled it and said, "My thighs!" I could see the light in his eyes as he fought against the laughter. His lips curled up in his signature scowl as he said, "That's enough, Miss Fiore. Sit." But as he turned, I could see a slight twinkle in his eyes. I got him.

I was in track and field, mainly for shot put and discus. I still had to run, though, and always wanted it to be the shortest possible distance since running was not why I was on the team. Sounds pretty silly to say you were on a team that ran, but you didn't want to run. Throwing was my jam. Senior year I made it to the state competition for field events. Even though I didn't place, I still felt a level of pride that 5' 1 ¾" of me made it to an event that used skill and muscle strength.

I ran the gamut from sports to music and everything in between. I said I liked to get involved! When I was in tenth grade, I had a boyfriend who played the drums. Our other two friends played the guitar, one of them was bass. They all knew I had taken singing lessons, and my boyfriend told them I had been in a few plays when I was younger. They decided they wanted to perform at the talent show our high school was hosting in a few weeks, but they needed a singer, so they asked me. Of course I said yes, I was excited to sing in their band!

In case I didn't make this clear enough: I LOVED TO SING! I never really was able to master that whole breathing thing my teacher stressed at my lessons, though. But the thought of performing in front of everyone outweighed the breathing thing, so I decided to give it a try. Besides, my music teacher always had me doing crazy high-pitched soprano songs like "Edelweiss" and stuff like that from *The Sound of Music*. I figured I could handle the cool songs we would do from U2! I clearly remember thinking, *I can totally do that!*

Heck, it doesn't matter, I was the lead singer for my boyfriend's band for two songs, and I sang it in alto (deeper). I knew it would be fine, even though I felt a bit nervous. A few weeks later, on a Friday night, we were up on stage, facing a packed house in our high school auditorium. I couldn't seem to hit the notes I wanted up there on stage. It sounded rough. I felt a little swoony when it was all done. I thought to myself, *Yikes, that was embarrassing not getting the notes the way I wanted. And boy am I hot. Is that stage sweat?*

Anyway, we did it. I did it. And when it was over, it was time to head to our friend's house for a party. My throat was sore, and I thought my breathing was off because of all the singing and practicing I had been doing. Maybe I strained my throat singing, but so what, I did it, and it was over. My dad taped the show and later said to me, "You really wanna look at it, honey? It was a little rough."

Wow, that bad, huh?

By Saturday morning, I was feeling yucky and had a fever. My throat and chest hurt. I went to the pediatrician on Monday, and it turned out I had bronchitis. Even though I had the answer for the epic failure on stage, I didn't ever revisit my singing career after that.

When I got the diagnosis, both my parents said, "Only you, Jen."

JOBS, DATING, AND WEARING THAT CROWN

I worked throughout high school. On and off for nearly seven years, beginning at the age of 16, I worked at our local drug store, and before that age, I babysat. I came back to the drug store even after high school to fill in since I was so familiar with the responsibilities, the owners, and the staff. I loved that little store and was sad to hear they just closed their doors recently. I also worked at the concession stands at the beach during summer months, at a seafood restaurant as a busgirl, and during my senior year of high school, I worked as a waitress at an event catering hall.

Throughout the years, I would also drive to my father's warehouse in Queens and help out in the office. Keeping busy, earning money, and interacting with people were right up my alley. I also loved to touch and count money. I remember a time when all I wanted to be was either an actress, a librarian, or a cashier. I was keeping all my options open.

I only had a couple of boyfriends, and yes, I did experience the ongoing drama of unrequited love that every girl experiences at one point or another. When the relationships were over, they were just that: over. But when the guy started going out with someone else after we called it quits, my radar went 'ping.'

I remember this guy I dated for about a year. He told me he loved me each and every day, wrote me letters and poems, and was a really great guy—gifts at all the right times and sometimes just because. Then one day, he broke up with me. That's it. From 100 "I love you's" in a single day to the next day, zilch. A few weeks later, he began dating someone else, and man, was I upset for a hot minute. It was just one of those things, and I needed to adjust. That was the crux of the high school drama for me: breaking up with a guy and being all right—until he found someone else.

If I had to describe my childhood, I would say that it was the "sweet life." Nothing could really take the shine off of that fact. Oh, how I loved the family parties and the float parties with friends where we would build the homecoming floats. Did I mention I was in the homecoming court sophomore year, and I was prom queen in my senior year? Yeah, well, don't be too impressed. My kids certainly weren't and hardly believed me until I showed them the pictures to prove it. Come to think of it, I do like wearing a crown on my birthday, the one time I am queen for the day without question.

Taking a ride in one of Dad's vintage cars with him, laughing with my brother, and eating genoa salami with my best friend after a party trumped the crown. I had a solid family base and friends to go to a party with or go hiking with in the woods. I had all the comforts I needed and so much more, and I knew it. I never asked my parents for expensive clothes or more than I was given because I knew they gave and gave, and I was happy with what I had.

Living in a small town, you think everything you do is simple. Looking back, it was reliable, safe, and special. Dad would work from 5:00 a.m. and be home each night for dinner, where we all sat and ate together. He never worked on the weekends. He and Mom were always around for us kids. I watched sunsets and sunrises in our beach town. I spent the days working at the beach and then returned in the evenings for bonfires. Talking on the phone to friends, sleepovers, trips to the mall, and school events filled the hours when there wasn't work to be done. The happiness I had came from all of these things combined. There was always something that could be found to put a smile on my face. It was impossible to envision life any differently.

"It is when you expect nothing in return than you receive everything.
Happiness is a state of being. It is a choice.
You ARE happiness. You live and vibrate joy without expectation,
then what you receive back has no measure or value attributed to it.
It is beyond measurements."
~ From Meditations with Jesus and Jen

Illness [ˈilnəs]

noun

a disease or period of sickness affecting the body or mind.

Illness wasn't even a thought in my mind. It was just a part of life.

CHAPTER 2

Issues with the Body

"What lies behind you and what lies in front of you pales in comparison to what lies inside of you."
~ Ralph Waldo Emerson

"Jennifer! I wish you would try to relax. There is nothing your father can do! We are heading straight home."

Here I was in a brand-new outfit I'd saved up for, special to wear on my birthday, crying and rocking in the back seat, begging them to go faster. My body curled tight in a ball so I don't lose my bowels. Special outfit and a side order of stomach pain, please. Happy birthday to me!

Since the age of eight, my stomach was a problem. I can mark the years with one nuisance that never failed to make an appearance somewhere in a week or month. It was always sharp, stabbing stomach pain that moved down my belly, ending with cramps that led me straight to the bathroom, usually for at least an hour. The pain seemed to happen mostly after eating. It was unpredictable, though. It would sometimes happen at every meal for days in a row, then all of a sudden, I would get a break and I could go days or even a week without a single problem. But when it did come, the pain was intense.

There were tons of mad rushes to the bathroom immediately following a meal, but I couldn't ever figure what the real cause was. My parents and I tried to narrow it down, looking at what I might be eating to cause this, but we could not nail it down to any one thing. It did seem to get worse as I got older. I recall a few times when the pain was so bad, I lost consciousness on the toilet: writhing in pain, sweating, and then out like a light. Erratic was the best way to describe the episodes. You never really knew which day it would happen.

Is this too much information? TMI, as my kids would say? Look, when you have this kind of shit happening (pun intended) to you for decades, you figure out how to defuse the topic. Yeah, maybe a little over-sharing mixed in with a small part humor and small part deflection . . . I knew it was a topic that most people could relate to and did talk about at some point in their lives.

Oh, but it's true. And it's one of the parts of me. No one else in my family had this pain and neither did anyone else I knew. Eating followed by unpredictable and painfully intense bathroom experiences: That is how I would describe it to the countless doctor's Mom took me to. It was a mystery to them as well.

"These things only happen to you, Jen."

I heard those famous words my entire life.

LEARNING TO ADAPT AND ADJUST

My mom took me to several different doctors through the years, but I never got any answers or relief. All of the medications they would ask me to try never helped. Suggestions of nervous stomach, spastic colon/irritable bowel syndrome, too much oil, food combining, and avoiding lots of raw vegetables or dairy were thrown at me. I tried every last one of the doctor's suggestions and guesses. Nothing worked. The pain and episodes never stopped. Funny how FOOD, the thing my family associated most with happiness and love, actually caused me so much damn pain.

Each doctor would tell me they were very surprised to see how healthy I was and how I still maintained my happy demeanor. I would respond, "What choice do I have?" That always confused me. I would say to Mom so often, "What am I supposed to do? Just sit in the house waiting for the shoe to drop and miss out on my life and having fun?" That was not an option~not one bit—since there was no rhyme or reason as to when I would be in pain.

Believe me when I say that I wasn't excited that there wasn't an answer for my stomach issues, but since the doctors couldn't get to the bottom of it, what the hell was I supposed to do? It just became part and parcel of who I was. Gosh darn it, nothing was going to stop me from living my life the way I wanted. If something bothered me, I dealt with it and didn't focus on lack of any kind for very long. I never could with my dad's motto always ringing in my ears: "Down time is wasted time, Jen."

Yes, Dad had this motto, and I lived up to it. He probably didn't realize how much those words meant to me. I clung to them and was not going to waste a moment of my life. So instead, I learned how to deal while still having a smile on my face and joy in my heart.

If I was going out with friends, I would eat hours before so that if I got sick, I would still be at home. I did not eat while on a date or at a big event. I would nibble on crackers. I would only eat a little bit of something if there were accessible bathrooms. I never ate in a place that there was as shared bathroom, one that had only one stall, or if it was right next to the dining area. I literally scoped out a place before I ate anything.

It's not as if I loved being stuck in the bathroom writhing in pain, but since it happened, I dealt with it. I couldn't allow it to steal my life, so I didn't let it. I grabbed the moments I could when I was able and tweaked my life when I had to. This didn't feel like I was avoiding anything. It just made sense to me.

With the unpredictability of my stomach, I preferred to eat big meals at home, especially dinner. After the food my mom would lovingly make for us, BOOM. Sometimes I felt so bad knowing how hard she worked to prepare the meal, that I would hold back tears until I was alone in my room.

If I had a homework assignment or a TV show that I wanted to watch, I was bummed that I was stuck in the bathroom. Since I was always adjusting my food intake when I went out in public, home was the one place I ate with abandon. Knowing I was in my safe place, home, if the pain came, was a relief. I didn't think or really care about when it would hit, until I was in the bathroom and it was messing up my schedule. I didn't bother my parents regularly because, let's face it, there was no answer, so what could they do?

LET THE SELF-ESTEEM ISSUES BEGIN

The physical result from my constant abdominal distress was an extremely small waist and flat stomach, but when I looked in the mirror all I could see was my thighs staring right back at me like a neon sign. Now many women would love a smaller waist, but I disregarded mine most of the time, because I was focusing elsewhere.

Nope, I never missed those legs. And yes, I wanted a different body - my body just sucked to me.

No matter how many leg lifts I did in that mirror, on the floor, and at the gym, there they were, taunting me. I would long for a bigger space between my legs. I think it is actually a social media trend today called a "thigh gap," and there are even exercises to achieve it. Well, this was before that came about. Anyway, this was my thing in the 80's, I would squeeze my thighs, pinch the inner part, and say, "Man . . . when will this be gone?" I thought I was the only one of my close friends with legs like this, so I considered it a disadvantage.

Being an active child, my days were filled with running around, biking up the street, and swimming. We all preferred being outside when I was growing up, and my teenage years weren't any different. We would still go biking and running, and as we got older. we added in weight training a few times a week. I wasn't a gym rat per say, but I did go to the gym when I trained for track and field, and in the off-season. I had a cheap YMCA membership, but most of my exercise came from activities outside. Yet, there I was fixated on the size of my muscular legs. Sure, I was defined and I could squat 180 pounds, but that didn't matter when I was trying to buy pants.

I didn't think how strong my legs were, or how they helped me to actually ride the bike or go for a run. I didn't honor them as part of my body; I actually despised them. I thought weight training would make them leaner, but instead they were muscular. All I wanted was legs like a girl. I guess guys get a bad rap, but I did have the nursery rhyme in my head whenever I would workout:

> *What are little boys made of?*
> *Frogs and snails,*
> *And puppy-dogs' tails;*

That's what little boys are made of.

What are little girls made of?
Sugar and spice,
And all that's nice;
That's what little girls are made of.

I so badly wanted to make it to the New York State Championship, so I had to put the image of snails and puppy dog tails in my mind and keep on squatting with the boys. I was grunting and sweating, grinding it out. When I was in that gym, there was no sugar and spice. Heck, I even made up a term when a guy was teasing me in the gym.

"You can't lift that much weight. You're too tiny," he said.

"I can too, so stop being such a douche nozzle," I said, as if that term was well known and not so dirty.

"What did you just call me?" my friend asked shocked. Yeah, that was me, the "shock jock", or "Just Jen", I rarely ever held back.

"A douche nozzle. I mean it's not a bag. It's a bottle with a nozzle and right now . . . you're being one!"

Yep, I made up the term *douche nozzle*-true story. But I knew once I left the gym, I could resume the sugar and spice. I always had that duality, the tomboy telling crass jokes and hittin' the gym who could also turn on the charm, bat her eyes, and smile wide. But no wonder my pants didn't fit as coach kept upping my weight with each rep. I couldn't fit in my pants, but I could squat with the football team.

Pants were a bitch to buy. I needed a larger size for my thighs and a smaller one for my waist, so the larger always won out. I would then have this sweet woman, a seamstress who worked out of her basement, take in the waist of all of my pants. Using a belt caused my zipper to pop out and make them "dicky pants" as I not so affectionately called them.

"Mom, I hate having to go to Ms. Maria for every pair of pants, I wish my legs were smaller," I whined as I loaded two new pairs of jeans into a plastic bag for my short trip to her house.

"Love yourself, Jen," was always Mom's response.

Just like it was the easiest thing, like it was nothing, I would nod my head, a bit ashamed that I must not be loving myself, but thinking that I did look different than my best friend, with her sleek athletic legs. I would go right to comparison mode every time my mom said "love yourself, Jen." It was like a reflex. The ideal figure was just a tiny bit outside of my grasp.

I remember one time, I was about sixteen years old, sitting with a group of older guys at our lunch table. I knew the front of my pants was sticking out since my pants were so taken in at the waist. I caught my friend Dan looking.

"Oh, pardon me, my dickie pants are saying hello." I was always good for some bawdy humor. I mean, I'm sure that's what he was thinking while looking at the awkward bulge in my crotch.

The laughs erupted and I was satisfied with the result. The dickie pants were my idea, no one else's. I preferred it that way. Elephant in the room acknowledged with a whole lot of giggles.

I was 5'1 and ¾" (I held on to those ¾ inches with both hands for most of my life). I had thick wavy dark brown hair, that had a mind of its own, brown eyes and olive skin. My skin was always on the darker olive side because of all the hours spent outside but never as tan as my brother and mother. Boy would they get nice and sunkissed. When I was younger, I guess you would call me a tomboy. I was always outside riding bikes or playing in the sand.

Hair, clothes, and good looks never really mattered, until one day they just did. Pretty much this began when I took notice of boys as more than a school yard crush, then the primping flood gates opened.

I began ironing my hair (with an actual clothing iron not one of these fancy and efficient things we have today) to be straight with a flip like Farah Faucet, or wearing clothing like in the teen magazines and envious of the older girls' busts. I never fully accepted what I looked like and always desired myself to have a different shape and smoother hair. I was just a bit unappreciative of what I had.

My dad would always call me his "diamond in the rough." When I asked him what he meant, he said, "Jen, you don't realize how valuable you are."

He continued to say that just like a diamond taken from a mine had incredible value, but no one realized it or noticed until it was cleaned, polished, and shined brightly for all to see. That's what growing up is like, polishing that diamond and then you see the value that was always there all along. It was the sweetest way to tell me to be patient with my body as it grows, and to know that I have a lot of value.

HIP SOCKETS POPPING

I was sixteen years old, and on one particular Saturday, I had been sitting, cross-legged, on my friend James's floor for hours with 20 of my classmates. We were all making paper flowers- hundreds and hundreds of paper flowers.

This year we will have the best float, I remember thinking. Well, that was our intention each year. Colored tissue paper was spread all over the floor, and I calculated how much more of each color we would need, wondering who was going to stick around to clean it all up when we called it a day. I turned my head to see my very best friend as she walked into the room, smile spread across her happy face. She was telling me to get up and take a look at the float in the garage, but I couldn't move.

Ahh, shit, not again, I thought. I had been on the floor for probably over two hours by that point, maybe even more. I told her I would be out in a minute and to go on without me. I tried to get up off the floor by pushing with both hands, but I was stuck there. I couldn't move my right leg; the left one only moved a little. I sure as hell didn't want to have to explain something I had no clue about. I backed into the couch and sat, wiggling my hip and leg. I knew if I gave it time it would go back into place. I couldn't wait that long because people were talking to me, asking me things. I began to walk as best I could, dragging along with a little limp.

"Jen, what's up?" my friend asked.

"Oh nothing, my leg fell asleep, I guess."

So, did I mention that starting at the age of 12, my hip would lock? Sitting in one position for an extended period of time or sitting cross-legged would make my hip freeze up. It felt like it was stuck, until something popped back into place. I thought it might be because of some exercise I did, but most of the time I thought it was because of the way I sat. While I was in school it wasn't too bad, because I sat and then changed classes, eight times in a day. Hanging around and sitting on the floor with friends or watching TV or doing just about anything for a long-extended period made it worse. By the age of 17, it had increased in frequency, and it took a longer to pop back into place. It was annoying me, and it began to worry my mom. She thought that we were ignoring it and worried it could be something bigger. This became another strange phenomenon.

Mom was concerned that it could possibly affect my future in the childbearing years. Meanwhile, I was thinking, *Who the heck is ever having a baby?*

While it was extremely uncomfortable, my hip would eventually settle back in place and I could move my leg. I just had to wiggled the leg and wait it out. The right side was worse than the left, although it happened on both sides. Finally, we went to see an orthopedist who told us that I did not develop complete hip sockets (what is called *hip dysplasia*), and with long periods of sitting or certain exercises, it would become unstable and cause pain. If it became a big problem, there could be hip surgery, and more than likely, that will be inevitable in my older years. To my mother's relief, it would not affect my ability to bear children. I had an answer, good enough.

"These things only happen to you, Jen," my mom said.

Ah, gee thanks.

REMOVING WAX AND BURNING A HOLE IN MY EAR

I went through a period where my face would be sore when I woke up. My ear ached from deep inside. I knew the pharmacy had a product that helped people remove earwax, and so of course, I assumed this was the problem ~ wax overload. I purchased an over-the-counter earwax removal kit and figured I would solve this problem on my own.

I plopped a few drops in each ear right before bed and waited for the magic to happen. About an hour later, I felt it burning a little, and I was so happy. I figured it must have been working, so I plopped a drop more in each ear for good measure. My thinking was, if it's working, then a little more must be better. Bewildered, I was awoken at 4 a.m. in massive pain with a stabbing feeling deep inside my right ear.

Surely this is not what people feel when wax comes out? I thought.

I put my hand up to see if there was wax. Nothing! I went to wake up Mom. I had school in a few hours so I wanted to see if she had a suggestion. I explained what I'd done, and she incredulously said, "Why would you do that on your own?"

I remember being offended and kind of annoyed. I said, "Because I have earwax, Mom!" I probably even rolled my eyes.

I reeled around in pain until we got to the emergency room. Turns out, I had 2nd degree burns in both of my ears. The young female doctor who treated me in the ER had the facial expression of both disbelief and scorn at the same time.

Geesh! I thought. *What is her problem? Mean lady!*

Then she said, with her nose slightly pinched, completely disapproving, "Young lady, never ever put something inside your ear without a doctor's instruction. You should know better at your age."

"But they sell it over the counter at the drug store. And," I stammered, "I know a lot of people who have done it before with no problem."

She exhaled loudly, and I didn't think it was possible for her nose to scrunch up any more but it did right along with her eyes, which were now pinched. Man, oh man, she was not pleased with me. "People use that product when they have been instructed to do so by THEIR DOCTOR. That means they went to THE DOCTOR, found out there was a wax blockage, and administered it according to the instructions on the package. You, my dear do not have a blockage. You didn't see a doctor. And as a matter of fact, there is no wax present. Have you ever had an abundance of wax before?"

"Well, no . . . but . . ." Yeah, I had nothing to say at this point. I shut up and took it on the chin. No wax, 2nd degree burns . . .

As we left the hospital, my mom said, "Oh my God, Jen! I can't believe you did this. Of all the things. Nothing is ever simple with you. You always come up with the craziest stuff happening, only to you."

DETACHED. COMPLETELY DETACHED.

After college I got a job with an employment agency placing people in jobs and making sales calls. I quickly learned what it was like to work with people who didn't take their job seriously. A guy my age was secretly "seeing" the manager, there was a ton he got away with. I was working here thinking, *did I go to four years of school for this?*

After talking to my father, he said that I didn't need to waste my energy there, and that I would be appreciated for my work at his business. He told me I could implement my marketing degree at his company. I jumped at the chance. I knew the business well since I'd worked during the summers in between my other part-time jobs. I began working at my father's stair business in the office where I did payables, receivables, payroll, phones, sales, and marketing. Five days a week, I traveled into Brooklyn, just like my dad started doing twenty years earlier, and got a ton of work and life experience. After several months of working at our family business, I noticed something new going on with my vision. I was seeing dots. I attempted to clear them by closing my eyes, but when I opened my eyes back up those black and gray dots were still there.

Man, they are really annoying. I've been seeing them so much lately.

Sometimes they irritate my vision. I wonder if they are the reason I have these headaches lately?

I was 24 years old, and I was over having my plans derailed. Having to address that part of me was an inconvenience to say the least, but I would grin and bear it so I could get to the part of my life that did make me happy. I dealt with the weird vision and dots for a period of time, and then was like . . . all right, enough wondering! I pulled out a yellow pages for Nassau county and looked up ophthalmologists. I found a doctor and immediately picked up the phone on my desk at work and placed a call. They booked an appointment with me for the very next afternoon at 4:00.

Perfect! I will have a full day of work and head there directly since it is on my regular route home.

The doctor told me that the dots were floaters, which are common for people who are near-sighted, but they do not cause headaches.

Hmmmm, wonder why I have headaches then?

He got very serious as he examined my eyes, and when he was done, he asked me to sit tight as he left the room. He came back into the room after about five minutes, and told me that he arranged an appointment to see a retinal specialist the next morning. He stressed how extremely important it was for me to make this appointment tomorrow.

What is up with this guy? I thought. He said that he saw something in my eyes that needed to be addressed by a retinal surgeon.

"Do you think that you can have someone take you tomorrow? The dilation may be a bit more than you experienced in my office today and you will need someone with you. Is there someone you can call to confirm you will have a ride?" he asked.

"Umm, I guess so, I can try my mom."

He suggested that I call my mother from his office so he could confirm my appointment. *Wow, this is strange*, I thought. I'd never had to confirm an appointment so urgently and intensely. I called my mom at home and she said she could do it. All was set, and I left his office a little concerned.

What is all the hoopla about and what is causing the headaches if it's not those gray spots? Well, at least my vision is fine, there is that, I thought.

The next day, we met a kind, young doctor who gave me a thorough and long examination in both of my eyes. I had never had my eyes looked at for such a long time and with such an agonizing thoroughness. He took this long metal tool and pushed on the space surrounding my eye, while shining this intense light at every single angle possible, as he looked through a specialized microscope he held in his hand. And when I say he pressed spots, I mean he pressed along the surface of my skin, near my eye, everywhere, to make my eye move and pop out a little. It felt like my eyes were going to pop right out of my head, or at the very least, wouldn't be able to handle all the poking and prodding.

He asked Mom and me to come sit at his desk where he went on to explain what my condition was. He said that I had *retinal detachments*, lattice degeneration to be specific, in both of my eyes— the level of it was very severe. This type of detachment involves the abnormal thinning of peripheral retina, which is the tissue that lines the back wall of the eye and is critical for maintaining good vision.

He continued to say that while floaters could be caused by nearsightedness, in my case, they were a result of my lattice degeneration. He explained that something must be decided immediately because he couldn't guarantee that when I walked out of his office, I wouldn't lose my vision.

What the F&*K!

He explained that if I did something that seemed benign, like bump my head in the car, I could become permanently blind as a result. I just stared at him in shock. Stomach issues, self-esteem crap, thunder thighs, hip sockets popping ~ all manageable. But now my eye might fall out of my head and I might go blind? Oh yeah, this was my body. This was a big part of me.

Then came the litany of thoughts that began to run rampant through my head.

I am newly engaged and planning a wedding, I want to see my wedding.

I want to see my future children. Wait, do I want children?! I guess I am starting to.

I wanted to continue taking acting classes in NYC.

I need my vision!

How could this be happening?

Before yesterday's visit to the ophthalmologist, the possibility of blindness was not even a tiny thought. I just wanted to know why I was having headaches. Losing my vision was never a concern when I made that appointment with the ophthalmologist. I didn't even know what a *retina* was! We didn't have Google back then, so I sat in the doctor's office, pulsating in fear.

One thing I thought for sure was, *I cannot lose my vision.*

The retinal surgeon said he wanted to call in one of the senior partners in the practice for a second opinion. He excused himself for a minute and returned to the room with an older doctor. The more senior doctor looked into my eyes with the same vigilance as my doctor did mere minutes before. I endured what felt like torture— more poking and prodding with the metal torture device. My eyes began to tear up and my stomach began to roll, but I did everything he asked of me, just like I did a short while ago with the other doctor.

The older doctor with his somber and serious expression, turned to my new, happy, bright faced doctor and said, "Buckle. Definitely. She needs the buckle, and she needs it immediately. That is my opinion." He turned to us, briskly said his goodbyes, and hurried from the room.

Oh man, now another thing I don't know~what's a buckle?

My new doctor explained the buckle procedure. The surgery places a material around the eye to hold together the retinal tear. It would need to be done in the hospital, and I would be required to stay for a few days. All these thoughts began running through my head. I would be in the hospital, at times without my fiancée or parents, and I would have no vision. How would I manage that? The thought of that brought so much fear. I could possibly be in a variety of situations and be completely out of my own control. I felt as though I was going to be sick.

They cannot be serious with all of this.

My doctor said that he did not agree completely with the senior partner. He did not feel as though that was my only option. He stated that yes, the buckle procedure would indeed work and work successfully, as it has for many years. But he was very enthusiastic about a new procedure they were using—laser treatment for retinal detachments. It was new but they were seeing success with it. They had the laser in the office and had done a few patients with some tears, but yet not as extensive as my case. He explained that the laser would "burn" the retina, causing a scar to seal and "glue" down the tears to the retina.

My doctor continued to tell us a few things we needed to think of in order to make this decision. He said my young age was a great benefit to healing with the laser. There was a possibility it would not work and we would still need the buckle anyway. If it did work, then we would avoid major surgery.

Also, another thing that we needed to consider was the large number of tears I had, so we had to make a decision as soon as possible. He gave my mom and me time alone to talk. After a tearful back and forth with my mother and calls to my fiancée and to my father, we all decided to take the least invasive route. Apart from the crazy ailments that popped up in my life, we agreed with the doctor that because I was healthy, the laser was a good choice. He was relieved to hear my decision, and we began treatment that very day.

The laser treatment was intense. I had to have my eyeball held in this contraption while the doctor tapped on a pedal on the floor for the laser. I became very dizzy, and we would have to stop every so often. We had a lot of ground to cover, so he would return quickly as soon as I gave the go ahead. I recall his stern voice telling me to hang in there when I would begin to feel faint, teetering on consciousness. He would keep coaxing me, "One more minute, Jennifer. One more and then I can give you some orange juice. One more, Jennifer. Hang in there, you're doing great." All the while, "Tap, tap, tap, tap!"

For years after, I had a Pavlovian response whenever I heard any sort of tapping sound. It would immediately trigger nausea.

After a few days of traumatic laser treatments, I was told to continue to rest at home with my eyes closed as much as humanly possible. NO movement of the eye. No sudden movements of my body. My future held no prospects of wrestling or jumping of any kind.

Lying in my bedroom, all snuggled up tight, there wasn't any natural or artificial light in the room. It was there, in complete darkness, that I would listen to books on tape, from the local library, on my cassette player. I walked with my arms extended and reached out in front of me. I walked to the bathroom with my eyes closed. Sometimes I found it easier to crawl so I wouldn't bump into the walls. I accepted visitors with my eyes closed. I ate my meals with my eyes closed. All in all, I lived with my eyes closed for over two weeks.

I had over a thousand tears total in my eyes, but luckily, that surgery held. I have needed no further repairs since 1992!

Unfortunately, I heard from a variety of people that phrase again, "Only you, Jen!" and the other one I wasn't too crazy about either, "All these crazy things happen to only you!"

Ugh.

"Belief in the body, not in True Self, perpetuates illness."
~ From Meditations with Jesus and Jen

INTERLUDE

A PART OF ME NO ONE
KNEW ABOUT EXCEPT ME

FACES IN TIMES OF NEED

*"For every fear that shakes your peace, for every night you feel alone, for
every moment you lose a little hope,
there is an angel who whispers . . . I am here."*
~ Anna Taylor

I can't take the pain, I thought as I was rocking back and forth. I
was 12 years old, and I had been in the bathroom so long my feet fell
asleep. *If I get off of this toilet, I will wind up right back here.* These are
the thoughts swirling around my mind. *Moaning helps. I'll moan a
little. Okay . . . that's not making it stop. Please stop so I can at least lie
down.* I closed my eyes and repeat please, please, please . . .

When I opened my eyes, I saw a face. I had seen this face before,
but not in this spot. More to the right once during another episode,
and before that, it was in my room. Come to think of it, they were
always in a different spot. I stared at it and forgot about my pain for
a while. I thought to myself, *I know these faces I see are sent to me. They
must be my angels.*

I was able to comfort myself most of the time, when I was in pain with a technique I developed. I would grab anything, a shampoo bottle, the wrapping of the toilet paper roll, a magazine in the rack on the floor, anything really, and I would read whatever I saw a sentence at a time. Then I would take each word, individually, silently spell it to myself. "This product is manufactured in the great US of A. T-H-I-S . . ." I would follow this pattern of complete nonsense until I was calm and I knew the pain would not suck me under. I had been doing this for myself since about the age of eight.

My parents couldn't help in any way. I knew it bothered them, and none of the medicines that the doctors prescribed throughout the years stopped it either. Some episodes were more than I could bear and I needed a distraction, a helping hand, to get through.

I found comfort in these faces. They seemed to always be around me when I was in great distress from stomach pain. I didn't freak out or go running to my parents. I never shouted anything like, "I saw something come quick!" It would have been understandable, but I didn't because I didn't feel that I was in danger. Instead, I felt comfort, just for me—all my own.

I can't recall where or when the first time happened, but I do remember, I was curious. Thinking something like, *what in the world am I seeing?* Quickly followed by a special sort of acceptance, then calm. At first, I caught myself thinking, *Am I making this up? Am I really seeing a face?* What I did know for certain, was whenever I was in pain, I was not alone, and I was being taken care of in some way. It was as if only God knew about my pain, and He sent angels to take care of me.

During so many of my painful moments, they were with me. As I mentioned, medicine couldn't stop the pain, nor lessen its severity, so I had to deal the best I could . . . with a little help. I knew I always had my parents if there was an emergency, but in the private of these moments, I had the faces.

A cold sweat would break out over my skin, blanketing me with this bizarre hot and cold sensation. I would need to strip off all of my clothes in an attempt to find relief. In those extreme times, I would almost always see a face in the rug. Yeah, it was the 80's and my parents had rugs in the bathroom. I would stare at the face and concentrate on the features. I would close my eyes and test if it would still be there. I would do this for a minute, sometimes a bit longer to see if this was just a product of my mind.

When I opened my eyes, each time, there it was in the same spot~exactly the same. But when I would look the next day, nothing. On the floor, the wall, the shower curtain, there was no limit to the places they would appear when they answered my silent calls of distress. They never failed to bring me the calm that I needed. They never spoke to me with words, there was no "show" that they were putting on, just their silent presence of support and peace.

One time in my bedroom, while I was lying in bed experiencing much of the same pain, I looked to the windows and the curtains fluttered, and there I saw a beautiful being. Non-threatening~just there for me. Love filled my heart and spilled onto my face in a huge smile. It felt as if my whole being was smiling at the sight, and like the light, I was filled with energy. I couldn't put it into words, but I could feel. I think I was feeling joy and it was overwhelming.

I had a great love of God, Jesus, and the holy family. In our family, our faith was a central part of our lives. Dad would always tell me that God would help us with the things we needed. I might not have known all there was of our faith, but I had heard over and over about God's help, God takes care of us, and God is with us. I knew the commandments and one of them was that I needed to attend mass every Sunday. As the good little Catholic that I was, if I went to a sleepover and missed mass with my family, I would get on my bike and ride the mile or so to the later mass, all by myself. That is what we were told after all.

Since we were also told to ask God for help, I would pray for help with my pain. I would beg, too. Once I got through each individual bout, it was like a new lease on life, a fresh start, and I didn't think on the pain any further. When I was in it though, I would take the help I was given.

I know it might seem like I should have looked into it more, maybe even gotten people more involved with what I was witnessing, maybe I should have even been afraid. Fear literally never entered my mind. This relationship was special between me and my angels. When I realized what the faces represented, and I knew the comfort I was given, it all felt exactly as I thought God might have intended it to be, peaceful.

I shared it with my parents once and they listened and were happy that I felt better when I saw them. I wonder now if they even believed me. Maybe they just let me talk about it as a means to cope with all the body issues? I didn't care one way or the other because what mattered to me was that my angels made me feel better. I accepted what was shown to me and what it brought into my life because I knew they were given to me to help me. Gratitude seems like such a small word when I think of all the times I was helped by the angels.

I didn't see the faces when I was out and about. It was always at home, when I was in need, or sick. But in time, once I knew completely that they were my angels, I would sense them with me in a room, even when I wasn't sick. When they were near, I felt loved and comforted, like the way I felt with my family. If I was sitting at my desk in my room, doing homework, I would turn around, and expect to see someone standing there plain as day. Nothing was there for me to see in a full body or form. It was the same feeling I would feel when I saw the faces. I was not alone.

When I was a child, I learned about angels through our Catholic faith. Here is what I knew: they were in the Bible, created by God to help Him give messages, and also there to protect us. I didn't have a reason before to figure out the details of how the protecting would happen. It wasn't until I first realized what I was seeing in the bathroom, that all I knew about angels was clearly true. Seeing it for myself made a believer out of me. There was no proof or stories that I heard of where everyday people were seeing angels. Regardless of the lack of stories, I believed!

It's kind of crazy because when I was even younger~around 4 or 5 years old~I began to have a real love of roses. I loved their look but, above all, I loved the smell of roses. I made some correlation with the smell of roses and peace and calm. The smell gave me a sense of calm at the same time a feeling of happiness~almost joviality! As I got older and started to experience these faces in times of need, I also thought the roses were connected somehow to angels. Was it something I'd read in a story? Did an adult say that near me? I don't know, but I just knew what I liked. It was from that age on that I desired to have rose water and floral scented perfumes. It wasn't until I learned a great deal more about angels and could hear them speak, that I learned that angels can be associated with certain smells.

Angels often send people the scent of flowers~especially of roses, which have the highest energy vibration rate of any flower (since angels' energy vibrates at a high frequency, they connect more easily with living things that have highly vibrating energy fields). If you smell a flower scent while praying or meditating, yet there are no flowers nearby, the fragrance is probably coming from your guardian angel as a sign that he or she is with you and wants to encourage you.

I still see these wonderful faces, but not as much as I did in my youth. One time I was sick with the flu, and I had a family and three dogs to take care of, but I couldn't leave the bed. There on the floor was a trusted friend. I sat there, probably in need of IV fluids, comforted once again by one of my angels. There was another time, in the middle of what I can refer to as my deepest time of need, I was sitting in mass praying, and I looked up and saw the angel's wings on the wall of the church, right behind the alter, as clear as day. I asked my daughter if she saw them and she did not. Another occasion around this same time period, I saw a face on the floor of the church. I knew that I could get through this stage of my life with the help of my angels and God.

I knew that the angels were watching over me, and I was grateful for my "friends" who helped me in the most difficult of situations.

"It has become a weight on your soul. But your soul is perfect,
cannot be tarnished, harmed, or belittled."
~ From Meditations with Jesus and Jen

Emotion [əˈmōSH(ə)n]

noun

a natural instinctive state of mind deriving from one's circumstances, mood, or relationships with others.

We learn what is acceptable and what is not through our experiences. We learn what creates a good response and what creates a bad one. Emotions can be displayed or stifled.

My emotions were simple. I felt happy. I felt love. I felt sick. I felt grief. I didn't feel much else . . . oh wait, I did feel scared to upset people.

CHAPTER 3

Feeling Emotions or Not Feeling Them at All

"Nothing can hurt you, unless you give it power to do so."
- A Course in Miracles

"You are so sassy! You got it, whatever you need, Jen! Salami! Haahaa. This girl kills me."

My co-worker was mumbling the last part as he walked away. Mumbling to me or himself, I don't know; either way, it worked as I'd hoped. I got a laugh. He called me sassy, but that was just me being me, my tell-it-like-it-is self, deflection completed. Bingo!

You see, I had a stomachache. Go figure. I knew the odor was wafting, so before my co-worker could beat me to the chase, I dropped a joke about eating too much salami and provolone for lunch. It's not the true story, but at work, in the pharmacy, where the only bathroom was directly behind the cash register in the back of the store, I needed to be quick on my toes.

So yeah, that's me. Well, another part of me, I guess. The me that used humor to deflect rather than feel the emotions that might have resulted in embarrassment. I never felt as embarrassed if I pointed it out first and we got a good laugh. I also would try to lighten everyone else's emotional load as well. I used humor and a little sass to get the job done. This is a part of me that speaks her mind, sassy me.

There was a little girl, who had a little curl, right in the middle of her forehead, and when she was good she was very good, and when she was bad she was horrid.

I remember this little poem, although I have no idea where it came from. I am however certain that according to my mom, I was that curly haired girl for sure. I thought that being the middle kid was the reason I got in trouble instead of my tendency to be "wide-open," 100% full throttle most of the time. I mean I wasn't always innocent, but my parents never saw how my brother goaded me. All anyone ever saw was my *reaction* to him, and his sly adorable smile behind my parents back, mocking me. That rat! He was my tormentor, but oh how I loved him. I was the kid who would mumble under my breath trying to defend myself, and then get in trouble for my "big mouth." And I thought I was being quiet! *What the heck*, I would bluster in my head, I was only speaking my opinion.

My brother would tell me, "You get in trouble because you argue with Mom. I just say 'Okay,' because I don't care~then I am free." He shrugged his shoulders with a carefree laugh, as if he had the world by the short hairs. I just didn't believe him. Nope, I thought I was picked on because I wasn't the oldest, like him, and I wasn't the lucky baby, like my sister. In my eyes they were like Teflon, not a thing sticking, the both of them.

"Oh my gosh, did she just ask the guests walking in the door where her present was? I think I will die. How rude?" ~ thoughts from 11-year-old Jen.

It was my sister's third birthday party and we were welcoming people in the house. She totally embarrassed me by asking for gifts at the door. And it got worse! When it was time to open the gifts, if my sister didn't like the present, she said so. I died every time. "Oh, she really likes it. She didn't mean that." I would apologize on her behalf. I had to make an excuse for how she behaved.

I could never get away with talking like that, I thought. But then again, I felt too badly to speak what might be on my mind and risk of hurting someone's feelings. I was secretly jealous of my sweet, tiny sister speaking her truth. I remember Mom scolded me that day. She told me not to "put what I think" onto the baby and let her be.

Wow, I thought, *wouldn't that be so cool to be the youngest and be free like that.*

BULLYING, PEOPLE PLEASING, AND LOIS LANE

As I cried all over the note paper, bearing my soul and all my heartfelt apologies, I listed, in detail, the reasons I was sorry.

"Dear Daddy, I am sorry you came home to Mommy mad at me again. I play after school and you work hard to make the money for our food that we eat. And we spend all your money. I am sorry, Daddy. I will try harder to be good next time."

Everything that happened with my family, well anyone really, that had to do with feelings, especially hurt ones, affected me deeply.

I remember, I had to be about ten years old, and I was standing with my legs over the middle of my bike, I began to scream, huge peels of screaming came out of my mouth. A kid I knew, who was a few years older than me, had his hands on my handle bars and was blocking my path on the sidewalk from Abe's Candy Store back to my house.

He said, "Get off and give me your bike. Now!" So I did what

I thought best . . . I screamed bloody murder. He jumped back in shock and I tore off as if I was being chased. When I got home, I told my brother and my cousin what just happened. And I told them who the bully was that almost stole my bike.

Within seconds, they were each on their respective bikes. All I saw were their backs as they tore off like bats outta hell. When they came back an hour later, my brother said, "Jen, that kid won't be a problem anymore." My cousin stood tall and proud next to him, both grinning that they got the bully good.

I could just picture what they did to the kid. I looked at them, my eyes so wide that they actually hurt. Then this feeling of sadness came over me for the boy who scared me so much I was in tears, just a little while before. I thought I would be happy they went after him, but instead my heart hurt for the bully.

That was me. I just never wanted anyone to hurt. And I always felt deeply, as if I knew there was a reason the bully was a bully or why someone was doing something hurtful. I didn't want to contribute to hurting others. My heart just didn't sit right with it. "Ohhh, I don't want to hurt his feelings." Or "I never would want to make her upset." I thought I was being nice. I always remembered Jesus's Golden Rule, "Do unto others as you would have them do unto you." I flat out disliked the feeling I would get when someone was mean to me, so I was on board with that rule, all the way.

I also didn't like to watch meanness being done to someone else, even a bully; it gave me a funny sinking feeling in my gut. I preferred to be a "people pleaser" to avoid that feeling. There came a point that my "people pleasing" went beyond just making me feel happy and spiraled into the land of not wanting to be judged.

I preferred a drama-free life. Positivity was my comfort zone. I knew what it felt like and I knew it's opposite. The opposite sucked.

I worked hard to please everyone, making things good for them, and keeping things peaceful, while not acknowledging my own feelings, which I held in place with duct tape and spit glue. It was second nature to me: dimming my own light each time I said I was sorry for something I didn't do, just to avoid confrontation of any kind.

All that I held inside of me would manifest into something later in life because, while I was doing it, I didn't realize I was doing anything wrong. It had no name. I was creating roadblocks for myself through my unending people pleasing. I was used to doing this to achieve the environment I wanted, and I didn't think it was of any detriment to me, it was just how I handled certain things around me.

I was 11 years old, and when I walked into class one day, no one said hello. All my girlfriends were looking at me with squinted eyes. I knew those eyes, they were giving me the evil eye. You give it when you are mad at someone.

What did I do? I thought incredulously. I put my book bag on my assigned hook and headed to my seat. I heard whispers behind me. I turned toward them. "What's wrong with you guys?" I asked. I got a harrumph and they both turned back toward the direction their seats were facing. I was being frozen out. It just went downhill from there. I had this horrible butterfly feeling in my belly. It wasn't the good kind, when you were anticipating something good. No, this was the sinking butterfly feeling, when you thought something really bad was about to happen.

Holding in my sniffles and widening my eyes so that the tears that threatened wouldn't spill over, I sat by myself at the far end of the lunch table. I couldn't touch my food.

What did I do?

Why do they all hate me?

No one would talk to me and just tell me; I had the plague.

We all headed back into class. I sat down in my seat and screeched. There was something painful happening to my butt. I felt around and there were tacks on my seat. That was it—I just burst out crying. The teacher, who I liked and knew thought fondly of me, came right up next to me in a second. I showed her and she was not happy. She brought me to her desk and asked me what happened. I was very hesitant to tell her about all the girls not talking to me, but the tacks hurt. I wound up telling her what had been happening that day. Let's just say, that didn't help make anything better.

At the time it was called, "kids being kids." Today, it would be classified as bullying.

It escalated from there. There were the dumb things at school, but then I became an after-school target, with constant prank calls, and pizzas being sent to my home. The pizza thing was sort of big. Since there was no caller ID to verify the order, when it got there, my parents had to explain they had no idea who ordered them. The delivery guy would just be standing there with three pizzas, demanding money. Being such a small town, it made it a little bit more embarrassing because that is where we would need to go for our pizza the next time we wanted it. To me it was the worst thing that could have ever happened to me in my short eleven years, and there was no way in hell I would ever let something like this happen to me again.

Only you, Jen, I began to think.

I did not like this part of me.

Many years later, in high school, a friend and I were talking about that time in sixth grade, and she felt so bad. She apologized all over again. I told her to forget it, but I knew how that time really hurt my feelings. I tried to tell myself it was all over. She told me what it was all about and I couldn't believe it. It all happened because I wouldn't do something with them, some really silly thing, that I thought was dumb. I didn't want to participate, and they were mad at me. That's why they called me "goody two shoes."

I forgave them all. And I had very close relationships with them as we got older. But I couldn't ever really shake what I felt when I was being ostracized. And no matter what, I didn't want to ever feel that way again. I never wanted to be the target of a perceived injustice again. Removing disapproval from my life felt imperative for my survival.

I never felt right in my skin if someone was upset with me. I was a people pleaser, through and through. If you were upset with me, I'd apologize. If you were upset at all, first I would think it might be with me, then I would go investigate what was wrong and try to help you not be upset. I was really hung up on how I was perceived, or thought of by others. I liked to be liked-simple as that. I also needed to rectify all angst.

Living in harmony was key. I would even go as far as apologizing for things I didn't do, just to keep the peace. Happy and calm is the way I preferred everything to be above all else, even at my own expense. Although I kept the peace with the whole world (so it seemed), the one person I gave a run for her money, was my mother.

I heard once that you fight with the person you are most like and closest with. You know they will love you no matter what you do. I never thought of my mother and I as being alike, but I do know she was the one person I freely and willingly butted heads with. I knew I was always safe. If she was mad, she would hold off attention because of her anger, but I always knew she would still care and provide for me. I guess that was the only time I wasn't in full people-pleasing mode because I knew I was loved despite her anger. But even with Mom, after I gave it sometime after a fight, and even if I believed I was in the right, I would say I was sorry to have peace restored once more.

But it wasn't just about my peace, I could deeply feel other people's emotions, too.

I wonder why my friend feels afraid to go home? I remember thinking. We were about nine years old and just moments before we arrived at her home, we were laughing and playing.

When I saw my friend look at her house, I immediately knew she was afraid of her father. His car was in the driveway and she was frozen. My heart was beating to a frantic and loud drum. I knew I couldn't help her but I wanted to make it go away for her. I think I mirrored how she was feeling, as my body went through a series of strange emotions. I asked her if she wanted to go back to my house and play instead. She responded to my question with fear in her eyes, shaking her head back and forth.

Where she stood it was wet, and there was a shiny wetness on her leg and on the bottom rim of her shorts that I noticed the moment before she began to run toward her house. She said she couldn't come back to my house. Nothing more.

I knew I couldn't help her; I knew I wanted to. I felt like I could feel her emotions as I watched her run up her steps to the front door.

My friend moved away a few weeks later. I never heard from her again. This memory sticks with me. I was an empath, through and through. And oh how desperately I wanted to heal what made her so afraid.

I was also a curious, inquisitive, and eager child but at the end of the day, I simply wanted to make my parents happy. I wanted to know about everything so I would ask a lot of questions, but I didn't want them to be angry or displeased with me for asking too many.

And as I got older, I wanted to share everything with them, but I didn't want them to be upset with me for speaking my truth.

Everything I did or said was almost always filtered under the lens of people pleasing and guarding other people's emotions. Any of the moments with my parents where I was simply "speaking my opinion" as I aptly called it, their happiness was important to me.

I was six years old. We were at my grandparents house with Mom, Dad, Grandma, Grandpa, Aunt Dee (and my cousin Michele on her lap), Uncle Jerry, Aunt Vicki, and Uncle Joe. *Man the table at Grandpa's is packed today*, I thought. Sunday meals at Grandma's were sometimes kind of boring, even when I was being chased and teased. I liked being pumped up, amped. I liked a lot of energy. And there was so much going on around the table on this particular day. I figured I could squeeze in between my mom and dad if I tried really hard.

What are they saying?

Who is it that went to work last week?

Where did he work?

Which uncle?

Where did Aunt Vicki get the cannolis from?

I was trying to keep up, so I finally started just chiming in, "Who was that, Dad?" and then another question and another flowed out of my mouth. It was like I couldn't stop it. But I really liked the grown-ups so much more than my brother and cousin at that moment. I liked to hear what the grown-ups would say and I loved to be part of it.

"Enough with the questions, Lois Lane. Go into the side room and watch TV or go play." Everyone laughed at Dad's joke.

"But . . . but," I stuttered. I didn't want to go in there and miss everything. Mad, I stormed off. I liked Lois Lane, she was cool, but I knew that Dad was sort of teasing me.

I loved being with the grown-ups, always. As I got older, and Dad asked if I wanted to go out with them for dinner, I would always go, then I would head off afterwards to be with my own friends. Growing up, my parents had fabulous family friends that we called aunts and uncles, and the kids, we called our cousins. I loved to be near the moms as they chatted over coffee. I learned my lesson not to ask too many questions at the "grown-up table." I never let Superman's sidekick, Lois Lane, stop me from being where I wanted to be. After all, I didn't want to piss them off, and then I wouldn't be able to sit there with them.

I might not have loved my nickname of Lois Lane because I thought I was being teased, but I thought when Dad called me "petunia" it was so special. Then when he began calling me Jenafoof, which morphed to Foof, I loved it. I thought it was hysterical the day I learned, from several Polish men at Dad's factory, that *foof* meant fart. We laughed about that forever. I am still called Foof by my husband, brother, and an aunt.

FRESHMAN BLUES AND TRAGEDY STRIKES

Let's jump to the beginning of my college experience. Freshman year. It was my first venture away from my loving family, who I was very attached to as you probably can tell. I had some pretty big life events happen, as well having been in a car accident.

Let me start with stating how I went into my freshman year at college: I was scared to death! I missed my family terribly, but was also excited to be making new friends and starting this new life. It was all going along pretty smoothly, if you consider crying every time you talked to your parents smooth. I also never wanted to miss a thing on campus which meant talking to my parent sparingly. This was even more traumatic for a daddy's girl like me.

During that first week of school, we didn't even have our phone hooked up. Yeah, in 1986, you had to wait to get your phone hooked up. The only thing you had to reach home was an AT&T calling card (or calling collect) on a phone located on the main floor hallway. There was just one phone for hundreds of girls. So, there I would find myself, in line, waiting to call my parents. This was difficult since what I really wanted to do was talk to my parents whenever I wanted to. Talk about taking a major "pacifier" right out of the mouth of this baby.

My family was moving on without me. I went back home for Thanksgiving break and there was a fenced in swimming pool and pool house in our back yard. No one mentioned a thing. All I could think was, *Wow, what other changes are happening without me?*

I didn't learn until years later that during the "no-Jen at home" stage of life, someone threw away a box in the attic that they believed was theirs. It is still a mystery to me how they thought that my Linda Ronstadt, Billy Joel, and Shaun Cassidy albums were theirs. Alas, gone were these memories of my youth along with an autograph from Billy Joel and Sylvester Stallone. Boy, if I knew about this when I was away at college, my FOMO would have elevated to 1000% and I would have packed my bags and hiked back home on foot!

About the second month of school, I received a call late one night from a friend telling me that our good friend from high school was murdered. I was absolutely devastated. How could that be? I'd just spoken with her a week ago. Her story was a sad one. Her ex-boyfriend (and a fellow classmate) was accused of her murder. The tragedy was very emotional for my eighteen-year-old mind to process. That kind of thing did not happen in our small part of the world.

I went home for her service and to be with my other high school friends. Every detail of that time back home was etched in such surreal devastation and sadness. All we could say to each other were things like, "How did this happen?" All of us were so sad for her parents and her only brother. We just couldn't imagine how they could handle the loss of our friend who was such a light in their lives.

No more than two weeks later, I got another late-night phone call, which delivered the news that crushed my heart. My beloved grandfather, who brought so much kindness into my life, my mom's father, had lost his battle to bone cancer. Since his diagnosis, I'd been home to visit him several times, witnessing his deterioration from my strong, virile grandfather to a frail man. My mind couldn't reconcile that he would succumb to this horrible thing. He was always burly in my eyes.

To this day I am not a big fan of the phone ringing in the middle of the night because it never is very good news. If it's ringing, then it is of some great importance, and all too often, news of a tragedy.

I was stirred by so much death. I went home for my grandfather's funeral. I also just felt I needed to be near my family. It was as if the bedrock of life was being shaken and I needed my touch stones, my family unit, where I was loved and accepted. I needed to see the life and vitality still vibrating in those people I adored, especially my parents.

HOMESICK AND HELPLESS

I didn't reinvent myself like some people do when they head off to college. I was me, just in a different geographic location. I was still the people pleaser, the girl who wanted to laugh and have a good time, the kid who did the right thing where school was concerned, and I did not dwell on my body. I enjoyed all the new experiences like going out to campus activities, or going to someone's dorm room with a group of friends to eat M&Ms, pizza, and diet Coke. I went out to parties and to the local bar. Even hanging out in the dining hall was fun, checking out all the cute guys! Making new friends and going out was never a problem. Enjoying people's company is what I lived for, but desiring to make everyone happy. . . well, that was where things got a little mucky.

I simply went through these times by not "rocking" the proverbial boat. That was no different for me than how I was at home. I only operated from what I knew. Of course, I took on college like most people do when they are away for the first time. I definitely attended class, did my work, and studied, but my primary focus was on experiencing college, friends, being on my own for the first time, sharing meals with others, boys, and missing home. Yeah, missing home was a biggie for me.

I loved to joke and be silly. I enjoyed making everyone laugh. I could be found most times, studying or goofing off with friends. I had a cute hairstyle shaved tight on the sides (as was the style in the late 80's), with the long tuft of hair sticking straight up in the air held together by a colored scrunchie. I looked like Pebbles Flintstone, minus the bone. Not holding back, from my style to my words, I let it all sort of hang out, which was a bit of a shocker for some of the girls from Massachusetts and Rhode Island. They seemed so proper compared to me and my outspoken, wide open approach to things.

I didn't tolerate anything to the extreme. But, I was never offended by a dirty joke and a frank manner of speaking; I thought it was just all in good fun. I took it as my mission to break these proper girls free, to help them have more fun in their own skin. My second-year roommate never even burped. I found this amazing. No air came from that girl's body, or so she proclaimed . . . ever.

How could that be? I thought. Isn't that painful?! I mean, we live together and not even a peep! Needless to say, before I left that school second semester Sophomore year . . . things had changed. She found that air that had been trapped all along.

I shared all of the parts of me with those at college, just as I did back home—that was just my personality. What you saw was what you got. I enjoyed things and was playful, but I could be serious when I needed to be. We would all sit around and share stories, joke, and laugh in between long hours of study. I would use a crazy high-pitched voice to tell a story, and again, we would all crack up. It was a great way to let off steam.

I have to say though, that the communal living was a bit rough for me while I was away at college. I mean I was the scouting agent for bathroom safety and stomach distress awareness. So for a year and a half, I tried to manage the stomach pains with as much dignity as I could muster. I would be so embarrassed when anyone would notice my frequent and long bathroom visits, so I would use humor to make fun of myself. Remember how I mentioned I deflected what was happening? Well I had to become a master of it living with a bunch of other people who shared the same bathrooms.

"Oh you know me . . . Give yourself a few minutes before you go in there!" What else could I do? It was so much easier to laugh at myself and initiate the joke. And the bathroom with this group of virtual strangers (who as I mentioned, I perceived as so proper and could picture them having tea with the Queen)…no, this was not the time I would give up the deflection humor.

God forbid someone came into a room and asked what happened to me in the bathroom. Yikes! I might expire on the spot. And it was worlds better for me to laugh about it so they knew I was aware of the problem, rather than worry that they were discussing it behind my back. Because let's face it, in close quarters like that, people had to know.

I know that professionals would say that I was managing conflict with humor. Or some might say it is a type of self-deprecating joke—where you are modest about or are critical of oneself, in a humorous way. It is how I handled the issue I had dealt with most of my life with new people who were not my family or lifelong friends. Even with those loved ones, I didn't bring it up~it just was.

It was in my second year of college, when I was pondering if I should transfer schools, that I had my first and only altercation regarding my stomach illness. It truly bewildered me because I was self-conscious about my frequent bathroom trips. I never wanted this issue to get in the way of my life. It was on that day I realized that living in close quarters with someone can bring about caa-razy stuff! My roommate at the time, came home complaining of a headache. I said that I was not feeling so hot either. That was the wrong thing to say that day for sure. She lambasted me. Screaming at me that she could never be sick because I always was; that she wanted to be sick without me being sick. I was standing there in utter shock.

She wasn't my lifelong friend or even my family so how could she know what I had to go through? Other than living with me and seeing me sick often, what was she to conclude? She was left to her own imagination on what was really going on with me. Well, it appeared she believed I was making it up.

There was never an official diagnosis for my frequent bouts, and I wasn't taking medication. I just got "sick" often. Here I thought I was doing a good job at hiding the semi-secret bathroom trips, but when living with someone, I couldn't hide the times it left me tired and drained and needing to lie down to recoup. I had no way to process this attack, other than stand there in complete bewilderment because I had never experienced it before.

I couldn't wrap my brain around someone thinking I would want to shine a spotlight on the real reason for my bathroom escapades (since I tried hard to fluff it off as no big deal with a laugh) as a way to thwart attention from her. We lived together and were friends, so we spent many hours together. It was inevitable that she would learn of some of my distress whether it was outright spoken about or not.

The incident was very confusing to me and hurt my heart. Was I sheltered by how my family and close friends dealt with me? Either way, I wanted back in that fold, where I loved and was loved in return, always.

I had a hard time processing some of these emotions. I liked the emotion of being happy, being joyful, but everything else was hard to deal with, that's why humor helped. There were parts of me I didn't always want to see, I guess.

But sometimes we have to get pulled backward to move forward. I went back home during Sophomore year, I had enough of long distance. That experience with my roommate left me shook, and no amount of covering up the emotions I was feeling would be able to bring me back to center. And I had to just go home, something was pulling me there, even if I didn't fully understand why as of yet.

Examining all the parts of me, the pull home, coupled with my mixed emotions, were too much to process on my own . . . I needed my family.

"Eventually, what you pushed down deep will resurface
when it is time to be addressed."
~ From Meditations with Jesus and Jen

INTERLUDE

My Own Glimpse of Death

*"Death is only an experience through which you are meant
to learn a great lesson: you cannot die."*
~ Paramahansa Yogananda

You might be wondering what happened. Well, this is a doozy that didn't feel like a doozy at the time, but man. I'll just get to it.

As you know, I was shook up by a lot of death during my sophomore year. Well, I had a glimpse of death myself during that time. One evening, just a few weeks after my grandfather's passing, I went to a local bar, right near campus, to have a drinks with some friends. Side note: My roommate would often get us into that bar because her brother worked there, and we were only eighteen. Anyhow, after we were there for a bit, me and a guy friend headed out to go back to our dorms. We had been at the bar for an hour, and it was now twilight outside.

As we headed out into the chilly night, garbed in our winter jackets, we were talking and enjoying each other's company. I can't remember my outfit, although I am sure it was something cute as I "liked" this guy. I do know no heels were involved because I wasn't that type of shoe person, so that means no tripping or stumbling was involved. I am also sure there was laughing and flirting going on, and

I am sure my focus was split between the road and my (hopefully) future boyfriend.

I was just two steps in front of him. I looked left. I saw nothing. I looked right, where the road bent slightly. Again, I saw nothing. On that night, my big mistake was not looking left again. Because it was at that moment of me stepping off the curb that I was right in front of a moving vehicle speeding down this small side road. It had to be going over 40 miles per hour because looking left, then right, then stepping, doesn't take enough time for a vehicle going the proper, slower, side street speed limit to be there.

But it was . . . right there.

What is happening? Is this car hitting me? How can this be happening?

Heat seared on the left side of my body. My hip, my leg, all the heat and impact.

Is this the front of a car? It must be the headlights. I feel the light. I see the light, so bright, almost blinding. But my eyes are closed though, how can that be? I see nothing but light.

But I feel. I feel myself changing locations on the car as I am elevating upward. I'm on the windshield. Maybe it is the top of the car, I can't be sure, but I feel motion and it is going up.

Next, I am airborne.

My head crashes to the ground, my body flies back up again, off the ground. The rest of my body, head, back and all, come crashing down once more, one final time, ramming me into the ground.

Darkness . . . literal lights out for Jen.

Other than light, I saw nothing the entire time, which felt like it lasted a second, yet I felt and went through so many things.

Were my eyes closed?

Or was I unconscious the whole time?

How did I feel all the details of the car on my body?

How did I recall exactly how my body hit the ground if I was out?

All the while my eyes were closed, but there was that light. *How is that possible?* I had no clue. I thought, *I must have cracked my skull open. I know my back is broken for sure.* Then there was nothing. All these thoughts ran together in one instance.

I died. I know this.

I don't want to die. I'm too young.

I am repeating this over and over to who? I don't know. Thoughts were popping in and out. *Am I saying this out loud? No, I am saying it to myself and to, and into, this light.* I felt a little panicked because I really didn't want to die, but then as soon as the panic came, it was replaced with me saying the words as if in a conversation, like I was discussing a choice. No other words other than the chant, over and over, along with an overwhelming feeling that everything was going to be all right. And there was that ever-present light since the moment of impact. I just knew I was being pulled toward it.

I don't want to die, I don't want to die.

There was a decision to be made, I just knew it. I think that is why I said the words. I was telling the light I didn't want to go because I had the feeling that I wanted to live and be **me** longer.

As everything was occurring, it seemed like lifetimes were passing in a split second. I can't explain that clear enough. It was like I had all the time in the world, but yet everything that happened, every word I said, and everything I was feeling was done in a split second. A snap of my fingers. Then it was calm; I was all right with whatever decision was made in that split second. It was like a dream.

It's not really happening to me, it's a dream.

The next thing I registered, was that I was back on the cold November ground, in the middle of the road, lying on my back. Still.

To this day I can recall exactly how my body bounced: first off my head then onto my back. If I close my eyes, I can feel it almost exactly, like muscle memory but there is no visual scene from my eyes that plays. The scene that plays through my memory is purely physical.

When I think about the whole event, I realize I must have been out a little while because when I opened my eyes and looked around, there were people everywhere, including police and an ambulance. My mind raced to panic, and I got up, and started to run. I apparently processed pretty quickly that I had no business being in that bar in the first place. That thought coupled with what I can only assume was a state of shock, gave me the idea to make a run for it.

Everyone around me knew better, as I was grabbed and kept down. People were talking but no words were registering. Apparently, no one else thought about the fact that I was in a bar (it was a college town, and I assume it was to be expected). The main focus was keeping me still because surely there were a lot of internal injuries. There was no way of telling the extent of my injuries. But it was strange, there was no blood.

I was rushed to the hospital by ambulance.

At the hospital, I must have been thoroughly examined, but I do not remember a single thing of their examining me, nor the ambulance ride, nothing. Tests were run, yet I have no clue which ones. The only way I knew I was at the hospital for a long time was that I can recollect when I arrived back to my dorm. It was the next morning, and we left the bar around 7-8 p.m. the previous night. I don't even know who came to pick me up and take me back to the dorm.

What I do remember was the choice to call my parents. Being eighteen, I had the choice whether or not to tell my parents. I could never keep anything from them. I was always an open book. Some kids that age might have thought that was a "get out of jail free card" but I didn't. Besides, wouldn't bills come home for them? There was no reason not to tell them other than trying to save them from worry, but honestly, I needed my family and their support. As the realization of what just happened began to seep in, I started to feel a little anxiety, and I knew I needed and wanted my parents. The need for them even overruled the thought that they might be disappointed in me. I made the call.

A scratch on my ankle (which didn't even draw blood and didn't require even the tiniest of Band-Aids), a concussion, and shock were all I the injuries sustained from that accident. To be honest, I don't even recall anyone telling me about a concussion or shock. Many years later, I concluded that that was the case when reviewing how my parents handled me the following days. They drove to Rhode Island to be with me. When they arrived at my dorm, they took me to a hotel where we spent the next two days. They let me rest and sleep and they watched over me. I was a little achy.

It was all like a dream.

My friends told me they thought I was dead, and the police couldn't believe I'd survived. I never saw the car, the driver, or anything else about the scene of the accident. Again, it all happened like I was dreaming.

So many people felt the need to share other accidents they knew of that were less severe than mine, where the people did not survive. I was truly grateful to be alive , but I couldn't help but wonder, *Why me?*

I had not processed the magnitude of what had happened to me and to my body—that fun November evening went astray. The honest truth is, I had never really taken the time to analyze all the minute details that occurred that night—the passage of time, the bright nearly blinding lights, the police, the brief time I thought I was dead, and the sheer depth of dying but then really being whole.

The magnitude of what occurred that evening was understated. I didn't write or wax on about how lucky I was. I knew it, straight up, and I thanked God and my angels, over and over for the next few days, weeks, and months, but I was also sort of numb by it. As if being saved that night meant not only was I not supposed to die, but there was more for me to do by living.

That's a lot to process at 18.

It was clear that I was not supposed to die, but I wondered if I ever really had a choice. Or was my chanting that I didn't want to die heard by God? Will He tell me what I am supposed to do on earth? Yeah, it was all too much, and I had more 18-year-old things to experience, so I placed it neatly in the category of God being with me and the angels saving me, somehow. I knew God would continue to take care of me. I didn't dwell on anything, or lament. I was grateful.

It wasn't until many years later that I began to think about the accident as a true near-death experience. I never called it that when it happened. I always called it "the night I was saved," or "the night the angels saved me." I suppose it is the same thing. Someone asked me, not too long after the accident, if it was a near-death experience and I couldn't answer them. I didn't know very much about near-death experiences at the time. I had no reference point, just some random things I'd heard. It was unclear to me what it meant, and what the person had to go through to have it be called that.

"Did Jesus sit with you?"

"Were there deceased loved ones greeting you?"

"Did you see heaven?"

"Did you hear a voice telling you to go back?"

I had no clue how to answer any of the questions people asked me about it, and since I didn't know or experience those exact things, I assumed it wasn't a near-death experience (NDE). I was content with the knowledge that I was saved.

It comforts me now to know,
"And there is nothing that the power of God cannot do."
~ Lesson 38, paragraph 2, line 3, page 58, *A Course in Miracles*

I was not ready, apparently, at this young age to understand the depth of my experience. Knowing about the angels and all that I learned from my Catholic upbringing was my great comfort (along with my family) at many times, and this car accident was no exception. Since I remained devote throughout college, attending mass every Sunday, and even teaching religious instruction when I was in my third year of college (and later in my adult life as well), I had a good working knowledge of my religion. I viewed God pretty much the way I was taught. Simply put, God is my Heavenly Father and Jesus is His only Begotten Son. Jesus died for us all—to save us. I knew I could always rely on them for assistance, all I needed to do was pray. As I heard most of my life, God would never give me more than I could handle, and that God would take care of my needs.

I knew they were there for me but is it normal for regular people to be saved from death? I didn't know, I didn't lose sleep thinking on it. Have you ever had a certain calm about something that happened? Like it is just there and you're not sure why, but you feel fine with being safe, calm, and reassured all is well? That was how I felt about that experience. I was truly calm about being saved; it was all right by me. Pondering the why of it all did not plague me.

My knowledge of God and the faith I had in my youth was of a loving God, who was my Father. But I thought He was outside of me, doling out the good and the bad. After all, He was God. This would all take on a completely different meaning decades after. There was no way of knowing yet, that when I did finally know the truth about myself and the wonder of God, it would change my life forever and the change would be amazing. Life saving.

"I AM *not* your intellect and body, and this Message is to teach that *You and I are One.* The words I herein speak, and the main burden of these instructions, is to awaken your consciousness to this great fact. You cannot awaken to this fact until you can get away from the consciousness of this body and intellect, which so long have held you enslaved. You must *feel* Me *within,* before you can *know* I AM there."

~ Joseph Benner, *The Impersonal Life*

It wasn't until later in my life that the true physical effect of this car accident presented itself, and the realization that it was truly a near-death experience that did happen that night.

"You already know I mean you no harm and would lead you from injury if you would so let me. It is now that I ask you to surrender to guidance in any form. You asked for a road map. I have provided it in faith. This leads you to where you need to go because no matter what you do to distract from it, I will lead you back. I need not lay out guidelines for you because your task is forgiveness in faith. Faith is who you are. Faith is my message, my Word. Faith in our God. Our Father. All that I lead you to was and is meant for the highest good. The journey is rich with rewards of God's loving bounty. Reach up to his level to know this bounty. Do not sink down to understand it other. For I see that agenda, and it does not serve Me."

~ From *Meditations with Jesus and Jen*

Relationship [rəˈlāSH(ə)nˌSHip]

noun

relationships (plural noun)

the way in which two or more concepts, objects, or people
are connected, or the state of being connected.

*Relationships were central to my life. They made my
humanness bearable, they brought so much happiness even
through the physical pain.*

*Friendships, family, the need for love, the need for connection,
finding my forever partner . . .*

CHAPTER 4

Relationships New and Old

"Some people arrive and make such a beautiful impact on your life,
you can barely remember what life was like without them."
~ Anna Taylor

"Ohhh no, Jen, that was alllll youuuu! You did that, Dice, not
this Jen." We were both Jen and only one of us was "Dice."

Ugh. I turned to my friend, the sweet girl I met in my business
101 class who quickly became a my sidekick, like wherever we went,
we went together. She swung her sleek and smooth bobbed hair
and pursed her perfectly lined and matted, mauve colored lips, her
signature, at me and burst out laughing.

Yep, after one-and-half years in Rhode Island, I decided to go
home and attend college back in Long Island in the middle of the fall
semester. I was always homesick—plain and simple—and I made the
decision and the move fast. The high phone bills and money spent on
travel were solid proof. Through those years, I noted how often I left
Rhode Island to go home or to be with my old friends.

Even though I might have enjoyed the college experience, it
was never more powerful than what I had at home. If there was a

party going on at my parent's house, I would catch a plane home. If my best friend from high school was having a party at her college, I would drive the five plus hours to be there. If I was missing the home cooked meals, I would freeze my tail off and take a bus to my parents' house.

Remember I mentioned this other reason for going home—that gut feeling that would not go away? Well, it was like I was going home for something other than fulfilling my need for family. I tried to ignore that nagging feeling and chalked it up to missing my family. I made excuses to everyone at college that the university back home had a better business program. I didn't feel comfortable telling my friends that I missed my parents. There was also an unnamed "something" that I couldn't explain, calling me home. I no longer wanted to miss out on family time. I just couldn't completely ignore the feeling that something else was waiting for me back home. I knew I wouldn't find it in Rhode Island.

NICKNAMES, NEW FRIENDS, AND THE REASON I CAME HOME

Apparently, my ability to volley a few jokes (more on the masculine side) the weekend before had these guys comparing me to the brash and offensive comedian of the 80's, Andrew Dice Clay. Hence, the nickname "Dice". I was not as bad as all that! But they must have thought it was funny that a "chick" could spar with them and not be too delicate to get offended.

So I was hanging my head out the window from the 10th floor of my friends dorm room, and I shouted, "Hey, where are you guys going?"

"Why don't you come down here and find out?" the group of guys answered. "It's hard to see who you are from down here. Oh wait, is that you, Dice and Jen? The two Jen's come on down!"

Oh boy, I was caught. Yeah, that was me. They remembered me from last weekend at the local bar we all went to right off campus. We had a rousing conversation where I threw in a quick "fogettaboutit" to a suggestive overture one guy tried on me, and then we all laughed it off. That was the moment I gained the name Dice.

I was just being me, wide open. Let me explain. We were at the bar the weekend before—it was smokey and loud. As I was weaving and bobbing through the crowd searching for my girlfriends, I felt a hand on my ass. *That can't be . . . oh yes, it is a hand.* It was squeezing! *Oh no, you didn't*, I thought as I whirled around to face my accoster.

Standing right behind me was a guy, not much taller than me, who was stumbling on his drunken words and spewing vulgar things. Okay words, who cares, but the hand, no freaking way.

I responded quickly, "Hey breast feeder, get your hands off my ass or I will break them!" I heard guffaws behind me where a group of guy friends were walking up.

"Holy shit! That was awesome! You just called him a breast feeder. I am so using that one!"

I squeezed my eyes shut. I couldn't erase that moment. I couldn't throw those words back in my mouth, but I sort of thought that guy needed it. The likelihood of him remembering it was next to zero, but the group remembering it, hell yeah, I could live with that.

That was pretty much how the fun began at my new college. I commuted, which was around 40 minutes from my family home, and on the weekends, I stayed in my friend's dorm room. Life was just a flow of activity. Like the young often do, we grabbed at every opportunity for fun while walking that fine line of balance with grueling hours of study and classes. For me it was a bit harder with the commute, juggling my work schedule, and being a volunteer teacher at church during the week. I loved doing it because I felt like I had the best of both worlds with all that college fun and being with my family too. I rarely missed a class and I was doing pretty well.

At least I thought I did well in college until my kids found my college transcript while we were looking through one of my memory boxes. They shuddered in horror that I could accept a C+ in a class. Being high achievers and excellent students, the fact that I said I was a good student and they saw evidence to the contrary, made my declaration null and void. I told them that grade *was* good for how hard that class was. They disagreed. I was glad they had higher expectations of themselves and their work.

I kept it to myself for a few more years that I was darn proud of the C+, in what I thought was a hard class—while socializing and extracurricular things, which more than likely wasn't as balanced as I had hoped. I absolutely went to class and did my work, but nowhere to the standard that they upheld. I let them hold onto their high bar of achievements and when they were nearer to college age, I had the talk about maintaining a good balance in the face of all the new and exciting fun.

Going out every weekend was so much fun, but I began to feel a little empty at times. I knew it was about time to have a real relationship. You know the phrase "you have to kiss a lot of frogs to find your prince?" Yeah, well, I was over it! I had kissed A LOT of frogs and threw them right back into the pond. I wanted to go on dates and have an adult relationship, and it was time to grow up in that respect. No one I had met or ever dated was that special someone.

I did what I normally did when I was faced with something that

I wanted, I asked God to send me an angel. This earth angel would be my partner. Someone who would accept me as I was because I just couldn't see myself changing my personality for anyone. Someone who would love all the parts of me - I was loud and loyal, and 100% Jen, so He better find me someone real special. I knew it would come to be; I let it go and carried on.

November 8, 1988, I met my husband—I was back home at my new school. Actually, we knew each other vaguely, through mutual friends, who later arranged for us to really hang out that one fateful night. They love to take credit for the serious long-term relationship and our eventual marriage.

My boyfriend (future husband) became the balance that I was craving and could not name. He was the "something" I came back to Long Island for.

I love the story of how we became a couple. Every detail is etched in my mind. I might not be able to find my datebook or my keys at times, but that day I remember.

On that particular Friday morning, I was walking from the parking lot, heading toward campus for a late morning class. I passed the dorm where all my friends lived as I was cutting through the parking lot, taking the shortest route. I looked to the left when I caught a movement. It was a guy carrying a laundry basket, wearing a brown bomber jacket and a baseball cap. I was struck with a bit of *Woowzee! That guy is really cute!*

He had the brightest eyes that really stood out against the scruffiness of his face. *Super cute*, I thought. We were nearing each other, as he was heading for the dorm. As I got closer, I stood there shocked. *I think I know this guy. Yeah, I do, he's a friend of a friend.* So, I said, "Hey" to him, all cool and casual like, when inside I was really thinking *what the heck?!* How could I have overlooked how cute he was for the last two months?

He said, "Hey, Jen." We parted, and I walked away shaking my head in confusion. When I got to class, where two of my good friends were, I said, "Guys . . . Fred is hot!"

The two of them were really close friends with him, since they all lived in the dorm. They would get together to party in the dorm and sometimes just hang out and talk. They were both so surprised that I said that. They exclaimed, talking over each other, but saying basically the same thing, "Fred? Our Fred? What? Tell us!" They were so excited to hear the story, so I told them exactly the play by play, and not leaving out how cute I thought he was. They were freaking out, and I could sense that they were already working up something as I watched the wheels turning in my one friend's eyes.

They told me that just the other night, they were hanging out talking, and he was telling them that he wanted a girlfriend. He missed dating and having that one person. I told them to stop whatever plan they were hatching, and told them not to act immature. You know, we were so mature at 20 and all. When I got to the dorm later that evening to have a drink with my friends before heading downtown, I walked into my two "scheming friends" plan. They set me up. There were about five guys and Fred, along with a few of my girlfriends all crammed into this room, playing drinking games.

We have been together ever since that night. Friendships and relationships are so important, and definitely integral to me. But this relationship was even more so, a huge part of me.

And let me tell you, it was a really good thing I listened to my mom before our first "official date" because we might not have been, if I let my thoughts carry me away. Here I was asking God to send me an angel and when Fred showed up, I thought, he was too good to be true. Remembering all the guys that came before him and who were less than stellar, I told my mom my misgivings. "He's too nice!"

My mother looked at me like I was an alien. She asked me if that was the sole reason for my hesitation with him. I told her it was. She was amazed that I would give up a chance to have a possible relationship with a nice guy because he was *too nice*!

I had a great time that Friday night. Fred was so attentive and sweet. It was all too good to be true. But Mom had a valid point. She said, "Give the date a try. You might be surprised." She reminded me that I *had* wanted to date a nice guy. "Don't ruin it with by overthinking it." What a smart little mommy I had. I gave it a chance and found out that he was the real thing. He came to the door and met my parents and the rest is history.

He took me to restaurants, plays in Manhattan, and he attended our family weekend dinners and any parties my folks had. We also spent time as college students, hanging out with friends with and without each other, studying, and getting our degrees. We truly enjoyed dating and he became my best friend. He was a Catholic also, and he attended mass with me whenever he was with me on Sunday. This clicked a box on my invisible serious relationship list because this was part of me, my faith.

We both graduated (a semester apart) and started adulting by getting jobs in our own home states—him in New Jersey and me in New York. The next four years we added some serious mileage to our respective cars. I was the tender age of 25 years old when he asked me to marry him.

He was the most supportive person I could have asked for. As I mentioned I had always wanted to be an actress. I saw visions of it dancing around in my head. I took acting classes in Manhattan. I was told by an agent once, that I was too New York. I guess with my thick curly hair, olive skin, and accent, I *was* pretty New York. I laughed about that years later when so many people were being cast for that exact stereotype, and I was too much of it.

I didn't have an agent, but I went to an open call once and got the job. I was in an STS commercial, and I was so proud of myself. I guess my Yankee was just the right mixture for them. That part of my life was fun and interesting, but what really stood out for me was that I had found a partner in life who was equally as proud of me. I truly knew there was great value in that. I was a lucky girl to have found this person to be in my life. He accepted all of me.

A PERFECTLY IMPERFECT WEDDING

"Remember that no one is where he is by accident,
and chance plays no part in God's plan."
~ ACIM, pg. 26 *Manual for Teachers*

We had our magical wedding in September of 1993. It was a wonderful big Italian wedding full of fun, amazing food, family, and great memories. There was an ice sculpture shaped like a circular stair (in honor of my father's craft and our family business), and on the very top stood a cream-colored statue of a bride and groom embracing. It was like a fairy tale for me, all decked out, in the current trend of 90's flare. I wish I could say that it went off without a hitch. Ah, but alas, my body issues did not take the day off just because I was getting married.

Before I arrived at the church, I had taken my beautiful princess-style wedding gown off four times. My father put his foot down in the limousine when I requested to make a pit stop on the way to the church. He emphatically refused my request to pull the stretch limo into the cramped back parking lot of our favorite Greek restaurant so that I could pop into the back hallway really quick (where I knew the bathrooms were located). Despite the gown removal, distraction of the body, before, during, and after the actual wedding ceremony, and the slight nerves about the magnitude of the foreverness of matrimony, I was still overjoyed by our marriage.

The beautiful old stone church in my family's parish was the most ideal place to get married. One thing I didn't take into consideration was the heat, and the lack of efficient air conditioning in the older building. There were a few wilting flowers, like many of the guests. My wedding party was trying to hold it together, all except for our best man. He sweat so much that it looked like flop sweat; you know the kind of sweat when someone is anxious or nervous in front of people and the sweat literally pours off them in sheets. Yeah, he looked like he was going to drown in all that sweat and my fiancé/ almost husband, was struggling to hold in the laughter each time he looked his way. That helped with my nervousness. I didn't feel the heat because all of my attention was on either the best man, the priest, or my future husband, as I attempted to be calm.

He would every once in a while, quietly whisper that everything was okay or that I was okay. I felt so much better when he spoke to me in his soothing tone. I learned, after the ceremony, that my father had sent someone out to the pharmacy to get smelling salts, and he made my husband keep them in the breast pocket of his tux because they were all convinced I wasn't going to make it through the entire ceremony standing upright. Geez, I didn't think I was that bad! Wasn't it normal to be nervous about getting married? How was everyone else so calm?

Flashback

6-Year-Old Jen

I wake up excited. I'm in my own bed. Mom and Dad went to a wedding last night and we went to our aunt's house while they were gone. They must have picked us up from their house late last night because I don't know how I magically got in my own bed.

I pull back the covers and run to the kitchen, in search of the one thing I love the most. They bring this gift for my brother and me every time they go to a wedding. Here they are! I eye them so greedily. I don't think I can wait for someone to wake up. I won't get in too much trouble if I just have one of these pastel colored almonds. The temptation is too great, after all this is my most favorite thing in the whole big wide world. They know this, that's why I think I will be safe. I'll just have one.

I place one in my mouth and suck on the crunchy shell. I close my eyes because it is so delectable, I have to savor it. But it's like that lollipop commercial I always see on TV, where they can't wait to get to the center, the sweetness must be mixed with the almond center. Crunch. The sweetness in my mouth along with the flavor of almond is my favorite. Gosh, I love weddings. I cannot wait for mine because this is what everyone will eat all night long. Maybe, I won't even have food! Just these wedding almonds and CAKE!

That night was everything I'd ever dreamt of when I thought of what my wedding would be! And more than just almonds and cake, but those were there too. That night hit it all. We had around 150 guests who enjoyed the meals and danced the night away. I remembered thinking that if I had to do it over, I would have chosen for us to be part of the cocktail hour because I knew what we had picked out for them to eat, and I was missing it.

When I expressed that I would rather be downstairs enjoying the food and fun instead of taking pictures, one of the staff brought us some food, but there was little time to eat it and no time to enjoy the full seafood smorgasbord that was set out for our guests. All that glorious food . . . and all without me. Dammit! I love good food!

SOMETHING OLD, SOMETHING NEW

"What a dream, Fred! It was the most magical night. It was everything I ever wished for," I said, while chatting with Fred as we changed into our after-wedding outfits. I was excited to wear my white pant set to the post party in my parents back yard and pool area. I was so happy they threw that party because no one wanted the reception to end. My parents went all out as usual. Fred and I laughed—they really do love to host a party. We both agreed that we wanted to thank them again for all that they had given us. We rushed outside as soon as we were done dressing to talk and hang out with our wedding guests. After several hours of more fun and festivities, we saw it was time to get to the hotel so we could sleep and catch our flight to our honeymoon.

We went in search of my parents. His parents left a little earlier since they were heading back to New Jersey. We'd thanked them for all they'd done for us, promising to call when we got back from our honeymoon.

The moment I saw my parents, I was frozen in place. They were walking toward us, and they knew it was time for us to leave. We were standing in the driveway, lined with bright lights, so we could see each other very clearly. I was thinking, *I will never forget this moment; it will be etched in my mind forever as the time I leave all that I have ever known of unconditional love and safety.*

Tears began to fill my eyes, and I took a deep breath in a futile attempt to prevent them from falling. I tried to paste a brave smile on my face. If I started crying, God only knew when I would stop. It would not be pretty. I could tell my parents had mixed feelings of being overjoyed for us, but they were trying to push down their sadness.

Looking into Dad's eyes, I saw that he was holding back the same tears as I was. Oh boy, that's it. I tried to speak; I couldn't get anything out. I stumbled and I stuttered on my words, because what I wanted to say was, "Noooo! I don't want to go! I don't want to really grow up and be married! I don't want to not call this my home anymore!"

What I said instead was, "I don't want to go! I don't want to be married." The tears flowed in earnest. My hours old, brand spanking new husband tried to make light of it by saying, "Ah, gee thanks. What every new husband wants to hear."

My parents were both sniffling now, hugging me telling me that it was a big day, with lots of emotions and excitement, a little bit of church drama, and a lot of changes, but it would all be alright. They reminded me that this is what I wanted, and how much I had been looking forward to this day—the day I would call myself Fred's wife. I heard what they were saying, and I knew it was true, but there was still this part of me that wanted to stay that little girl, who lived in this house with my entire family, and sleep in her childhood bed.

I knew there would be changes that were good, but the life I knew and the closeness I had with my family would change once I left that driveway. I knew that was what the next step in life would be, but right then I didn't feel very logical. I felt very "whack-a-doodle" and emotional. The next step felt so difficult.

In that moment all these thoughts flooded me at once. They were crashing down on me like a 2x4 as I was standing there on the sloped driveway, among the lights and decorations, shining and lighting up the background. *Did I make the right decision? I am madly in love with this man. I want to live with him and start a family with him, but I can't move from my family, hell even off this driveway!*

In my heart I knew that I could not ever live without my husband. He really was my other half, but leaving my family felt so gut-wrenching. I wanted my husband, yet I wanted to stay the same.

I needed a few moments of being enveloped in my parents loving arms; sharing my words of love, gratitude for the life I was given, and thanks to them that words really couldn't express. I let them go and stepped into my new life.

I walked to our car, tears still flowing, knowing I would make it all work. I needed my family in my life still, I just needed Fred and our new life more. I knew that. After all, God and the angels orchestrated us together. I would be alright. I was so grateful for them. For their love. For my life. I was saying goodbye to one part of me and opening the gateway to another.

I love(d) being married. It was an adjustment to live closely with another person, and having that person be a boy person was harder still. It helped that I was in love. The adjustment of cohabitating with a male was expressed in my first book I ever wrote called, *My Pet Peeves*. It was a joke and I never published, but it chronicled the things I noticed when living with someone else. But pet peeves didn't hinder our life any as we began to carve out life as a married couple. All felt right with the world; as Jen, just herself and as Jen, the wife.

I continued to work at my father's business, which had moved to Brooklyn, and I commuted into New York City for acting classes once a week. On all the other days of the work week, my husband and I went to the gym together after work. Then we went back to our cute little apartment in Long Island and made fun home-cooked meals. Weekends were for friends or family visits. I was in the groove of the married life.

"In this dream, you use the body as a tool to allow the expression of LOVE to shine to all. All living things will feel the vibration of love."
~ From Meditations with Jesus and Jen

PART TWO

My Brokenness

brokenness [ˈbrōkənəs]

noun

> having been fractured or damaged and no longer in one piece
> or in working order.

Brokenness: that part of you that is full of shame, is lost, is feeling unworthy.

Brokenness: that part of you that sees yourself as irrevocably damaged. That no amount of help can bring you the peace that you long for or that could be the needed balm to your soul. Brokenness is the part of you that can't hear past the pain, and that tells you that you are incapable of being loved.

Fear ['fir]

noun

an unpleasant emotion caused by the belief that someone or something is dangerous, likely to cause pain, or a threat.

Fear is the belief that you are not safe, you can be attacked, you are alone and separate.

CHAPTER 5

Learning Fear

"To live is to suffer, to survive is to find some meaning in the suffering."
- Friedrich Nietzsche

"Jen! Is this for real? Does that say what I think it says?"

We'd been married about 9 months when we found out by way of a drugstore pregnancy test that we were going to become a family of 3! Of course, I had to confirm it for real. When I went to the doctor, it was not as simple as I'd imagine confirming a pregnancy would be. I had to go back a few times in the beginning without any real understanding as to why. I was so green to this stuff, newlywed and all. Beaming with excitement, I would dress up for these doctor visits, and made a day of it.

I remember at one of the appointments, I was sitting in the office chair in my short skirt and a floral blouse. I bought this cute outfit when I worked at a small privately owned boutique. It was just a town over, and man, did that put a dent in my wallet. What can I say? I had a love for nice fabric, patterns, stitching. Well-made, eclectic, unique clothing was my jam. I was always willing to pay for something fun. I wore that outfit because this particular day was special. Smiling secretly to myself, I'd placed my hand on my belly, wondering how long it would be before I had a big round belly, and the outfit I was wearing would have to find a new place in my closet buried behind bigger outfits.

My foot was bouncing up and down. Trying to distract myself, I looked at the magazines piled on the table and thought that I would have so much to learn, once the doctor knew what was up with our little treasure. I figured the doctor would explain what was going on, why they were doing all the testing, and she would get to the bottom of what was happening with our little one. I trusted her.

Oh, and Fred. Fred was my prince charming, that's for sure. He was excited, loving, my rock. Have you ever read a love story or watched a romantic movie and gotten fully invested in the happy couple's life? I mean, I remember yearning for that when I was younger, but dismissing it. Like those stories could not be real, right? Just so full of love, so much so, that I would find myself getting a flitter-flutter in my stomach thinking about the joys of that kind of relationship! Well, I can say those love stories are true. Because, with Fred, that was the way I felt nearly every day, before and after we got married. I was living the life that I dreamt of with a great guy. It felt like we were in the prime of our lives and we were both loving it. Then, as I mentioned, around nine months into married life we found out this love story had a baby on the way. We were so young and carefree. I had no idea how much this would change our lives.

HAVING NO IDEA WHAT TO EXPECT WHEN EXPECTING AND GOING WITH THE FLOW

Let me backtrack a bit. We weren't trying to get pregnant. It wasn't something we were planning. There was no counting ovulation days going on here. I did go off of the pill once we were married, but I thought it took years to get pregnant.

Well one day, I was having lower stomach cramps, and they were pretty intense. They sort of reminded me of the menstrual cramps that I had when I was in my teens, before the doctor put me on birth control to help lessen their severity. And since I was off the birth control, I assumed these cramps were related in some way to that change and therefore had something to do with my cycle. After a week or more of these cramps I was wondering where my period was. I hadn't run across any problems since I came off the pill, but it hadn't been that long since I'd stopped either. After waiting for over a week, my period never came.

The weeks prior to this "mystery of the missing menses," I was sort of feeling blah. I was tired, but not to the point that it stopped my normal scheduled activities. What I was doing, which was totally out of the norm, was eating salt like a lunatic salt junkie. I even went as far as hitting the grocery store for Spanish olives, pimento and all; loading up on them like there was going to be a shortage in the near future.

After discussing my situation with some gals at work, then running it all by my husband when I got home that evening, we agreed, unquestionably, that we should go grab a pregnancy test and find out if we should celebrate or not. I ran up the street to the local CVS, came back home, and 30 minutes later was looking at a positive test in my hand. We were going to have a baby!

A little bit surprised, but extremely excited, I scheduled an OB/GYN appointment, where the doctor confirmed that I was pregnant. I told her about my symptoms of cramps and feeling tired and well, just all around yucky. She said these were all common symptoms experienced during pregnancy.

The doctor explained that she liked to perform a sonogram for newly pregnant moms so that we could see the baby and how tiny it was. I was excited to see this, although a little bummed out that my husband wasn't there to see too. The doctor reassured me there would be another opportunity in the future. She was a little confused by the absence of a fetus and the amniotic sac during the sonogram, but she did mention that it could simply be too early and for me not to worry. To be on the safe side, she had the nurse draw my blood that day to detect the level of the pregnancy hormone, HCG, in my system as pregnancy tests that use urine can only detect the presence of the hormone (by showing positive or negative) and not the hormones actual level. The doctor also scheduled for me to get a second blood test in two days (waiting 48 hours) to see the HCG level at that point as well. She thought scheduling the blood test at a lab would be easier and more convenient than at her office.

Now, I knew absolutely nothing about any of the terminology she was using. She didn't seem worried, so I wasn't worried. And, remember, there were no cell phones to perform an immediate check on the information that was given, like I would do today. We were in her office, just the two of us, she was throwing out some words, but was completely relaxed. I wasn't thinking there was a problem. I didn't bring a notebook to take notes. I was a young newlywed, excited about becoming a first-time mom. I did not question or check anything she said. Through everything she was saying, I was still glowing with excitement.

I wonder if that is why today, I am so reliant on checking information I am given, because I can remember, so vividly, the time when it was not available to me. In 1994, Google was not even a verb. I don't think the phrase, "I'll Google it" came about for years after. There wasn't a quick and easy internet computer search that I could do when I returned home. Researching the information that the doctor had mentioned would have required a trip to the library or me relying on someone else's knowledge.

I did recount the story to a few friends and family members. But as it turned out, no one that I spoke with in my family knew anything about the timing of the sonogram, HCG, or anything the doctor had mentioned that day. They did tell me about a book called *What to Expect When Expecting* that I could pick up at the bookstore for information throughout the pregnancy. I placed "run to the bookstore" on my mental to-do list right alongside of "trust the doctor" since I had no clue about the technicalities of pregnancy.

It never occurred to me to do anything other than what I was instructed to do. I assumed the tests were to help figure out how far along I was in the pregnancy. I felt no need to be concerned at this point because, although it was unchartered territory for me, it was also very exciting. I had zero details or facts about pregnancy, other than the obvious ones you pick up just from living life and being observant. My husband and I believed everything was good, and it was great news that we were pregnant with our first child.

Now that I had an explanation for my off the chart consumption of a wide variety of olives, it also solved another mystery that I hadn't figured out . . . the Burger King's chicken sandwich. I saw someone at work the week prior eating that sandwich, and could not for the life of me stop thinking about the damned thing. I had never had one, but it smelled so good and looked even better. So on the way home, I found myself in the drive-thru of Burger King. Needless to say, during that week, I went from having never ordering at Burger King (much less a drive-thru) to someone who had learned all the dos and don'ts of drive-thru ordering! I guess this would be right in line with what people meant when they said they had cravings during pregnancy.

As the days moved along, I noticed that I was dizzy very often, so darn tired, and I was feeling increasingly yuckier with each passing day. I guessed those were more of those pregnancy symptoms that I didn't know much about, but was confident that I would learn everything I needed to know once I bought that book.

SOMETHING IS OFF, WAY OFF . . .

A few days after my second blood test at the lab, I got a call from the doctor's office, and the nurse asked me to go back to the lab and repeat the blood test. So, I left work a little earlier that day to get the blood drawn and headed home afterward. I set an appointment with the doctor for a few days later. At that appointment, she just simply explained the purpose of so many blood tests was to detect the actual levels of HCG hormone in order to determine how far along in the pregnancy I was. To me, that made sense. I was never given any results, and besides, even if I was given them, it wasn't like I would know what they meant anyway. Even though there wasn't a great amount of detail and explanation, I trusted her and her process. I relied on my doctor to know all the details. After all, she was the medical professional.

At that follow-up appointment, she asked me how I was feeling, and I told her honestly, I was feeling increasingly crappier. Again, she said it was all normal symptoms for pregnancy. The doctor told me to return to the lab and have more blood drawn as it was part of the process of detecting levels and timeline. She said she wasn't yet confident that it was a "viable pregnancy." But, she delivered that message kindly, not overly dramatic, and so that was how I took it. I was just listening, wide eyed.

In my heart, I knew the baby was coming—I had morning sickness and all the early pregnancy stuff. That was when a little radar started to go off. No, it wasn't blaring "red alert," but it did bring something into my attention that was not there even just moments prior. Calmly, matter-of-factly, in the casual conversation-like tone my doctor used, she continued to tell me that it was possible that the pregnancy might abort on its own. But in the very same breath, she told me not to worry, and that we would have better answers after a few more blood tests.

My brain felt a bit of a ping pong match going on. Viable or not viable? Healthy or not healthy? Carry this baby or a miscarriage was coming? But, instead of buying into worry, I followed my doctors lead, and decided this was no big deal. The baby was fine, they were just being overly precautious. She arranged for me to have several more lab appointments to draw blood over the course of the following week. I felt like Norm from *Cheers* because I became really familiar with the lab and the employees. Since the pregnancy was confirmed, in just a few short weeks, I had gone to that lab for bloodwork 12 times!

But, when I had a quiet moment to sit and think about this pregnancy possibly not being healthy, I remember feeling a great deal of sadness. Even though we weren't trying to get pregnant per say, once I found out I was pregnant with this little one, I felt even more bonded to Fred. He always looked at me always with so much love, but I felt it even more so, if that was possible. I was so ready, and really looking forward to being a mom and starting our family. It was a neat feeling to be included in the time-honored group of pregnant women, where we all have similar symptoms and are part of the amazing experience of aiding in the growth of a new life.

I was having conversations on a whole new level with friends who had babies. But, as much as I wanted to be as excited as I pumped myself up to be, I was not looking at tiny baby clothes, the adorable soft shoes and socks, planning out what the nursery would look like, having conversations with my belly, and I still was not shifting into full on "nurturing mode". Inside, I was scared. I was sad thinking that the little one growing inside me might not make it. But I'm not sure I believed it fully; the sadness didn't run so deep that it made me depressed, like so many women who have miscarriages. It was more of a quiet sadness when I was alone and in my head.

Besides, all of this going back and forth to labs and doctor visits, while feeling so sick, was very confusing. I was being introduced to a new part of me~the part of me that felt broken. I desperately wanted to nurture and help grow a healthy life, but I couldn't help but wonder that maybe this baby was ill, just like I felt.

From the first second of finding out about that pregnancy, it was shrouded in surprise and confusion. Even my first visit to the doctor never clarified anything other than confirming I was pregnant. We seemed to be in "investigation" mode the entire time. While the prospect of losing the baby was very sad, I knew there was a possibility of an unhealthy pregnancy not surviving to become a healthy and thriving child. So, I had to wait.

HCG, A D&C, AND PAIN BEYOND BELIEF

Before that pregnancy, I'd never even heard the term HCG. Now it was all I could think about, mainly because they were testing my

HCG levels so often. And that number held the fate of my little one. So, yeah, I began to put a lot of stock in it. In the 1990s, it was believed that the level of HCG in a pregnant woman's blood should be double when tested after 48 hours. Today, it is thought to be more accurate to look at the numbers doubling in 72 hours. There are ranges for this hormone during specific weeks of pregnancy. Based on my last cycle, my numbers should have been anywhere from 7,600-29,000 mIU/ml and rising. Again, I had no knowledge of any of the facts about pregnancy hormones and their role in a healthy baby until much later. I just knew mine were being tested often, and I wasn't seeming to pass.

After another week of ongoing blood tests, I returned once more to the doctor's office. And after another sonogram, where we still couldn't see the sac, the doctor concluded that the numbers were not rising in the manner and pattern they should with a healthy pregnancy. It was presumed I was around seven weeks pregnant. The doctor said the only option was to have a D&C (also called a dilation and curettage procedure where the cervix is dilated so the uterine lining can be scraped to remove abnormal tissue) to remove any part of the pregnancy that remained and which she had determined was not viable nor healthy.

We were so sad that the pregnancy didn't take, but since it all happened so fast, I was more stunned, confused, and very disappointed. But I had this slight thread of understanding that helped me to hold it all together. I hadn't even purchased my book yet.

I scheduled the D&C and was kind of in disbelief mode. Going from imagining my belly growing to removing the unviable pregnancy in just a matter of weeks threw me into a little tailspin. We were a family of three for a blip, but for most of that blip, I was confused and in pain, and now sad. In the days leading up to the D&C procedure, I got sicker and sicker. I was tired all the time—I truly had zero energy. I was sleeping pretty much 24-7 at this point. On top of that, I was bloated, and the cramps got so much worse. The doctor, once again, chalked that all up to what was happening with the pregnancy.

A little less than a week passed, and I went in to have the D&C. After the D&C procedure was performed, she informed me that I would still not feel 100%, and many of the same symptoms would probably continue for a few days, maybe even a week. She said if it got much worse to call her. I felt as though it couldn't get much worse than feeling like total crap, so there's one upside. I was not able to go to work or drive, not only because of the outpatient procedure that I'd just gone through, but more because there was no way I could perform any task, much less drive a vehicle. I was asked to return to the lab for one more blood test two days after the D&C, and I needed someone to take me there.

I stayed at home in bed for those next two days. On the third day, Saturday, my husband and I had plans that we arranged months before. We were scheduled to go and meet with his parents for a great night with a fabulous dinner, and then off to see a play on Broadway.

Now, remember, growing up I dealt with pain and discomfort all the time. I was flexible, I made it work, and I never let my pain stop me. It just became a part of me I joked about. This brokenness I was beginning to feel was very unfamiliar. I didn't want to not be me. I didn't want to lie in bed missing out on life because of a little pain. That was never me before, and that sure as hell wasn't going to be me now. I was going to "Jackie-O" it all the way to the theater. Put my lipstick on and a gorgeous outfit, get out of my pity party head, and have a beautiful evening in New York City.

I gathered up as much oomph as I could to get dressed and get through the evening. I called for Fred to come into the bedroom to take a look at my stomach because I thought I saw some light-colored red dots, like a rash, and I wanted his opinion. He agreed that he saw a rash and wondered if it could be the same as the eczema that I always suffered from on my legs and occasionally my hands. This rash on my belly didn't itch and looked a little different than the one I was used to seeing on my legs. We agreed to just watch it to see if it changed or got any worse.

The energy that I was able to find was fueled only by knowing that I had my husband with me. He was always the strength I found myself depending on. Even though I really dreamed of nothing more than lying down and sleeping, I had him to help me carry on with that evening. Before this mess I was SO looking forward a night out in the city.

We drove to New Jersey to meet his parents, where we all took a ferry to a famous steak place before we headed off to see the play. I had absolutely no energy to enjoy anything and wasn't able to eat a bite. I could barely move, and the pain in my abdomen was so bad. The doctor told me I would continue to be uncomfortable, but I couldn't even determine if the pain was *more* uncomfortable, or if it was just pain compounded by grief over losing the baby. I had no barometer of the pain level. It was as if I had shut down and was on auto-pilot—moving and thinking like a zombie. What propelled me along was the fact that the doctor told me I might feel poorly, and that if there was any concern from the procedure or extra blood work they had drawn, that obviously she would have called me.

Not eating at dinner, and being limp and lifeless at the play, my husband was concerned and attentive. He asked me what he could do for me as he held on tightly to my hand. I assured him I was fine.

He saw that I fell asleep several times during the performance. One of my waking moments, he asked what was all over my face, but I had no idea what he meant because I hadn't looked at my face all evening. Hell, I hadn't moved from that theatre chair.

It seemed like the same rash that we saw earlier, on my stomach, was now on my cheeks, chin, and a little on my forehead. The bumps didn't itch. We had no explanation for that either, but we were really curious. We didn't have a tremendous amount of alarm because other than looking a sight, they didn't have a "feeling" to them. We assumed they must not be a horrible thing.

During intermission, my mother-in-law told my husband that she was worried about me. She had noticed the rash as well and asked if there was any bleeding. He told her there wasn't. My mother-in-law then used a term that I hadn't heard before, or if I had, I didn't really know what it meant. She said everything I had gone through and with these rash like dots on my body, I could have an *ectopic pregnancy*. She warned that if I started to bleed, it would be really bad, and I would need to go to the ER. My mother-in-law didn't jump immediately to rushing me off to the hospital, and in light of the fact that I just had that procedure, she thought she could be wrong, and it could all be related to the D&C.

My husband and I had no idea what an ectopic pregnancy was, but since I wasn't bleeding, surely it must not be that *thing* she just mentioned. We also chalked some of her concern up to being a bit paranoid since she was an EMT for over 20 years and we were family. We were also a little defensive of our naiveté and told his mother that if it was an emergency-level problem, surely the doctor would have told me to stay in bed. It brought us a touch of comfort that I was under the care of a doctor, and we mutually agreed that I would call the doctor on Monday if I was still feeling badly.

SILENT CRIES, AN ANGEL IN THE GAS TANK, AND APOLOGIZING TOO MUCH

That night I slept deeply from sheer exhaustion. The following day, I slept the whole way back to Long Island and stayed in bed for the remainder of the day and on into the night. Later on Sunday evening, while we were both asleep, I woke up suddenly with horrific stabbing pain. I felt like I needed to go to the bathroom, so I slowly stumbled out of bed and managed to get there. The bathroom was just across the hallway from our bedroom, but even that felt far. There was a lot of white noise in our tiny apartment. Being a hot summer night, we had a box fan on the floor and the A/C unit blasting on high in the bedroom window, plus there was added noise coming from my husband's snoring which required earplugs to drown out.

I situated myself on the toilet, and then tingling began. There was a numbness in my legs that made me feel as if I couldn't move from that spot, even if I had the energy to do so. The pain was killing me. I thought I was dying. In fact, I knew I was dying. Deep inside my being, I knew that if I couldn't get to my husband, and I couldn't move from that spot, that I would not make it.

My energy was completely zapped and I could not summon my voice above a whisper. I knew there was no way for him to hear me above all that noise, but I still tried. I said his name over and over, trying each time to breathe a bit deeper to put some force behind the whisper. I hoped and prayed that he would come to me so I could see him once more before I died. I wanted to tell him I was sorry that this had happened and that I had to leave him this way. I felt like I was losing consciousness. I felt desperate to see him, but that whisper was all that I could do.

Finally, Fred must have sensed something or heard my quiet cries for help, because he came running into the bathroom, shouting my name. He saw me and he looked so frightened. I told him I was in such horrible pain. We needed to call the doctor or go to the hospital right away. Although I was no stranger to pain, this was so much worse than anything I had ever experienced. He called the doctor's answering service, but deep inside, I thought I was going to die before we got anywhere. I couldn't share this feeling with him though; it just wouldn't have been fair to scare him further.

The doctor called him back immediately and told him to get in the car and rush to the hospital, where she would meet us. She told him not to call the ambulance because the time it would take for it to get to us may be too late, and she thought it would be faster if we drove ourselves. We quickly threw our shoes on, and Fred helped me to the car.

As Fred drove down the hill from our apartment, he saw the red glow of the low gas light blaring up at him. There was no way we could stop. Firstly, in 1994, on this stretch of road from Glen Cove, Long Island to North Shore University Hospital there were no all-night gas stations. And secondly, if there was one open, would we have been able to sacrifice those valuable minutes to put gas in the car if we were instructed by the doctor that we didn't even have enough time to wait for an ambulance?

Since Fred walked to the train station, just down the road from our apartment, for work, and I wasn't going to work Monday based on how I felt, there was no rush to fill the gas tank earlier that day. We thought we would just get it done sometime the following day. We only had that one car between the two of us. We never thought we would have needed the car in an emergency in the middle of the night. It also showed how we never thought or expected I was in this sort of danger.

The hospital was 30 minutes away from our apartment. There was no traffic at 2 a.m., so Fred sped well over the speed limit and we both silently prayed. Those valuable minutes flying down the road, seemed to be crawling by, further cementing in my mind the unrelenting thought that I would not make it.

Oh God, please let me make it before I die from this pain, whatever the hell it is! I hope that not any one of these single extra minutes isn't the one that would be one too many, but there is absolutely no way of knowing.

We were trying not to focus too much on the fear that at any moment the car would begin to sputter and stop, because if that happened, then it would all be over. The entire drive I continued reciting the mantra that I began in our bathroom, what seemed like hours ago. "I am okay. I am okay . . ." I was trying hard to convince myself.

When we got to the emergency room, literally against all odds (an angel must have gotten us here on that empty tank), we saw my doctor immediately upon arriving. She was standing behind the registration desk where she jumped into action and took me in a wheelchair, straight into the operating room. I was in the OR for over four hours.

What I had all along *was* an ectopic pregnancy in my left fallopian tube, and it burst. I had an emergency tubal ligation. I was eight weeks pregnant. The teary-eyed doctor told my husband that if it took us 15 more minutes, I would have bled to death. Had we been forced to stop because we ran out of gas, or had we been able to stop for the needed extra gallons to get us to the hospital, I would have died.

The following morning, when the doctor came into my room to check on me, I thanked her. I was so grateful to be alive, and I believed, at that time, that she saved my life. "Jen, you should have told me what you were feeling. This could have killed you." She scolded me and I shrunk into the hospital bed even more. She was actually angry with me, and so I apologized and thanked her again.

I *apologized* for something I had *no idea* I needed to report.

The pain was nothing different than what I had been telling her about all along, until whatever it was burst inside me. There I was, in the hospital, recovering from a near fatal pregnancy, and *I* said *I* was sorry! And I was. At that moment, I thought I should've known something horrible was happening. It hadn't computed yet that I had zero details or information, nor the education, to figure out what was going on inside my body. I only knew what I was told by the medical doctor who did have the education for this sort of stuff. I trusted that she would take care of me.

This part of me, of brokenness, of broken trust taught me the world was unsafe. I was not safe. I was the only one who could protect my body. Looking at the world through new eyes of fear was horrifying. It was like I woke up from the surgery and nothing could protect me from danger.

Remember in the *Wizard of Oz*, when Dorothy's house landed on the Wicked Witch, and she opened the door completely boggled by what had just occurred, scared of this new land far from home? That was me. I had to navigate this dangerous world with this broken body and it was terrifying.

TAKING "ONLY YOU, JEN" TO A WHOLE NEW LEVEL

After coming home from the hospital, there was not much else I could think about. I talked about the ectopic pregnancy, the weeks leading up to it, and everything in between over and over with my parents and my husband for days.

How did this happen?

Why did this happen?

Hell, it was more like—

What the "F (&^" happened?

That was the most excruciating experience, I was scared to death, and I wanted to make sense of it all. I needed to know what this all meant so that it never EVER happened to me again.

As you may recall, when I was growing up, and even leading up to that pregnancy, I experienced pain and medical stuff. Every time we would leave the doctor's office or I would have an embarrassing bathroom episode, it was always, "Only you, Jen." And we would shrug our shoulders. I would make jokes. I learned how to navigate my humanness even when it was hard. I had angels surrounding me when I needed them, too. I mean, I went through a near-death experience and still was not as fearful of the world as I was immediately following the four-hour tubal ligation.

It wasn't the procedure that made me afraid. It was my lack of control for what happened to me. It was me, naïve little me, putting 1000% trust in a doctor, and almost dying again because of it. And even though an angel got us to the hospital on time, and an angel amplified my voice so Fred could come running to the bathroom, I felt all alone. I couldn't feel their presence the way I had in the past. I went numb, and all I could feel was my broken body riddled with pain and worry that pregnancy could kill me.

New life could cause death.

Doctors could not be trusted.

These messages filled my mind, but I dared not speak them aloud.

I had to get to the bottom of why this happened to me. If I could solve that riddle, I could take back control of my body and my fate. I was learning fear in a whole new way. I was learning that my happy bubble was not enough to protect me from the dangers of this world. I could feel my shell cracking a little more each day. My perfect love story marriage had its first bit of tarnish. Although my husband was supportive beyond compare, what kind of wife was I, so broken that I could not have a healthy pregnancy?

Guilt and shame set in, along with growing fears and the need to take control. No one but me could protect me. And, of course, these things only happen to me. I had so many friends enjoying marriage, pregnancies, and family life. My pregnancy from the start was a ball of stress and confusion.

Only me, I thought.

And to top it off, Fred accepted another job and we had to move to New Jersey. I had to get us packed for the move, and the Jen I was before ectopic would have done this with love and excitement. I mark this period as "BE" (before ectopic) and "AE" (after ectopic) because of the distinct difference in how I reacted to the world AE. This newly discovered part of me, the broken part, was throwing our belongings in these boxes without any regard as to what was what. I was angry.

Why the F$#K do I have to pack right now?

All I wanted to do was crawl in bed and forget. I wanted to wake up and realize it was just a nightmare—I was the same, we were all good, nothing to fear. But, it wasn't. It was my reality. And I had to take our physical belongings, pack them up, and move them out. Well, let's just say there was zero love and care. Boxes were filled with a mish-mosh of stuff, no rhyme or reason. I remember pushing my wild, out of control hair from my face with a frustrated hand and looking at what I'd done.

Who did this? Why did I do this? Should I organize it so there is more order when I unpack?

I couldn't bring myself to care. I attempted to shake away the tears that were flowing in earnest down my face. I cared about very little at the moment. I was numb to the world except for two things:

1) I was leaving Long Island and moving to another planet— New Jersey, and;

2) I was almost murdered. The doctor had my life in her hands and forgot me without a backward glance . . . until she realized her grave, monumental mistake. *She almost killed me.*

I couldn't understand how I got to this place, and it seemed to happen so fast. Our things flew into the next box with a little more force than moments before. I reached deep inside, and tried to muster the courage to care, or at the very least be excited for Fred being closer to his job. The frustration that boiled inside me was being taken out on the belts I was hurling into boxes. How horrible was I to not want to leave Long Island to support my husband with a smile on my face? 3 days prior, I would've been more supportive. My head was again guilting me, shaming me.

Jen, you are the worst person. You are selfish. How could you feel this way?

I was being scolded by my thoughts, just like the doctor scolded me. Holding my head in my hands, I let the tears flow. I couldn't stop them. I couldn't do much of anything. Looking around at the bedroom that was our first as a married couple brought me zero joy. I would be leaving these walls that would always know the terror of that night. The next people to live in this space would not know what these walls and I knew—that Jen would never be the same.

THE NEED TO KNOW AND ANGER
REACHING NEW HEIGHTS

We moved to New Jersey exactly one week after I returned home from the hospital. That move had been planned well before any of the craziness happened in our lives. Every day, I would unpack a box or two, but what I did most of the day, was think a whole lot. My mind would spin with questions about the ectopic. My thoughts would banter back and forth, yelling at me for my stupidity in trusting a doctor with the pregnancy. How could I not know more about ectopic pregnancies and what really happened to me?

I hit the local library. I needed facts and I had to find them for myself. With each book I pulled out, my blood would begin to boil. I sat there in those uncomfortable wooden chairs for hours. I learned so much and none of it was pretty. Often times, I couldn't read the words on the pages through all the tears that welled up in my eyes. And those that weren't in my eyes, were falling down my face, soaking the collar of my shirt. I was a mess.

I made hundreds of copies of each and every detail I could find on the subject of ectopic pregnancies, pregnancy in general, fallopian tubes, and pregnancies after an ectopic pregnancy burst. I over worked that antiquated photocopy machine. The first glimpse I had of anger was nothing compared to the raging inferno of anger that I now felt, having uncovered all the facts. All I could see was red when I contemplated how the doctor could have let this happen to me. The facts were the facts; and there was a blatant disregard for my well-being. I was the victim of negligence, clear and simple. I nearly died as a result, and I was definitely different because of it.

In my quest for answers, I learned that ectopic pregnancy was the leading cause of maternal mortality in the first trimester, and accounts for 10%~15% of all maternal deaths. I sought out other doctor's opinions about my health and hoped they could give me good news about healthy future pregnancies. I was told, by a few different doctors, that it would be difficult to become pregnant with one fallopian tube—the chances were reduced by half. Also, I needed to be hyper vigilant with tracking my period and to be super aware of how I was feeling to avoid another ectopic pregnancy, since I now had a higher chance of another occurring.

As I absorbed all these facts about ectopic pregnancies, and thought about all I went through, I realized I didn't handle anything wrong. Ohhhhh, when I thought of the apology I gave to that doctor, I would vibrate with anger. I did the best I could with what little I knew, and all the fault lay at one person's doorstep . . . and it wasn't mine. As I learned more about pregnancy and ectopic pregnancy, I grew angrier and angrier.

All of the books pointed to the chances of a viable birth being greatly reduced after having an ectopic pregnancy. It seemed like I now had so many new things to battle with. So at the age of 26, I became solely dedicated to becoming a mom because everything was telling me that I wouldn't be able to become one.

I was angry and lost and I didn't like this new way I was looking at my life. I felt panicked about it all. So many people had brought up the topic of depression, and that I might be experiencing it. Many of my friends and family said that having depression would make sense after the loss of the baby. I heard their opinions but for some reason I didn't feel that that was an accurate way of describing me.

I wasn't sad, I was bitter. I was angry. I could put it aside enough to put on a "happy face," but I would always end up going down the rabbit hole of blame, and inside I just felt beaten down, broken, worn out, and abused. I wasn't thinking "poor me" or sulking in self-pity, although I guess I was learning what it meant to become a victim of my life because I would often find myself asking, "Why me?" or "Why do these things only happen to me?" or saying to myself, "Only you, Jen!"

DESPERATELY SEEKING SOMETHING

My husband and I agreed that it might be a good idea for me to talk to someone. I remember the very first evening I went to speak with the counselor. I went by myself because I felt it was something I had to do for myself, alone. It was just about dusk outside and the parking lot was pretty empty that time of night. I recalled sitting in her waiting room, wondering what to do since there was no receptionist to greet me. In the waiting area there were just a few cushioned chairs, a coffee table with a few old magazines, and a door to what I assumed was her office. Above all the musings about the space I found myself in, were the thoughts of why I was even there in the first place. *How and why am I in this position to begin with?* I thought.

The counselor did, in fact, come out of that one door, which opened directly into her room. I sat there in her comfortable office, in an extremely comfortable chair, where she talked to me about some stuff that was very uncomfortable, focusing mainly on the grief of losing a baby.

As she continued, it became very obvious to me that I was not grieving the loss of the baby, as she described. As soon as I learned that the pregnancy was not at all viable, my feelings of grief shifted. I grieved the "thought" of having a baby being gone, but in my mind, the formation of the baby never happened, so there was no baby to actually grieve. I know this may not sound rational, but I guess you can say my grief was overshadowed by anger and sadness; I felt anger towards the doctor for taking the joy of pregnancy away from me due to her negligence and sadness for the loss of being in control of my life. I felt like I lost my freedom.

I explained to her that my choice was taken away from me. I was right there all along with that doctor every step of the way. I was part of everything, but I didn't have a say in anything because I wasn't knowledgeable enough or even aware of what was happening to me. She was, though, and I almost died.

I expressed that I would continue to suffer, every single day as I tried to have a baby. I remember saying to the counselor, "Every month I will wait for my period with anticipation and anxiety, and I will have to think about its results for all the other days. If my period is a day late, I will suffer all over again with thoughts and pleading, "Oh please Lord, this cannot happen to me again."

"And late at night I will pray and, in my praying, I will ponder the same question, over and over, 'Why did this happen to me?' This is not how I want to live my life, but I don't have a choice. This was the hand I was dealt at the hands of a doctor who just didn't give a crap about the peripheral damage of her neglect." I took a deep breath as if all the air was being let out of a balloon that almost burst into flames.

In her tiny office with no windows, I purged all the feelings I felt about what I'd lost. I also shared with her the strong feeling and driving need to prove all those doctors and the statistics wrong and become pregnant with a healthy baby. It was what gave me strength to move forward but also it kept me stuck in my mind, in my thoughts, and trapped in a body that was a mess. And being in my mind was being stuck in a tunnel that was focused firmly on loss, life, pain, and even death.

You see, in my quest for justice and answers, I found out that my doctor knew on that Friday (nearly three days before the fallopian tube ruptured and before I went to the Broadway show) that I had an ectopic pregnancy. She received the pathology report that stated there was no fetus found in the D&C. There was no baby in my uterus! And the last blood test that she sent me for, a few days after that procedure, showed that I still had elevated levels of HCG, above what is present in a non-pregnant woman.

With the absence of a fetus in the uterus and the presence of HCG level higher than a non-pregnant woman still in my bloodstream, the baby had to be somewhere else. One can argue that she didn't put two and two together. But later, we found out, through her court subpoena patient records, that her notes reflected that she was aware of all of the above details and in her own hand writing she wrote "*Ectopic Pregnancy*" alongside of the facts shown in my reports. She never called me. Did she forget to? Whatever the reasons for her large oversight, they would:

a) never be shared with me, and;

b) not matter one single bit, because hearing any reasons for her negligence would never change what happened.

With all the knowledge I gathered from my extensive research, I knew that my numbers should have been in the thousands and rising at a steady rate. The fact was my HCG level never crested over 1,000. As a matter of fact, the levels were going up and down, never steadily rising at any given point like you should see in a good pregnancy.

Also, they were not decreasing steadily, like you would see in a pregnancy that had aborted on its own. The up and down nature of my levels was a red flag. My numbers were never in the range of a viable pregnancy in the 6-8 week range. If I did miscarry that pregnancy, as she believed, then after the D&C that she did, I should have had a HCG level of less than 10 mIU/mL. Mine was somewhere around 800 mIU/mL on my last blood test. Another red flag.

The doctor never thought to investigate the results further, let alone the evidence found in the pathology report stating no trace of pregnancy tissue in my uterus? Any one of those things alone would have been reason enough to call me into the hospital for an immediate investigation. I knew that all from my research.

And to think, my fallopian tube could have burst while I was out on the Hudson River (either time—on the trip heading into NYC or leaving it) that Saturday evening and I would have died for sure. The time it would have taken to get from the point on the water to get to a hospital would have been virtually impossible. I shuddered at the thought of that possible tragedy.

I had pieced it all together and to me it looked like the doctor played a mean game of Russian Roulette with my life; placing that lone bullet in a proverbial gun, and then she ruthlessly pulled the trigger—the trigger to my life. So yeah, I had a lot of anger inside of me, and a lot of blame that I first put on myself, but quickly transferred to the doctor.

I could not get out of my head, my spinning mind, and this thing that happened. And, it could not possibly have happened "for me" but rather "to me" because these things only happen to me, and it happened tragically to me because of neglect. The counselor may not have been prepared for me coming in, as she thought it was going to be a grieving session. I felt grief, of course, but my mind channeled all of that sadness, all of that pain, all of that loss into anger toward the doctor.

After I met with the counselor, I felt even more determined to get justice. I think my husband and family were hoping it would bring me peace. Instead, it just fueled my fire even more. No one could understand how I felt on the inside. As much as I tried to explain, everyone around me wanted the old Jen back. This new part of me was unfamiliar, and the Jen that would people please, the Jen that wanted everyone to feel comfortable and happy, that Jen people pleased herself into an apology with a doctor who almost killed her.

Looking back, I think that was my breaking point really. That Jen was replaced by the Jen striving for justice and fairness. Don't get me wrong, as you read, I was a feisty one even when I was people pleasing. I would speak my mind, make people laugh, and I loved to laugh, too. But now, I felt cheated. I felt afraid. And I just buried my head in books and researched to get to the bottom of it so it never ever happened again.

TELL ME I CAN'T AND I WILL DO EVERYTHING TO PROVE I CAN

I was thrown another doozy—a confirmation that I wanted to counter but couldn't in all the reading I'd done. The research mentioned the difficulty I would face getting pregnant again, like the other doctors confirmed, and I could see that this doctor had a hand in all of it.

In my quiet moments throughout each day and all throughout the night, I prayed about that horrible experience. I felt I needed to do something so that no one else would ever suffer like I did. I might not be able to have a baby but maybe someone else's chances would not be jeopardized if I spoke up. I was fueled by anger, a desire for justice, and an even larger need to help other women who may be faced with the same condition. We filed a lawsuit—medical malpractice—against that doctor less than a month after that scary night.

It was the angriest I have ever been in my life to date. It would also be marked as the scariest time as well because I had no idea if we would ever be able to have children. I had to try, though. As soon as I was cleared and everything was safe for us to try to conceive, we began our attempt to have a baby. Although the lawyers did mention that our fervent desire to have a baby should be cooled slightly at least until after the lawsuit was complete, so that it wouldn't bring up any complications. Yes, it might take years, but it would be best for the case and could possibly bring a higher settlement if I wasn't pregnant.

I couldn't hear of it. Were they nuts? I couldn't fathom the idea of not trying. My mind was so muddled with what I might not be able to have that I was a woman on a mission. Besides, I wasn't suing for money. I was suing for justice and to protect other women.

The most important thing to me was having a family, something that this doctor might have taken from me. I wasn't going to let a lump sum push off my desire to be a mom. Besides, the courts would have to see all the suffering she caused regardless of my ability to get pregnant again or not. I was traumatized. My whole entire worldview changed. I was neglected. Fear became my operating system.

We had to go to Newark and speak to the lawyers, have our depositions taken, and answer any other questions they had for us. Everything regarding this case was in our favor. Well, at least that was true, right up until we got the awesome news that we were pregnant for a second time.

The lawyers told us that this successful conception placed our lawsuit in jeopardy because it took away the "permanent damage" aspect. Well, that took the value of the lawsuit down by over 98%; from millions to a couple thousand dollars. Even though this wasn't about money, I was so angry that the doctor's negligence, and all that horrible pain that I endured (along with the side order of the "brink of death" I faced), weren't more of a consideration in the eyes of the malpractice law.

And while this all really pissed me off, and thinking of her getting away with no more than a slap on the wrist brought me to angry tears, all I had to do was focus on the baby growing inside of me to ease that pain. As the months carried on and the and the baby began to move, the anger subsided. Being pregnant was helping me to heal in so many ways and it helped to ease the anger inside me.

All I had wanted since that dreadful night was for us to have a healthy baby, and that is exactly what we got. We called her the million-dollar baby for so long. We wouldn't have traded anything in the world for her.

There isn't much more to say about what happened to that doctor because I haven't a clue. I never looked her up after the case was settled. To be completely honest, I can't even recall her name and if it wasn't for chronicling this story, I haven't thought of her for quite some time. I prayed that this served as a lesson for that doctor, the practice, and anyone else that was associated with her.

Hopefully, the young doctor learned to have diligent accuracy with testing and reading the reports. I hoped that she would listen carefully to the symptoms the patient provided. And last, but definitely not least, that she handled potential ectopic pregnancies with the utmost reverent attention, care, and laser focus.

The thing is, at the time I was so busy being angry I had no idea that I was also learning a lesson. I was so used to controlling my humanness that when I lost the ability to do so, I became a fear-filled victim of my life.

I was over the moon about the baby. But while I had this wonderful new part of me to experience in my life, and I wasn't nearly as angry with the doctor as I once was, I had a crap load of new fears. A vital element of that ectopic pregnancy was how it all affected me and the person that I became. That tragic event in June of 1994 served as a key component to my severe attachment to the body.

THE FEAR TAKES OVER

Who I was before 1994 was a woman slowly beginning her journey into fear with each event that would pop up in her life. There wasn't one particular memory standing up and shouting, "You should really be afraid now!" until the ectopic pregnancy. Once that fallopian tube burst, it was like everything in life just magnified. I was on the fast track of fear, and I didn't even know it. That experience was life-altering to say the least. Not all events are life-altering to our advantage— at least not at first.

The near-death experience (NDE) nearly six years before, never brought any fear, but instead a type of calm or a knowing. Even when I was going through the actual accident, I knew I wanted to live. It didn't feel anything like the fear brought on by my ectopic pregnancy, or by the horrible night when my tube burst, or the pain that led up to it. Instead, the NDE was dreamlike; it happened to me so suddenly, and then I survived. No real pain, no drama, just trust and knowing. That ectopic pregnancy was completely different. I experienced levels of pain to the likes that I have never been able to adequately articulate.

What was obvious, and magnified with great intensity in my life, was that I could (and would) be hurt and there was no two ways about it. Jen had a body that was frail, and could be harmed, and I had to protect it because it could be attacked. And when it was attacked it would hurt like hell. I had to be ever vigilant in order to live and I had to look out for myself.

Up until that point in my life, I had experienced many things in the body, but I didn't identify with them and there was certainly no fear that hit the level I was experiencing now. Before this point, it was like the body was going through some stuff, but it never had any bearing on my life with any lasting horrible effects. It was like I was a "go with the flow kinda girl" and I just kept on swinging—I didn't walk around and have thoughts that limited me.

My stomach pain, I handled it. My follow-up visit to the retinal surgeon was handled without any anxiety, but rather an alertness to pay attention. Before that June in 1994, I just found happiness in life, despite what was going on with my body. I did all the right things to ensure my best care and trusted that it would all be okay. After the ectopic, that was no longer the case.

I became a person who *thought* a lot. I thought about what happened to me. I thought about what I'd lost. I thought of all the things I might not have. I thought about how someone's error almost cost me my life. I thought about pains I felt and what they meant. I thought about the future. I thought about the babies I wanted that people were telling me might not be ours. I believed a lot was *happening* to me; and I also believed it was all so unfair. I believed the doctor pulled the trigger that jump started a real fear of death. I feared the possibility of that intense pain happening again; I knew I could never endure it a second time.

Up until this point in my life, all that I experienced with my body, was dealt with but was never my identity. I didn't dwell on the difficulty or sit in fear of anything that happened— that wasn't living as far as I could tell. I didn't walk around having thoughts about when my belly would hurt next. I didn't run around worrying and crying in my room about my eye sight. I handled life with a sort of presence and definitely without anxiety. Before the ectopic pregnancy, I found joy and happiness in every aspect of life and certainly never allowed my body to hinder any part of it. But that was no longer the case. I became different.

I allowed my mind to take me to places I had never thought of venturing before. I thought about this body of mine and all of its failures. I began to get frustrated about things that I once simply glossed over. This person I became reminded herself of her own frailty at every turn. I shared these feelings only with the closest people in my life—my husband and sometimes my parents. No one else got a look behind the curtain at how my thoughts began to ravage me. I had become very good at keeping it all stuffed inside of the gregarious packaging called Jen (or in years to come "Fun Jen").

No one else got to see the dark side of fear deep inside of me. Those closest to me always were amazed at how they I handled things, because on the outside I kept smiling. They did the very best they could to love and support me when all "these horrible things" happened to "poor Jen."

I am astounded by the young woman I once was, because in spite of all the fears that were running around in my mind, I hid it well and continued to grab what I could out of life. Beginning at the age of eight, I experienced stomach issues and pain which were just part of the fabric of my life. And once I had a near-death experience and a near-fatal pregnancy get thrown in the mix, I had the beginnings of a made for TV miniseries.

Unfortunately, it wasn't a potential TV show, it was my life. Many times, I would wish I was a hypochondriac because I felt that if I was, then all the things that happened to me wouldn't actually be real. But I wasn't and they were. Instead, I hoped and even prayed for relief. I absolutely loved the good days, and a bunch of them in a row was so incredible.

As the years rolled on, and I accumulated more life experiences, more pains in the body, and I also had taken on the mindset of someone who believed she was a victim: a victim of her own body. The view of my own life seemed to have an undercurrent of fear and victimization. It was like I was in a never-ending battle with mysterious issues.

When I was out and about, I was not like I used to be; instead at this time, I was extremely aware of when I got sick to my stomach. There was no way anyone knew of my unidentified hidden fears, 'cause I certainly didn't share them, and I was still close to the vest about my stomach issues, so I continued to suffer in silence.

My once jovial bathroom hunts, that provided my husband and me with a ton of jokes, were becoming a bit more stressful. I was no longer taking them in stride as I always had before. I discreetly continued to do my bathroom guideline checks; how many stalls are there, are they located far enough away from patrons, and so on. If the criteria that I had set up was not met or seemed a bit too sketchy for my liking, then I would tell my husband that I was not that hungry. I avoided a big meal and just nibbled on the bread basket.

I avoided all food in general at the places that I was not

comfortable. If everything looked good at the restaurant, then I just avoided too much oil, fried foods, and lots of veggies because the gastro doctors told me that these things could be a cause of some of my stomach problems. At the time, I figured I could make some small attempt to follow their suggestions when I was out in public, even though not one single doctor had a real valid idea or diagnosis for why my stomach always hurt and why I would experience such severe reactions after I ate.

I can't even count the times that we stopped off to the side of the road or that I had to run into a gas station. I am amazed that my partner still wanted to marry me after all that he witnessed over the five years of dating. At any one of those mad dashes to a restroom he could've said, "Wow, this chick has too much going on . . . I'm out." But instead, he went through it all right alongside me; my shelter in all my storms.

Many times, I would be in the passenger seat of the car, in tears from pain and embarrassment, rocking back and forth clutching my tummy in pain, my forehead covered in perspiration, and I would hear him say, in a steady voice, "Hang in, Jen, we are almost there." It was like a balm to my mind and to my soul knowing that I didn't suffer alone. He always tried to reassure and support me because he knew this pain was real. He was and is the best friend I've ever had, and I was as close to him as I could be to another human being.

But even as close as we were, and even though he witnessed a whole bunch of things through the years, having a stomach issue in front of someone else is a mortifying situation to be in. I don't think anyone ever really wants to have every single experience in front of the person they love. Kinda takes a lot of mystery out of the relationship and shows a bit too much humanness, if you get my meaning. Anything and everything that you could think of bathroom related happened—use your imagination, or don't. Agh! To help lighten the embarrassment, we made jokes about the different scenarios we found ourselves in. Deep down, I would have traded all the jokes for not having to experience it at all, if I was ever given that as a choice.

And the other thing that became a constant ache in my heart, each day, no matter what was going on in my life, was pregnancy. I always kept close vigilant track of my body. I was not going to miss any signs that might show up, because I was going to avoid the possibility of another ectopic pregnancy at all costs.

I was driven by a secret undercurrent of fear of death and of horrific pain, but I was alone in it. I hid that secret while I went about life with a smile on my face. My poor husband was the only one in on the secret life of Jen. What a heavy burden to remain calm when partnered with someone who is always in discomfort in body and in mind.

I became a victim of so many things. I believed that everything happened to me. I was a victim of the body I was given. I was the victim of the doctor's error. I was a victim of my stomach mystery. The way I saw it, so many things happened to me and no one else experienced the magnitude of things that I did.

When I thought about myself, I missed being the carefree person I once was. I thought I had no choice but to remain in this state because of the lousy hand I was dealt. When life throws you lemons you make lemonade, or so the saying goes, but unless you have a crap ton of sugar, it might be too bitter to swallow. That was how I felt about my body, a bit more than I could swallow at times.

"It is when you expect nothing in return that you receive everything. Happiness is a state of being. It is a choice. You ARE happiness. You live and vibrate joy without expectation, then what you receive back has no measure or value attributed to it. It is beyond measurement."
~ From Meditations with Jesus and Jen

Worry [ˈwərē]

verb

give way to anxiety or unease; allow one's mind to dwell on difficulty or troubles.

noun

a state of anxiety and uncertainty over actual or potential problems.

Worrying was my mode of operation. It was just how I went through life. It was a part of me I could not shake.

CHAPTER 6

The Making of a New Kind of Worry Wart

*"Worry is like a rocking chair: it gives you something to do
but never gets you anywhere."*
~ Erma Bombeck

"Another Caesar salad? They know you by name, Jen! As soon as they see me, they know exactly what to make for you."

Yeah, that was me, craving Caesar salad. Pregnancy would seem to be a focal point for a few years, and for as long as I had a reproductive system. I was equal parts afraid of it happening, not ever knowing if the pregnancy would end up in my uterus, and then of course really desiring a bunch of kids. I would battle against these mixed feelings, month after month, for years. And yes, fear was my new tagalong, and I learned to live with her.

Ultimately, I would have 3 babies, making us a family of 5. But with each pregnancy came its own set of new fears. Learning how to navigate those terrors and the fears that came along with being a mother, gave a whole new meaning to the term "worry wart."

No honestly, I gave a new meaning to it. I was the vigilante of our problems and all my fears, with a bit of angst mixed in for good measure. I never worried over imagined things. Nah, I had enough on my plate. Instead, as issues arose, I had to take the preverbal bull by the horns. So . . . don't go calling me a "worry wart" with the image of someone sitting in a room by herself, wringing her hands, and wasting time over worrying about perceived problems—there was literally no room in my life for extra!

I hit each problem by not letting anything slip through the cracks, with the great fear that in doing so it could lead to catastrophe. When each new thing arose, I had the quiet creeping fear that would lead me down the path of responsibility. I needed to be responsible and figure things out for those I loved, and myself, or we could be harmed. I had great angst over certain things. Where there once was trust and faith, now there was present moment anxieties that required me to be the detective that figured out why we all were sick. I would cry about it in private, where I let most of my stuff spill out.

I didn't borrow problems. More accurately, problems, well, they just showed up—uninvited. The world had no accurate term or label for me, I was quite unique. I wasn't sitting at home thinking of things that could be happening to me that hadn't yet. I was worrying about the things that were right in front of me, and how in the f#$k was I gonna handle them and control them so that no harm came to me and my family! I wasn't worrying if the kids would get a cold from someone else or if they'd fall while playing. I wasn't worrying about the "possible stuff" that might happen. I was dealing with the stuff that WAS happening. I wasn't the classic worry wart.

"You have no idea what I have to deal with. It's not worries! It's called responsibility and survival. Things can happen to me, and now to my kids, who I'm responsible for. I need to make sure they're safe." I would say to justify my actions. It was as if I was a mom version of a superhero, and under my shirt I wore a leotard with the letters VM boldly across the chest, standing for "Vigilante Mom". At a moment's notice I would turn into her, fighting for my kids to protect them.

I had been living in fear mode ever since the first ectopic pregnancy. Every month before my first pregnancy and then in-between pregnancies, I worried about my period. The possibility of a baby growing in my tubes shook me to my core. I remember the feeling when I first got pregnant after the ectopic. I felt like this was it— the big race, the 9-month haul, baby #1 was on her way. At first there was joy. But panic didn't take long to follow. I needed to know that baby was growing in its proper home, my uterus. There was no room for a mysterious ultrasound, and I had no desire to play detective. That baby needed to be in position and fast. Every moment I did not know for certain where the baby was growing was a moment of fear.

Once we were over the hurdle of locating the baby, and then waiting to make sure it was healthy and thriving, it still wasn't smooth sailing from there. Don't I wish! Instead, I was very sick, especially in the beginning, and lost around 15 pounds from morning sickness which lasted all day. The doctors only concern was that I hydrate and try to eat crackers. They said that weight loss was common, and if it continued into the second trimester than we should address it.

I am sure that I was slightly dehydrated, because I was weak. I missed a whole bunch of work, and a few times my husband had to carry me to the bathroom. I was so drained. But if anything could be said about me, I did have a tenacity, and so, if I got sick, I returned immediately to sipping water, juice, or anything I could find to stay hydrated.

Hyperemesis gravidarum (HG) is a pregnancy complication that was characterized by severe nausea, vomiting, weight loss, and possibly dehydration. I learned about it on my own, because HG was never mentioned to me. The doctor just said to keep trying to eat and drink and to rest as much as I could. Thank God I worked for my father or else I would've been out of a job when I was feeling better.

I had cravings. I mean I was hungry, often, but once the food got there, well you can only imagine how sick I got. I begged my husband to get me that Burger King chicken sandwich. Yup, it made a repeat performance, that little ole sandwich. I hoped it would work because after all, it was so wildly successful the for a bit. Ah, but alas, not a success for long. Actually, nothing was until around the third or fourth month when food began to stay down. And then it was game on and I gained weight with a vengeance.

I knew that this baby was going to come out loving Caesar salad because, strangely enough, once I could keep food down, that was it for me. The dressing needed to be freshly made, and with anchovies, the right way, and there was a nice Italian restaurant down the road from us that made it perfectly.

One night, we bought food from them and brought it home to eat. I finished that salad, and I looked up into my husband's eyes, and he knew immediately what my eyes were telling him. "You want another one, don't you?" I bobbed my head up and down, a tad embarrassed. He said, "I'll get it! Hell, I am just glad you are keeping it down. But you're sure it won't be too much?" He saw how bad it was for months and now that I could eat and it stayed with me, he gladly ran out to get me whatever I craved. He was astonished at times what I packed away.

DILATING EARLY AND ANOTHER
NEW SET OF WORRIES

It was about my sixth month of pregnancy that I was told that my cervix was dilated. That was strange because I never experienced any symptoms or contractions. My new OB/GYN told me to restrict my chores, and by all means, pay attention to any cramps or pains, because they might be signs of premature labor. You know by now that I would do whatever it took to make sure this baby was healthy and that I didn't endure any surprise horrific circumstance. Therefore, I did what she suggested—I rested as much as I could.

I didn't do any strenuous exercise. I did only small chores around the apartment. I went grocery shopping and made dinner. I stopped driving into Brooklyn for work because I just didn't have the energy, and to be honest, I was worried I would cause a further problem with the baby. My father agreed that I should stay home. After all, I was carrying their first grandchild and I was his baby, so he said they would manage without me returning to work. I was at home throughout the day—just me, our growing baby, and my angels, who made a return. I went from an active working girl, to sitting around being bored. Each and every day I was so excited to see my husband when he came home.

As I mentioned, I was so full of anger and fear during the ectopic and right after, that there was no space for the angels to come in. I was too clouded mentally to feel their presence or see them, and as a matter-of-fact, I forgot to even ask the angels for help for a while. But once I was pregnant and we were sure the baby was not in my tubes, my heart opened a little bit again for a short while, allowing the angels to come through.

Coming to better understand our angels, right at the beginning of that pregnancy, was one of the luckiest things to happen. I think believing they were around, protecting us, helped me to not allow my new thoughts and fears to take over my life (and mind) completely. But, oh just wait, this doesn't last too long.

At each checkup appointment, I found out that I was dilating a little more each time. This increased dilation brought up a lot of fear and worry. I wouldn't do much of anything out of fear that it would harm the baby. Light chores turned to no chores, leaving a bigger burden on my husband. On occasion, I would stroll through the town, explore where I could, but I didn't know anyone in New Jersey. Fred was working from when he left early in the morning until 6-7:00 at night, so needless to say I was getting a little stir crazy. It left a lot of time for my mind to wander and the anxiety took over again. I asked a million questions every time I went to the doctor, the slightest pang warranted a phone call, and I stewed in my worries day and night when Fred was working hard to provide for us.

IT'S GO TIME

By week 36, I was four centimeters dilated, and the doctor thought it had gone on long enough. She said that much dilation might cause problems with the placenta, so they were going to induce labor that day. The doctor told me to head home and pack a bag and to meet her at the hospital at 6:00 p.m.

I got back to the apartment and called my husband. He said he would get home right away. The next call was to my parents. They were in the car, on their way to Virginia, for a wedding. As we were excitingly talking, Dad said, "I am already off the exit, turning around, and heading to New Jersey!"

I exclaimed, "Oh, I am so happy, but I hate for you to miss the wedding."

He responded, "There is no way we're gonna miss our baby having her first baby!"

The most beautiful baby girl joined our life at 8:43 p.m. I also got one of the nurse's leftover turkey sandwiches she had in the refrigerator, because, let's face it, once we knew the baby was safe and healthy, I needed to eat. We were over the moon to have successfully gotten pregnant and given birth to a healthy child, who, by the way actually did turn out to be a huge lover of salads.

Nothing out of the ordinary happened post pregnancy, although nursing proved to be a bit challenging for both mommy and baby. But, we persevered. There was one thing that I learned a whole bunch about that can still bring a slight chill to my bones, and that was sleep deprivation. So many mothers know the struggle. People who have to work long hours know how hard it is to survive with little sleep. But holy cow, there wasn't enough information in those pregnancy books to warn you on how bad it could truly be!

I know that I would have still wanted to have children even though I would be missing a ton of sleep—the struggle was real. I would have endured anything I needed to get the family we desired so much. But man, oh man, I still remember sitting and dreaming of the day when I could sleep for four hours in a row. I knew my regular sleep pattern would return one day, but sleep deprivation can sap the joy out of just about anything. I knew I signed up for this journey, so I had to suck it up.

ANOTHER BUNDLE OF JOY
AND A NEW SET OF WORRIES

Our first born was a year and a half when we got pregnant with our second child. I was even more tired than I could have ever imagined, but I figured if I'm not going to get any sleep anytime soon, might as well just keep on keeping on!

My stomach was giving me a whole bunch of problems. We could definitely see that this pregnancy had intensified my stomach issues, but since they have always been part of my life, I knew I needed to just deal with it. It was like I had a break for a window of time, then it was back once more. So no big deal, I could cope.

At my first visit with the OB/GYN, I learned I was already dilating. I was just 12 weeks pregnant. It was with a heavy heart that I realized this was way too early; we feared for the survival of our second child. This was just like the last pregnancy, except a lot earlier. The doctor knew this had happened before, and decided the best option for this baby to make it to term was for me to be on complete bed rest at home.

Being given that advice by my doctor, my brain heard the "high alert" sound. It was like internal bells and whistles were going off. My mind was a landmine, and I was so worried every moment of every day. They told me to do my very best, to try really hard not to pick my daughter up, and especially not to push the vacuum around. Basically, I was told to just remain on the bed or couch for as long as I could manage. The doctor said that if I had a hard time with that, or the cervix dilated more, I would have to consider hospitalization.

To say I was upset would be a drastic understatement. I was so devastated because I didn't think I could be the mother I wanted to be for our first child. But, I am a rule follower, and when someone tells me to do something, I do my very best to follow through with all the rules or instructions.

I was the person who sat in the dark for 2 weeks so I could ensure my stitches in my retina were secure. I also followed instructions do well, that I only had to have my braces on for nine months instead of the year or more that I was told. The orthodontist told me, "If you can use this night brace as often as you can, you can reduce your time in the braces!" That was all I needed. I wore that night brace contraption during the day, whenever I was inside the house watching TV or doing homework, and faithfully each and every night. Even when it hurt like crazy, I wore that darn thing. As long as there weren't friends over, I was in that thing and it paid off. I told myself I needed to approach this bed rest with the same tenacity even if it broke my heart daily.

Family pitched in. I felt so bad and guilty for it, but it was very helpful. My wonderful mother came to live with us from Sunday evening until Thursday afternoon. God bless my father for having to do without her and her company for those days. My mother-in-law took up the time Thursday afternoon to Friday evening until my husband finished work. My state of mind oscillated between acceptance to flat out pity party. I knew deep down inside I really wanted to have several kids, but I couldn't help wondering why it had to be so darn hard.

Only me. Ugh.

Why me?

Why can't I enjoy the experience of pregnancy, without the worry of losing the baby?

Why can't I do this and raise my first child from somewhere other than the couch?

By the way, I made my husband sell that darn couch at a garage sale because I couldn't look at it after countless months of lying on it.

I was exhausted and my head felt fuzzy most days. I often wondered how I was so drained from doing absolutely nothing. I looked forward to the day that I would not be so tired. That pattern continued until the 36th week of pregnancy.

The doctor mentioned her concern with the baby having lung issues if she came too early, because I continued to dilate a tiny bit each time she checked me. She was baffled when I told her I didn't have any contractions, ever. With the condition of my cervix and the doctor's concerns about the baby coming too early to survive, she ordered steroid shots. I had to get them every week from week 20 through week 36. The doctor's orders were that I remain horizontal at all times. In fact, they would prefer I crawled to the bathroom rather than stood up. Gravity was not my friend. So how was it even safe for me to make the weekly trip to the doctor's office? It sounds comical now, looking back, but at the time, I took these orders to heart, and they weighed so heavy on me.

The world I once knew was completely gone, and I couldn't even stand straight and tall in this new reality. I was at war with my body and literally doing an army crawl just to get to the bathroom. Cortisol pulsed through my body day and night. I worried that even standing up once would risk the baby's life. I was not taking any chances whatsoever.

So, in order to not have to drive in the car, we came up with a plan. A fabulous friend of my husband's family, who was an RN and lived in our town, came to our home and gave me my weekly shots. I was so grateful that she did that for us, and for our baby. And this was the life I lead until our baby safely joined the world.

I was petrified day and night. I wasn't noticing angels. I had forgotten to trust in God's plan; I just lived in the body, in the mind, and worried that it was all in my hands. I was deathly afraid I would do something wrong and lose this baby. I could feel her kicking and moving, and I wanted to make sure I brought her into this world safely.

Fear was a very powerful thing. I would think and worry as I laid there on that couch. Worried about my first daughter not getting what she needed from me, and then I would worry if I had too many stomachaches or crawled to the bathroom too much. As I was alone in my thoughts and fears, I could not have those angel interactions. I was pretty consumed with what was going on to see anything else.

I didn't blame people for saying that tired phrase I wasn't a big fan of, "These things only happen to you, Jen!" What else could they say? That was what they saw; I just didn't like to be reminded of the things that I seemed to be the only person suffering from. There were other things that occurred during this pregnancy and it comes as no surprise now, that it all revolved around the body, pain, and fear.

NEW LEVEL NUMBNESS AND A BABY IS BORN

I was at the end of the bed rest. I could soon be free and vertical without worrying about our unborn child. One night as I attempted to get out of bed to use the bathroom, I couldn't move. I reached over and shook my husband and he couldn't seem to get me to move my leg either. He wound up calling his mother, who was an EMT. She got the ambulance to take me to the ER. They couldn't get the gurney up the stairs, so I had to go down the stairs, with help, on my rump.

Once we were registered at the hospital, and I had been seen and had whatever tests they could perform on a pregnant woman, they determined that our stubborn child in utero was sitting on a nerve near the vagina and causing the pain, tingling, and leg paralysis to my right leg.

Can you believe this? *Only me*, I thought once more.

I didn't even know this could be a thing. I believe it was called pudendal neuralgia, and the doctors at the hospital said that when the baby moved it would eventually get better. They told me that the baby looked perfectly fine. I was sent home with medication that was safe for me to take with the pregnancy . . . and a cane! I was unable to walk without a cane for a week.

So, we finally made it past week 36. The baby we all worked so hard to keep healthy and safe didn't make her debut until exactly WEEK 40, in October of 1997! Our wonderful second daughter was born in all her stubborn glory. She was the tiniest and sweetest little thing with lungs like an Olympic swimmer.

It took a little adjusting to get used to taking care of two kids after being inactive for so long. I was still experiencing exhaustion and dizziness. I just chalked it up to getting acclimated with activity again, and to being a mom of two babies.

Two months later, my husband had an opportunity to have a business in Georgia, so we packed up our little family and moved. It absolutely broke my heart to leave my parents and all I knew in New York and New Jersey, but I knew this was what my husband wanted. He was sure this move would be a great opportunity for our family. Our little family of four was my focus now and I needed to be onboard with what was best for all of us. We agreed I would be a "stay at home" mom, and if this was the work he wanted, starting his own business and becoming his own boss, then I needed to be a team player like I agreed.

In Georgia, we were able to achieve the goal we set up as a family. Fred worked and I would stay at home to be with the kids. My parents were wonderful and came to visit us nearly every other month. My children grew very close to them. My in-laws also came to visit several times a year. We were so lucky to be able to spend each holiday and birthday with family.

FEARS AND FEVERS AND SURPRISE #3 TRIGGERS WORRYING ALL THE MORE

From the first few months in Georgia, our second daughter began to have fevers and a bunch of reoccurring ear and throat problems. We were familiar with unexplained fevers from our first daughter. The pediatrician always said hers were due to a virus or one of those "pesky" childhood illnesses like fifths disease or hand foot. But our second child's fevers were being chalked up to being related to specific things. Unfortunately, as soon as we thought we had it under control, it would return. That poor baby would have to deal with fevers, tubes in her ears, and be on antibiotics, time and again. Thank goodness she was the type of kid who wanted to play and laugh and keep busy no matter what was going on because it helped her to manage the pain better during the day.

Me on the other hand, oh how I worried about her. And although it was a relief to watch her play during the day, nighttime was a whole different can of worms. Like many parents know, nighttime was when all illnesses come out to play. Nighttime was so hard on her and in turn me. No matter what we tried, the fevers along with her ears, caused a bunch of pain, so I was up, on and off, all night trying to soothe her. I never showed either of my daughters my feelings when they were sick, I remained upbeat in front of them despite how I felt inside.

My husband and I agreed to stop at two kids. We thought that we were lucky to get these babies through the rough pregnancies and into our lives. Even though they were sick often, the doctors could never find anything seriously wrong with them, so not to be crude, but we honestly felt in our hearts we should not push it. We were in agreement to not try for a third, and we felt so blessed to have the family that we had. Let's be honest, we were really tired too. We talked and talked about it, and we were convinced that two kids would be just fine even though we always thought we would have three.

God had a different plan for us and our little family though. Because against all odds, and contrary to all the biology lessons I had ever learned to date, and regardless of preventative measures, we became pregnant with our third child when our second daughter was only 10 months old. It's funny, because when I was growing up, my mom would always say to me, "You want to make God laugh? Tell him your plans."

Now I knew exactly what she meant. I knew that was definitely the case with us deciding we were not going to have a third child. Our son entered the world and completed our family one year after our move to Georgia, in 1999. He was such an amazing blessing for sure and clearly the will of something much greater than our own.

Having the history with pregnancies that I did through the last five years, you have already figured where I am going with this story right? We prayed for an uneventful pregnancy this time around and that was not what we got.

At my first visit to the OB/GYN, I explained my past pregnancy history. Since we now lived in a new area, I had to find a new doctor and begin all over again. She said she would not take me as a patient unless I had a cervical cerclage at 12 weeks. Here I thought there would be a chance this pregnancy would go off without a hitch and she said *not a chance!*

She told me that the advice she was giving was exactly what she would advise her own sister if she had a history with pregnancy like mine. She believed that since there was no real rhyme or reason for the dilation, she was sure it would happen again. She told me in detail what the procedure was, and was as thorough as could be. I was a little nervous, but I remained hopeful that this would keep me off the couch and in my two little girls lives as an active, albeit pregnant, mom.

For those of you who were as lost as I was at first, a cervical cerclage is also called a cervical stitch—it is when a suture is sewn into and around the cervix. Its function is to help prevent preterm birth. But if it was successful, I could live a normal life, they'd remove the stitches and just wait for the baby to naturally make his/her debut.

A PROCEDURE AWRY
AND EVEN MORE FEARS

I had the procedure, seemingly without issue. In the recovery, there was a slight delay of the spinal block wearing off. I expressed to the nurse that I needed to urinate (of that much I could feel, but I seemed to be unable to do anything about it), but the block hadn't worn off. She didn't believe me and just told me repeatedly to relax and it would simply happen. It didn't. I felt this pain in the bladder, no matter how hard I tried to simply be still and relax. My bladder began to quickly distend, and she was now on a mad rush to catheter me. She was so alarmed at the amount of fluid she withdrew—so much that she said she needed to stop at a certain level so as not to cause a problem.

Yeah, she believed me after that, but unfortunately, it was a bit too late. It was not too much longer after the bladder/urine incident that I developed a fever and had to stay in the hospital an extra day.

Unfortunately, by week 18 of the pregnancy, at my routine doctor visit, we found that I had been dilating once again without contractions through the cerclage. I couldn't believe it. The doctor placed me on mandatory bed rest. Here I was again.

Why is this happening to me?

Why can't I just have a normal experience with pregnancy?

Only me. Ugh. Ugh. Ugh.

We had no family near us. We didn't know anyone well enough to help us with our little family, since we had only been in Georgia for little under a year, at least no one we felt comfortable enough to care for two girls under the age of three.

Once again, my mom, who was now called "Mimi" by the girls, came to the rescue. Mimi came to Georgia to live with us. We were too far away to do the few days here and back home, so she stayed with us until week 36. I know it was hard on my parents to make that sacrifice for my family. I was and still am to this day so incredibly grateful to them both. Without their assistance in helping us raise our girls while I was bedridden once again, our son would not have made his happy venture into the world. The way my husband and I view it, without their assistance and sacrifice, we would not have any of our children.

Even with my family's love and support, to say that that experience was difficult was a wild understatement. I was frustrated, lonely, and I felt broken and worthless. Shouldn't pregnancy and childbirth be natural for a woman? Why were mine so extraordinary, and not in a good way? I was in a continual loop of worry, and in "on the edge of my seat" fear mode, just trying to keep our baby safe. At times I felt like a statue, trying to just stay still.

In general, I felt like crap most days, fuzzy in the head, and exhausted every day. I would run the laundry list of "Why Me?" complaints daily. It was so hard to never show the girls that I was miserable. I read them books while they laid near me on the couch.

In the beginning of the pregnancy, they would ask me to come with them to their playroom, pleading sweetly or pulling at my arm to get me off the couch to play. I would explain to them that Mommy has a big job to help the baby grow, and I needed to lie down so he is safe. I think that one of the saddest days on that couch was when the girls didn't ask for me to come and play. What beautiful, well-adjusted souls they were—accepting that their Mommy needed to be where she was. They were so accepting of having Mimi there for them, and they were happy.

What more could I have asked for? Knowing all of that didn't stop the pain in my heart; I wasn't part of their play or their lives the way I wanted to be. Of course, my husband and mother would corral them at some point in the day to be with me, and although I appreciated it so much, I would cry into the pillow when they were out of earshot. I would never let them see my hurt; they didn't need to bear that. What my entire family needed for me to do was to be accepting of their love and their help; they didn't need to feel guilty or bad when they were doing it.

Our son entered this world fast. The doctor broke my water then told me to relax. I thought that was kind of odd. Was that what they normally did? I didn't remember hearing why she broke my water, but my husband said that she did it so that we could have this baby all before her lunch break. I wasn't too happy about rushing the birth of my son for her feeding schedule, but it was done already so I just had to deal. She figured all would be on a particular schedule once the Pitocin, a drug that causes the uterus to contract and is used to either induce labor or to speed it up, was fully administered. Ahh, but things with Jen hadn't gone as planned so far, so this should not be any different.

I instructed the nurse that whatever she was trying to put in my arm was leaking all over and not actually going into me. She took the needle out and tried again. Still no cigar. I called her in and told her again, and asked her to stay right near me until she saw that it was actually going in and not leaking. Well, remember what we said about plans, it was minutes from when that needle was in and the Pitocin was flowing, that our son decided to come . . . and fast! The doctor was called from her practice to run back. Maybe she would get her lunch break after all, or maybe not.

And there was another complication. He was delivered as a meconium birth so there was a mad rush of lots of strangers running into the room to help out our baby. Fred was placed outside of the room because there were so many people in the room helping our son. To be honest, I was lost. I had no clue what all of the concern was about, other than they told me it was vital they addressed the meconium (stool, or early feces) that happened while he was still inside the uterus. They did not explain anything more to me at that point because of the urgency to address the baby. It clearly seemed to be an emergency. My heart was beating so fast. *Where's the panic button?* I just wanted everything to be ok. You know, like those peaceful moments when a mother first sees her child in the movies? I wanted one of those childbirths. No dice.

It wasn't until about an hour later, that they told us he was good and they would monitor him closely to ensure no problems arose. They explained that since the meconium happened while he was still in the uterus, it could cause the baby stress, affect his oxygen, or cause other problems. Thankfully, he was fine and had no problems as a result of how he entered the world._

I wondered what it would be like to have a carefree and uneventful pregnancy.

"Every new beginning comes from some other beginning's end."
~ Seneca

FUN JEN EMERGES, HIDING THE WORRY WART FROM THE WORLD

After several months of living in our cute little Augusta neighborhood, in our very special first house, the new friends I made began to call me "Fun Jen." I was having a good time to say the least, and I fully embraced my hard earned new moniker. I spent most of my time at home with the kids or taking my oldest on playdates or to Gymboree classes. In between I made time for me and us as a couple. We found trusted babysitters, and went to events in the neighborhood.

I was getting involved in my life as a Georgian. I played Bunco with a great group of women once a month. In case you're wondering, Bunco is a really fun dice game commonly played in the south and an excuse to eat appetizers and drink wine with friends...kind of like a ladies' version of Poker Night. I was also a co-chair on the Social Committee, and we ran fun events for kids and some for adults. We raised money for our neighborhood through many different events. The one event that I loved was a dinner fundraiser. We would cook the dinners at the clubhouse. Each family pre-paid with their order and on the big date, would pick up their family dinner at their scheduled staggered times. It was a great fundraiser.

In addition to our Easter egg hunts, and community garage sales, and an occasional wine tasting here and there, a large group of us would host parties at each other's houses. I would hide my worries by having fun, reminiscent of my college days except with a family in tow and not as much alcohol. I would joke about the things that weighed heavy on me, and I didn't even realize it; I just thought that's how you dealt with the hand you're dealt. And so "Fun Jen" lived for fun and laughter to hide the rest. No one realized that when I wasn't laughing at a party with them, I was fighting for our survival. Yep, the other 99% of the time, I was in my "Vigilante Mom" mode.

We were in this new town for a little over two years when I got this wild business idea. I bought several hand-painted glass beaded bracelets I found in an "off the beaten path" store while in Florida visiting our close college friends. They were incredibly affordable , too! I thought since they were so different and cute, if I bought a bunch, I could re-sell them. That was exactly what I did, and it was a big hit at the kids' nursery school and in my neighborhood. I even took it a step further—I began creating my own. I had this one bracelet that had glass crosses hanging off it, and it inspired me. So the search for materials began.

In 2000 and 2001, there wasn't a ton online yet, and although I found beads to make my own designs, what I also found was the world of costume jewelry. Costume jewelry was affordable jewelry that people really wanted. This was a time in my life when I was ahead of an idea. Costume jewelry was just starting to take off and I was able to sell these costume jewelry items to all the people I came in contact with, and on top of that, all within the restrictions of my stay-at-home mom life. This was a great convenience for me, and the people I was selling to.

That jewelry business was a side job really, because my first job was already spoken for. But boy oh boy, did I work that one when I could. If the kids were napping, at preschool, or even for an hour right after they went down for bed, I was researching new items or tagging what I had already purchased.

After a while, I needed to form a company because I wanted to be able to purchase wholesale. Getting the best price was my first priority, right up there with getting adorable designs. I chose to never do the triple markup that was suggested by the companies. I wanted repeat customers, and since I had no real overhead, I could always have new items to offer. It made sense to me, and God knows I loved a deal, so I figured so did the next person. I felt so good about this aspect of my new business, giving people a great deal. It was exactly the way I would hope to feel when I was buying something that I probably didn't really need, but just wanted.

For holiday events, I would rent out the clubhouse, give each customer a brown paper lunch bag, and they would walk out with the bag full of jewelry. Wow, thinking back on the days of costume jewelry and how much fun I had buying and selling sure made it all worth it. I loved being a mom but I also found something I loved to do that wasn't 100% about my family.

The company morphed a little as time went on, and I found other things to provide my customers. I bought and sold pre-made jewelry, I made jewelry, painted glassware, and made wine glass charms. After a while I started to dabble in sterling silver. Years later, I increased that sector of the business into finer jewelry with semi-precious stones and handbags.

I named the business *All Nice Things*. The name came from our first daughter who loved (and still does) anything jewelry related, really more specifically anything pretty. A few years before, when she was around two years old, we were in a store picking up a few gifts and she began to have a little bit of a tantrum. She was holding two items in her tiny toddler hands, and I just told her she could get one toy. Ahhh, but she wanted two. I told her I wasn't happy with the way she was behaving. The tantrum continued.

Being a new mom trying to navigate parenting, expectations, not spoiling my child, and keeping tantrums at bay, I wasn't loving this behavior. I remember saying something like, "Now you know mommy doesn't like this behavior. It makes it hard for mommy to want to get you anything at all. Be happy with what I was going to buy for you, or we can just put both of the items back and you can get nothing." I tried to have a calm tone as I spoke these strong words, but as you could imagine, she heard something different, as an actively tantrum-ed up toddler would.

She began to cry, "No nice thing for me, wahhh. But, Mommy . . . wahhh. I like ALL NICE THINGS!" It was so hard to keep a straight face when the kids would say adorable things and a tantrum was attached. I maintained a level head, but I absolutely loved her words. So stinking adorable! I never forgot them, and used the words a few years later for that company that I ran for nearly thirteen years. Oh, and in case you were wondering, she never did get either of those toys.

THE BODY ISSUES DON'T QUIT JUST BECAUSE YOU'RE MOM

Keeping up with all the fun, the kids, the business, I never had a pause from my body. I had so much to look forward to in my life and to feel really blessed about having, but there was this nagging stuff that always lurked in the background of my FUN!

Family of five: birthday parties, playdates, dance classes, Gymboree classes, meeting customers, making jewelry, visits from grandparents, nap schedules, and doctor's visits filled our days. Through it all, I still experienced my life long stomach pain and discomfort, which seemed to be getting worse if you could imagine that. There was now a twist to the experience, I had the issues in front of three spectators.

Hey kiddos, umm. You see, Mom has to rush into the bathroom, and can't even stall to put a movie in, because you're toddlers and need to be supervised. So, umm, coloring books, crayons, and a picture book into the bathroom with me!

Poor babies. Thank goodness they didn't have a problem with my tummy ailments, because as I said, they were really easy-going kids. What I felt horrible about, what I couldn't rectify in my head, was when they began to experience the same distress with their stomachs as well. Bathroom time was an issue with every one of the kids. Talk about mom-guilt; I couldn't get answers for myself, and now I have all three kids with one problem after another.

Even as infants they were such happy babies, but eating time and potty time—oh, the misery. We noticed that each of them had their own gastrointestinal distresses as infants too—lots of gas pains and just overall discomfort. Each year, the pediatrician would comfort us, but it was always brushed off as "it happens."

That is until our son gave everyone (including the doctors) a bit of a scare with his belly issues. We noticed, like our girls, his belly would distend and hurt him. I breastfed each of the kids, but I never equated that to being a problem. It was supposed to be the best thing to give them, right? I began experimenting with my diet to help our son have some level of comfort. I reduced my food intake to boiled chicken and bread for weeks to see if anything made a difference for him. His little body was in such distress, and was accompanied by blood in his stool. This was scary.

He was referred to a pediatric gastroenterologist. With extensive exams, and a colonoscopy, you would not believe what the doctor diagnosed him . . . an allergy to my breast milk! Yup—at the time, only one in a million babies had this allergy—it was extremely rare! I mean I know my kid was special and all, but one in a million!?

But again, I found myself in the position of listening to the advice of the doctor, because I had no knowledge of what else could be wrong with our six-month-old baby. I felt that I had no other choice, because what other option or reason would explain his pain and bleeding? I didn't have a clue and neither did the medical community. He became a bottle-fed baby at six months and the bleeding stopped, but his discomfort and constipation just continued.

Now who was baffled? Everyone! *Only me. Only my child. Ugh. Ugh. Ugh.*

A REAL SCARY AND GROWING CONCERN

Not too long after we had our son, I had a surreal conversation with our middle daughter who was less than three years old at the time. Both my girls had the normal childhood viruses, stomach issues, and high fevers. And now our son had gastrointestinal problems as well. Being a mom added a whole new level to worry. Even though I masked my fears with laughter and fun with friends, I don't think my heartbeat ever slowed down.

There was a bunch of visits to the doctors. Sometimes it felt like we were there each week. We even had a scare with our oldest child because she often had high fevers Sometimes her lymph nodes were so large, the doctors became concerned. They sent her for scans and blood tests to rule out lymphoma. There were so many horrifying and panic-inducing times when the kids were real young; it was a time of worrying about a lot more than just myself. I had the fear with my own issues, now spilling over into my children.

I was nervous about their health often, but I never spoke about my concerns in front of them— not on the phone, not with my husband, never when they were in the room much less in ear shot. I had the belief that the kids would pick up on what they heard and would take on worries you had—that would make them worry as well and even make them feel worse.

So, I did what I thought was best, I downplayed it. I reserved my tears of fear for my closet, or my master bathroom after the kids were put to bed. Since the kids never heard me express my fears or saw me cry, I was pretty taken aback when our middle daughter, on this one particular night in her bedroom spoke with such clarity and in an unearthly demeanor about afterlife. I had no idea what to make of it.

I was singing to her while rubbing her back. She turned on her side to face me, and calmly said, "Mommy, I love you. Don't worry, you know we will always be together in heaven. Just like before." I didn't know what I know now, so where I went, and really, really quickly, was a place of fear. *Ahh, fear, my new companion. Glad you could join in.*

I told her, "Yes, we will always be together no matter what.

Mommy loves you and I am so happy I have you as my sweet and special daughter." Then I went into our master bedroom and sobbed. Was my daughter telling me that she was leaving me? Was she so sick, and I couldn't figure out what was wrong with her, so she was preparing me for her death? I didn't know what to think.

As the days passed, I held onto the idea that she could feel how worried I was and just said what she instinctively knew. I have heard that kids are more open and connected to God and angels when they are really young. While I didn't go out to the bookstore and buy anything about this to learn more, I just assumed that was how she knew to tell me this. I thought she just had some kind of knowing. I had one foot on the side of believing that she was connected and in fact reassuring me that no matter what happened to her, we would never be apart, and the other foot was too scared to contemplate any of it!

I lost an unborn child, and as you know that ectopic did a number on me. But the thought of losing these three precious gifts, I couldn't wrap my heart or mind around that happening. It planted a worry so deep that everywhere I looked became a maze of danger. In that maze, I found myself in the same pattern that I went through, again, but this time for all of my children. I researched every doctor, followed every medical guideline, took every test. I tried anything and everything available to us in the medical community to make us comfortable. But no one gave us answers—sound familiar? I could not allow my children to die, so I decided it was my job to protect them from any sort of threat to life.

Living life in this matrix of fear made everything that much more challenging. Hiding these fears did a number on me. One part of me was laughing and "Fun Jen" while another part of me was sobbing in a closed room. I couldn't bear to put a burden on anyone, other than my dear husband (and even on him only sparingly), so I had to carry the weight of this worry alone.

AS NORMAL OF A LIFE AS POSSIBLE

Life continued on with these bouts of gastrointestinal distress for the majority of our family, except my husband. I tried to navigate life as normal as possible, because I just couldn't take the valuable time away from our family. I did not want to focus on the drama of it all. Instead we continued to trudge through this difficult but beautiful life, raising these fabulous human beings, and dealing with all our health issues. I mean, what else was I supposed to do? I'd lived with that my entire life, and had to survive it, and I would be damned if the kids couldn't live a happy life too. Lots of time was spent in our bathrooms. I had the cleanest bathrooms in America!

It was about four years after our move to Georgia that my health took another decline. I was getting so sick that I wound up in the emergency room on more than one occasion with horrible pain, headaches, and dehydration. I had debilitating migraines, worse than before I got married, and I had no clue what was making them so horrible. This happened a few times and I was over it.

One afternoon in the beginning of 2003, while our oldest daughter was at school, the two younger kids and I had just gotten home from errands and a trip to Chick-fil-A—a huge favorite back in the day. It was no more than ten minutes before the pain began. I was running to the bathroom. The kids were playing in their playroom not far from where I was, but today was different. I felt really different. I was able to leave the bathroom, and I gathered them up to head to the doctor. I was feeling so poorly, but I couldn't make it out the door. I took their hands, plopped them in front of the bathroom with some toys, and I headed back in.

A long while later, I was able to make it to the doctors. I had placed a call to my husband and told him what was going on. I explained that something felt really off. He said he would meet me at the doctor after he got our oldest.

While we were in the waiting room, I noticed my vision was going gray. I really started to get nervous. I got up out of that waiting room chair with as much energy as I could muster, and headed toward the receptionist window to tell them I needed to lie down or something because I was not right . . . then bam! I was on the ground, out like a light!

Next thing I knew, people were pulling at my arms to get me through the examining room doors. I was saying, "No. My kids, my kids." They were towing them behind me. The stomach pain was so bad, but it felt like so much more was going on. My husband got there within a half hour and we were told to go to the hospital (I didn't want to go by ambulance because I knew that was an expense I didn't want to rack up). Thankfully, a friend came and grabbed our kids.

After hours and hours at the hospital, and many exams and tests, they told me that it looked as if an ovarian cyst burst, causing pain and fluid in my ovary. Well, that did sound plausible, because I have had ovarian cysts through the years. It had happened once before and it wasn't pretty, but I couldn't stop the feeling that there had to be more to that.

Maybe it was because I was so fed up?

With so many visits to the ER, and now this, I was at the end of my rope and I knew that something needed to change. I didn't think I could honestly keep going on like this; great for a few days and then pain in some form or another knocking me out of commission the next. *What the actual hell?* How could I run my family, my marriage, my business, and whatever else popped into life when I never knew when the other shoe was going to drop?

Other people could live life normally nearly every day. I, on the other hand, was on a rollercoaster. *Only me.*

ANSWERS FINALLY AND MORE TO WORRY ABOUT

It was through the guidance and advice of a dear friend that I learned about celiac disease, also known as Celiac Sprue or gluten-sensitivity enteropathy. This is an auto-immune disease where there is an immune reaction to eating gluten; a protein that is found in barley, wheat, and rye. In 2003 I had never heard of gluten, and honestly not many had.

My friend had been watching her children experience a large variety of health troubles and she was helpless in finding an answer. Her kids were very ill and had some truly odd things happening to them. Yeah, I was raising my hand in agreement while on the phone with her that day, because she was virtually telling me my life's story. She took them repeatedly to the doctor. Finally, after much testing, she was told that all three of her children, herself and her husband, all had celiac disease.

It is not very common that every member of a family has celiac disease, since celiac disease is hereditary. What are the odds that these two people found each other, married, and both had celiac disease? Well, like attracts like, I guess. Isn't that the phrase? Anyhow, it sounded promising to uncover an answer to our medical drama.

My friend was well aware of my health and what had been going on recently. She had to take me to the ER once. So yeah, she was quite familiar. As we were talking she said, "Jen I think you need to go to the doctor and get tested. You check so many of these boxes. We were only tested because of the kids, and we have only a few symptoms. It's nothing like you are going through. So, please go and find some relief for yourself."

If it wasn't for her and her family's journey, it might have been many years until I even heard of celiac disease.

After talking at length with her, I was in. There was nothing that was going to stand in my way if there was a possibility that I could feel better and be more present in my life and that of my family. Whatever it took I was committed. I did some research and found out a bunch of shocking facts. The most obvious one being that everything I ate had this thing called gluten in it.

I mean, all my go to things that I used to soothe my stomachaches and stomach distress were riddled with gluten—number one ingredient, gluten! Any time my stomach hurt, what did I eat? Crackers or pastina with butter. Let me tell you what pastina is, or was, because I haven't laid an eye on pastina in 17 years. It is a really tiny pasta shaped like a star. My mother lovingly made it for me as a child all way up until I got married, and then I made it for myself and my kids when anyone had a sour stomach. Pastina is loaded with gluten!! No wonder it didn't help.

I learned, that with celiac disease you can heal yourself by taking the gluten out of your diet, and in time heal your intestines. I called a gastroenterologist and had an appointment scheduled for a month from then. I couldn't wait that long with the hope that I could begin to feel better. It was within my grasp. I began to remove gluten all on my own, even without a diagnosis, the very next day. I hit the grocery store hard, and found an online store in Canada that had gluten-free options. I knew this was going to be a life change to say the least. No matter what though, I saw light at the end of the tunnel. For literally the first time in my life, I had hope that I could be normal.

If this potential diagnosis was true, then I in fact had answers to things I just thought was my crap luck. The way I saw it, after having to live with stomach pain and distress for the better part of thirty years, knowing what was causing it was an answer to a prayer.

It was amazing the results I saw after just a few weeks of a strict gluten-free diet; I was feeling so much better. Like a new person!

I began to wonder if the kids had this since it was hereditary. I so desperately wanted them to feel how I felt. They deserved to feel the relief that I was now feeling. It was a whole new world for me.

Celiac disease was the reason for so many of my physical day-to-day problems and for some of the medication I was prescribed. The obvious and biggest was my stomach, but the others were rashes, sinus pain stuffiness, headaches, random skin reactions to just about anything, pains in joints, agitated (because, let's be honest, who isn't agitated when they are always feeling like shit?), dehydration, and a bunch of things that I would later figure out. For my babies, much of the same! I knew those poor little things needed the same relief, and so Fred and I decided to take the step. We agreed that this would be the hardest thing yet, but the idea of them suffering brought us both to our knees. So we got everyone the necessary tests, traveled down that road, and arrived at the answers we each needed.

I saw a difference within a couple of weeks. The stomach pain and urgency I experienced for most of my life were gone. My headaches reduced by more than half. The eczema I battled with my whole life that no cream or steroid would ever clear up—gone. When we switched the kids, the differences in each individual child was remarkable. We have been dedicated to a gluten-free diet since 2003.

Each of the kids had a new lease on life. I am not going to sugar coat it and say that it was easy, how could it be when I was no longer buying Publix birthday cakes with cool decorated themes on them, or giving them cookies from the bakery counter when we shopped, or the fried chicken strips they loved, or the semolina bread we would grab for sandwiches after mass on Sunday?

Everything in life changed. And I had to hold it all together because deep down inside I knew what a life of pain would mean to them if they continued to eat gluten. I couldn't even try to explain to a four-year old why his cupcake looked so different than all the other kids cupcakes in pre-school. Or why none of them could have pizza at the parties anymore. I tried to make life as normal as possible, as I watched them strive more and more each day.

Do you know that my daughter who had 4 sets of tubes in her ears, and her adenoids and tonsils removed, never got an earache ever again? And her first noticeable "cold" wasn't until her 2nd year in high school.

Knowing we all had this disease, I went into "mama bear" protective mode on ultra. The danger I saw in the world trying to keep our bodies healthy was now magnified even more because anything they ate or touched could be a potential enemy of their bodies. I had to protect them, so I created a special box for each of the kids for their respective classrooms. In it, was emergency "fun" snacks in case some parent came in with treats I wasn't aware of. I was going to do all that was within my power to make them still happy in their lives while being healthy with a gluten-free lifestyle. I would prepare whatever they were having in the classroom, as close as possible. I believed it was my responsibility as their mom, not the teacher or friend's mother at a playdate, to give my kids what they needed to be happy and well adjusted.

I spoke at length with each of their teachers and explained what needed to happen from paint and glue, to food and cross-contamination. I asked that the teachers inform me of parties and any celebration they were having, especially the secret ones. I would prepare whatever they were having in the classroom, as close as possible. There was a bunch of research and experimenting happening.

There were many days I was so overwhelmed, but all I had to do was think of them thriving and I pressed on. I would think about our daughter who they thought may have ADHD. When we removed certain foods we saw a completely attentive and energetic eight-year-old. I knew I would never revert back no matter how hard it became.

I went all in. And in going all in, I created more stress for myself to trade off for the reward of our health and well-being. I had to recreate everything. I got wise after a while and always had a stash of really special cupcakes, both vanilla and chocolate, in the freezer, along with the ingredients for a quick frosting, sprinkles and all. I made our special gluten-free pizza and froze several slices, wrapping them individually. I went to the teachers once a month, or earlier if needed, to replenish their boxes. I gotta say, I never really thought about all the celebrations and treats when the kids were at school until I had to be aware of it. Wow, I was well aware of it now! Those kids were celebrating a lot.

We had some problems in the beginning with cross-contamination and some tears because the bread was too crumbly or the other kid's pizza looked so good. I tirelessly created treats and food, until I perfected my recipes so that they tasted just like the old ones they remembered, and in just a short time, they preferred me bringing their special treat. Years later, my son came home from school happy.

The class went to the park and had a picnic, and he said, "Mom! My friends all wanted my brownie instead!"

I got a huge hug out of that.

On occasion, especially when they were younger, they had meltdowns and there were a few times where I would have to sit down with them and talk about their celiac disease. They would plead with me to not have to deal with being different. I would ask if they remembered how they felt before we made the dietary changes, and they did. Then I would ask how they felt now, and they would tell me they felt great. That was all I really needed to hear themselves say before their faces would light up again and they were off playing.

After several years it became old hat. It was just how we ran our house. We built big pantries in the house to accommodate the baking goods and the treats I would have on hand.

Our kids were the best though. Honestly, I know it has been echoed by many mother's the world over, but I'll say it also. I was so blessed when I was given these three beautiful souls as my own children. They were always grateful. They recognized the efforts I made to ensure their happiness and that they were always included in all the activities. They never let a day go by without thanking me.

I would worry about possibilities of cross-contamination, 24-7, but they didn't see or hear me worrying. I would pray that they would stay in good health throughout their lives, and I would do everything in my power to keep them healthy and well always.

AND THE BODY STRIKES AGAIN

Once I had this lifestyle change well in hand, I thought all my prayers had been answered. I had never experienced life without stomach distress and it was a cool new world to be living in. I had successfully adopted a gluten-free lifestyle, but suddenly, just a short while after, I started to get stabbing pains in my neck, numbness down my arms, and excruciating stinging in my upper shoulders. DANGER with this damn body again? How could this be? I was rolling.

My doctor sent me for an MRI of my neck. The results painted a clear picture. I was told I had arthritis in my neck, from C2-C7, and that because of disk degeneration, I would have to have my neck fused. I was dealing with the kids and my stomach problems so this new development needed to take a back seat. I was not in the right mindset to deal with this, much less even fathom this type of invasive procedure.

By now Google *was* a thing, so I saw all I needed to see to know this was a biggie. I was well informed that there was arthritis in my neck, and it came as no surprise that it was the result of the trauma my neck and back experienced during the car accident NDE in 1986. I figured it was a small price to pay in this body for the fact that I lived through it, and it was showing up now nearly 17 years later. I placed it in the 'win column' and dealt with the pain through anti-inflammation meds when needed.

Sometimes it would knock me out of commission for a while. I would have to make adjustments; like not lifting the kids too much, or avoiding doing a repetitive action for a long time like crocheting or jewelry. I was told, by the medical community, that until I treated it surgically, it would continue to be a limitation and gradually get worse. I chose not to address that at this time in my life.

Only me. Only f*cking me.

As much as I knew everyone had their set of struggles, I felt mine were beyond my control, mine were worse, and I couldn't catch a break.

"With every struggle you are shown, and every hurdle that is thrown in your way, know you are where you were led to be, and with some perseverance miracles will unfold for you."
~ Meditations with Jesus and Jen

Pain [pān]

noun

physical suffering or discomfort.

Pain is when, in either mind or body, you experience discomfort that grabs your attention, "zaps" your energy, and has the ability to stop you from experiencing your "normal" life.

CHAPTER 7

Pain, Loss, and Questioning
if Life is Worth Living

"It all goes away. Eventually, everything goes away."
~ Elizabeth Gilbert

"Jen, your dad just passed away."

2003 was a big year. We changed our diets, and we were preparing to move. My husband had an opportunity to expand his business to coastal Georgia. Several months before this big move, the unthinkable happened, an event that would forever change who I was in this world and how I saw this world as well.

May 1, 2003, my father passed away, suddenly.

We were all at soccer practice for our two younger kids when my husband received a call. He looked ill when he closed his cell phone. He turned to me and said that we needed to leave now. I asked if everything was all right, and he said it was fine. I asked again because he looked so gray. He told me, again, that we needed to go home. We immediately gathered the kids and left the practice. We had separate cars since he met us at the field after work. I had all the kids in my vehicle. I was so concerned with why he looked so ill. *What couldn't he tell me?* I thought maybe he was sick.

I found myself also fantasizing that my parents were coming early to help with next week's birthday party and communion party. I thought maybe my husband didn't want to get into what the call was about too much because they wanted to surprise me. We had a lot of celebrating to do the following weekend, and we always went a bit overboard on food and festivities. We really just love to have a party. My worrying was quickly replaced with excitement.

Cooking, food, and the sheer joy of working together in the kitchen was always part of my life with Mom and Dad, even as an adult. Preparing a beautiful feast for ourselves and tons of friends was an important key to the celebration as far as my parents and I were concerned. We were building the kitchen in our new home in the coast of Georgia to have the space to honor this tradition of huge cooking parties. My husband and I would marvel at the design and say things like, "Oh, Tony's gonna love this counter space." Tony was my father. He loved cooking, and he loved his espresso. He had a special machine that he made it out of, and he loved that thing so much too, that he he bought one for our house for their visits. "Maybe we can set his espresso machine up in this space here," we would say as we looked at the architect's renderings.

When we got home, Fred told the kids to go watch TV, but asked me to stay in the garage. I told him he was scaring me now and to tell me what was up. His eyes filled with tears and that's when he told me my dad passed away.

I screamed.

I felt like I couldn't breathe. It was such a surreal experience—like I wasn't in that garage but rather watching myself experience the tantrum. That's what people did on television shows when they heard horrible news. That did not happen in my family. I had both my parents. No one was dead! That just didn't make sense, and it could not be true.

If it was true, then I knew I would never be the same person again.

My father was my best friend. We spoke several times a day. He was the person that we ran things by when we needed advice or ideas. We all did. Tony was our rock, our leader, our mentor, and our friend. My children thought he hung the moon, as did my husband and I. He would light up a room with laughter and was never down in spirit. He would always say, "Down time is wasted time! There is no need to waste time being upset or sad. God will provide for all that we need, always." He lived by this motto, even when things were tight at his business.

I treasured our relationship. At the time, I had no idea how Dad would impact my life even after his death.

After the news of Dad's sudden death, I was a zombie; not from physical pain but from mental and emotional pain. I don't remember anything of the day or so before we left for the funeral in New York. I know that Dad was in New York and Mom was in Florida. (They were setting up residence in Florida in preparation for Dad's immanent retirement.) The plan was for Mom to go to New York, and they would come to Georgia together for the birthday parties and big communion celebration.

My mom was all by herself when she learned of Dad's passing. He was not ill. His death was completely unexpected. My father was driving from work in Brooklyn to join a lifelong friend and his wife for dinner at their house. It was told to my brother, who went to the side of the highway to see Dad and identify him, that his vehicle was slowing down and simply steered off the side of the road and stopped.

A gentleman had followed Dad's vehicle, because he saw that Dad was in need of help. That gentleman called 911. Then the kind stranger called the last number on his phone, which was his office. The office immediately called my brother, who went immediately to the scene. God bless my brother, and the job placed on him.

When my brother arrived, the gentleman was nowhere to be found. As a family we later discussed what the probability of a stranger stopping was under these circumstances. He stopped to follow a vehicle that was simply slowing down to go off to the side of the road, in a controlled fashion, at 5:30 p.m. on a busy New York City highway. I mean, New Yorkers are nice, but often in too much of a rush to notice things like that. We all decided that the person had to be an angel.

My brother told us all that Dad had definitely passed, but he had a smile on his face. That fact was such a comfort to us all. What Dad saw upon his death brought a smile to his face. We all knew that he was faced with a type of rapture we could only imagine you would see when faced with Heaven. (Dad would later tell us of this rapture, and how God and His love could really affect my life).

SIGNS, SIGNS, EVERYWHERE SIGNS

I became unglued on the way to the airport for our flight to New York. I was unsuccessful in my desperate attempt to keep my uncontrollable crying under wraps. I didn't want to make my confused children any more upset, so I prayed for help. I prayed for God to help me, then I prayed to Dad. With my eyes closed, tears continually streaming down my cheeks, I asked him to give me a sign. I asked for any sign that showed me that he could hear me and was still with me. I felt that if he could at least show me that, I could handle the next several days of greeting hundreds of people, seeing him in a casket, then having a mass to say goodbye. I stayed quietly in prayer, with my eyes closed, for a few more minutes then I opened my eyes.

There was a large tractor trailer to the right of us. It was keeping time with our vehicle, but what I saw immediately was the writing on the truck: "It's Me. It's Me. It's Me . . ." I took a shocked inward breath to confirm I wasn't losing my mind (any more than I thought I had lost it the last two days), and I asked my husband what the writing on the truck said. He read it exactly as I had and said, "Oh, that is funny. I have never seen that company or slogan before. Wonder what company that is?"

I was frantic to tell him. The words were coming out so fast, I could barely believe I was saying them. I told him my prayers, and he had tears in his eyes and on his cheeks and he said, "Yes, Jen. I see the same thing. I knew your dad would not leave this earth without communicating with you. It will be all right, honey. We'll get through this."

And as a confirmation of what we just saw, my husband turned on the radio to relax us, and a new song we had never heard came on the radio called, "Calling All Angels" by Train. It spoke of needing signs to let us know they were here. We were learning what it truly meant when things were divinely in order. These signs helped soothe the pain, as we knew he was with us. I just couldn't bear to completely lose my father. But his passing did open up a part of me I was not prepared for, a part of me in deep pain that I had to stuff down for the duration of the next few days.

We landed in LaGuardia airport in New York and received another sign from Dad. As we were walking to the baggage area, our oldest daughter found a penny on the ground. This moment was so important to her. It is forever ingrained in her mind; she even remembers the tile on the floor of the airport. When she reached down for the penny, she was so excited. I explained to her that we can get signs from heaven, people sometimes refer to these signs as "pennies from heaven," and that might just be Grandpa's way of saying he was with us all. She looked so happy and relieved.

The wake happened much like I thought, with the majority of the time spent trying to hold it together. It was wonderful to see all the people who came to pay their respects to our dad, and it was nice to hear their words of kindness. At the dinner break between visitations, we all went to an Italian restaurant not far from the funeral parlor. My brother and I were so excited to see that they had cold seafood salad. It was a favorite of Dad's.

Growing up, we always honored the "no meat" on Christmas Eve tradition—known as the feast of seven fishes or The Vigil (La Vigilia). This was a tradition from Southern Italy dating back to Roman Catholic tradition of abstaining from eating meat on the eve of a feast day. Our family made a cold seafood salad on Christmas Eve for as far back as I can remember. I continued with this tradition when we began our own family and always made it with my parents, when they joined us for Christmas in Georgia.

The only thing in the salad that was not my favorite was scungilli (a large sea snail). It had a tough consistency, but luckily for me, since moving to Georgia, it was impossible to find. This became a running joke with Dad and me. We would talk on the phone each day and plan our meals well in advance of their arrival with great excitement. I would joke with Dad and say, "Thank goodness we can't find scungilli in Georgia, we obviously would have to make the salad without it." He went so far as to bring it in a cooler one year. We always got a laugh at the scungilli.

So there we were in that Italian restaurant in Oyster Bay, on the first day of Dad's wake, concentrating on ordering and talking to keep our minds off of the reason for us all being together. My brother and I were excited to see the family favorite, so we both ordered it. When we received the salads, I burst out laughing and crying, tears flowing down my face. In front of me was a seafood salad that was comprised of 75% scungilli. My brother's plate was a beautiful, even distribution of all the proper seafood for this culinary delight, but my plate was a joke from Dad.

That evening my mom asked if I wanted to say the eulogy. I said yes, but inside I was screaming *NO!* I could not speak to hundreds of people about my best friend and father without having a complete breakdown. The morning of the funeral was a blur. We were trying to get three little children ready for something I didn't even want to be present for. I was praying, rather pleading, for strength all while I was thinking *I can't do this.* I would have to say I couldn't, and we would just carry on with the rest of the mass. Then a wave of warmth came over me, and I heard, "Of course you can do it. You will be happy that you did." Was that God I heard, or was it what I wanted to feel my dad tell me? Whatever or whoever it was, I felt calm. That was it.

I gave the eulogy at my father's funeral. I choked up once, but I got through it, expressing my love and admiration for the man who raised me and my siblings, and who everyone there felt a special connection with. I told the people sitting in the pews in honor of Tony, that when they felt special talking to Tony and having his undivided attention, well, they were special and they did have his attention—that was his gift. Dad always truly loved everyone he was with.

Returning home to Georgia and resuming life was my next challenge. I began the task by pulling the suitcases into our master bedroom to begin the laundry. I found a surprise from Dad. You see, when we were preparing to leave Georgia for the funeral, our youngest child was in a frantic search for the toy airplane that Grandpa gave him the year before. He loved that little plane that made the sound of taking off when the little red button was pushed. We all searched everywhere. Every bed was looked under and all the toys were taken out and looked through. It could not be found, and he was very upset because we were getting on a plane, and because Grandpa had given it to him.

My wonderful friends had helped me pack all of our clothes and helped me straighten up, so that when we came home, it would not be a mess. Walking into the house that way helped me so I didn't have to see all the chaos that occurred when we were preparing to leave. As I numbly walked into our bedroom to place a suitcase on our bed, I stepped on something smack in the middle of our floor. It was the toy plane. I smiled knowing again my dad was sending those signs.

One week after Dad's passing, we had our oldest daughter's First Holy Communion and our youngest's fourth birthday celebration. The Communion would be the first event without my father, the first event without Grandpa. This was the first time we had a big party without cooking with him. Well honestly, it was the first of anything without him. We were all having moments of crying on and off.

As we sat in the car in the church parking lot, our daughter cried. She explained that she was so sad that Grandpa wasn't here for her big day, and she could not make herself be happy. We talked, and I told her I understood. We got out of the car and began walking from the parking lot to the church. As we walked onto the sidewalk, there was a penny. My daughter saw it right away and picked it up. We all said that it was a penny from heaven once again. Grandpa was with her. It was amazing how that helped her and all of us adults as well. It was now the second time we received a penny since Dad's passing. Little did we realize that there would be years and years of pennies.

As I write this book, over sixteen years later, our daughter continues to find pennies. The pennies come when she needs the reminder that she isn't alone, or a reminder that she is loved, or when there is a reason to be excited or happy. Sometimes she finds many pennies in a week.

Much like my oldest daughter, my middle daughter and I find pennies as well when we are in need of the reminder of love and that we are not alone. The best part of everyone's penny stories was that they were never with any other coins. They were in the strangest places right when they were greatly needed.

A few days after the big party weekend, I woke up with all the words and pictures for my book *Heaven Cent*. I had never thought of being an author before, let alone a children's book author. But Dad gave me everything I needed. He nudged me gently, and in my heart I felt someone might need those words. Who was I to hold back Divine inspiration?

A DARK, DIFFICULT, PAINFUL PLACE

The following months following Dad's death proved very difficult. So many things had happened, from the ectopic pregnancy, to viewing everything as a threat, to the health issues we all had, to the unexpected moves, and the sudden, untimely death of my dear dad. I thought I was losing my mind. I would describe to my husband that it felt like I was in a dream. I could not fully make anyone understand how disturbing this feeling was.

Often upon waking, I would feel like what I was experiencing was not real—the surroundings, the actions, the movements. It all felt like I was dreaming. It didn't make any sense at all. While I was awake, tending to my family, going through life, I would think to myself that this cannot be a world where the magnanimous personality that was my father was no longer around. It just couldn't be. In my heart, I felt like he was still with us, but maybe on vacation. The thing is, if he was on vacation, he still would have called me. He would never not call me. This realization reminded me I was not dreaming, and this was not a vacation. My father was gone.

I would have dreams where Dad was speaking to me. In many dreams, we were on the cell phone much like in real life. He would tell me everything would be all right. Other times in these dreams, I couldn't find him or I was upset with him because he left us all for another family. Each time I would awake in a numb haze, having to remind myself that this was real. The life I was in—the one with three kids and a husband—was real. It was the same world where I was alive and Dad was not here anymore. This was the life where I couldn't talk and laugh with him. This was the life where I was alone.

I truly thought these things. In my grief, I actually believed I was alone. Meanwhile, I had a wonderful husband, three amazing kids, my incredible mom, a bunch of family, and friends. I also had Jesus and God, but I believed them to be just outside my reach. As I lived my everyday life, my mind flitted along with thoughts of despair while this hole in my life felt like it would never be filled again.

"Hey, Foof!"

"Hey, Dad. What's up?"

"I'm driving home from a Rotary Dinner and thought I would say

hi. I just want to make sure you are going to have what I need to cook when I come in 2 days with Mom for a visit. Sorry for all the calls today, just didn't want to forget." We'd spoken earlier today, as we did every single day. He then asked, "What are you up to?"

I looked down at my outfit of sweats, and a big night shirt. I'd been soaked from the kids' baths and had just changed. No bra because hell, I was over it at that time of the day. The baby hadn't nursed in forever and a bra 24/7 was no longer a requirement.

"Well, I am standing at the sink washing the dishes and the floor at the same time—in my current post baby body!"

Only my dad would get my joke immediately. He started to howl in laughter. The bellow quieted enough for him to say, "Jen, you crack me up like nobody can. The things you say, you are so my daughter!"

"I love to make you laugh, Dad, but I can't tell you how scary close to the truth it could be . . . Weight Watcher's here I come!"

Besides having my dreams, besides the many memories of the many conversations we had, I began hearing Dad right before I would wake up and before I fell asleep. At first, I thought I was hearing him because I wanted to communicate with him so much. I thought I was making it all up in my mind. All of the signs I saw after his passing came as such a comfort to me. I saw these outward signs as justifiable and believable signs he was there with us. But hearing him, I was very unfamiliar with. Even the time before his funeral, I thought the greater possibility was wishful thinking on my part.

One night, before falling asleep, I got a crash course in hearing Dad. And so this new relationship of communicating with Dad began. At this time, I would lull myself to sleep by reading a love story, nothing too deep or mind stimulating. On this particular night, as I was reading I heard Dad thanking me for taking care of Ronnie, my mom. I heard the words as clear as a bell in my mind. (This was a bit different than anything I had heard before.) He continued to say that I would be doing this for him, and he knew that, and he was very grateful. I felt his love for my mom. I saw hearts and hugs. I sat there in my bed, with my eyes closed, astonished and bewildered.

Did I just really hear actual words from Dad while I was awake?

Did I feel his love and see images? Again, while I was awake!

I was happy but I still held onto a tiny bit of doubt. That nagging thought came immediately—did I just want to hear him so badly that I made it so?

I opened my eyes and continued on with my reading. I turned the page in my book, and in several spots on the page a new character was introduced. The woman's name was my mom's name. It was spelled just like she spelled it: "Ronnie", which was short for Veronica. There, in that moment, hearing and feeling my Dad's words and feelings, then seeing the words on the page in that love novel was when it sunk in that it was truly Dad. He was making sure I understood that the communication was real.

I had never before had the need or desire to see the depth of connectivity with spirit. Never before had I sat in deep contemplation of God's love that flowed from us forever, even once the body was gone. These concepts were something I think I just took for granted. I assumed all was well with my soul, so to speak, since I had a devotion to God, the Trinity, and life itself. I prayed daily and I went to church faithfully, but that was the extent of thinking about what would happen once I left this body. Yet, here I found myself in deep contemplation of "What happens to us when we die?" It just was not in my wheelhouse of thought or understanding. I guess you could even say it was a mystery to me. But at that point, it appeared that it was one I should face because I was communicating with my father!

"Foof! What are you up to?" Dad's voice crackles across the phone connection this morning. *I love to hear his voice in the morning.*

"I don't know, probably about a buck sixty at the rate I'm going!"

His loud guffaw comforts me as I push down the thoughts of how close I am to my joke. The baby is a complete surprise and this weight is not. Damn bed rest!

These conversations replay over and over in my mind. *Did I speak to him about everything I wanted to speak to him about? Did he know how much I loved him?* I think he knew. I know he did, but it still would swirl in my mind a bit. I just felt a hole in my heart so very deep, and I wanted him to know how much he was missed.

I knew that God was God, and He loved us all. I trusted in that fact, but I never delved deeper into it. I had no clue that the deeper I dove into knowing about that love, the better I would feel about myself, about death, and about the world in general. From 2003 on, I went down a road of uncovering things in the life as "Jen" that would rock the foundation of all that I thought I knew. Things were showing up in my life in the physical body, in my thoughts (in the metaphysical), and spiritually. I was pretty oblivious for a long time of all that was playing in the background of my life.

I learned, unfortunately not quickly enough, that in order for me to be truly happy and have peace, I had to uncover the lessons I needed to learn one way or another. My lessons ran deep and were plentiful. And it all seemed to tie together for me. Eventually I would see that this communication with Dad would propel me into a more rewarding, love-filled relationship with God and myself. You will learn all about that later.

Five months after Dad passed, we moved into our new home in coastal Georgia. My mom sold just about everything and moved in with us. Once she felt settled in, she would begin to search for her own home in our new town. We all went on with life. Dad was always on my mind. I was raising the kids and enjoying the new life we'd created in that new area. We became very involved in church, and I began to teach religious education again. I was also happy with what I thought was a close relationship with Jesus and with God. We had many friends, and we hosted lots of parties; we became part of that new community.

NOT SO FAST, SWEETIE

I loved that part of me that still was able to have fun and be with friends. But the other part of me kept tapping me on my shoulder saying, "Not so fast, sweetie. You still have pain. You are broken. Your body is broken. And no amount of partying will change that."

When I would feel moments of joy, the damn body would cause me pain again. And I lived in it. I lived in that pain deeply, behind closed doors of course. No matter how hard I tried to brush it off for many hours of the day, I could not get out of that attachment to my body, felt deep inside that it was only happening to me.

And so a few years after my father passed, some particular health issues became more and more noticeable. Let's just say I was a bit young for *Depends* and just couldn't figure out what was going on. Turned out, I had to get a bladder sling, and I learned after the operation that other organs needed to be "tacked" as well. That news would have been really good to have before the operation. But alas, no dice.

The urologist told my husband and me, immediately after the surgery in the recovery room, that he should have called for an OB/GYN, but there was no one on call that he knew. He said that I would need to address the problem of my severely prolapsed uterus very soon. He expressed how he hated to leave it like it was, but it was not in his scope of expertise, and it needed to be fixed or else more issues could arise. He was, however, able to tack part of the colon that was prolapsed.

Wait, what? My colon prolapsed?

My uterus prolapsed?

*My **body** is <u>literally</u> trying to come out of my body?*

My body is in so much pain that it literally is trying to exit the building which ironically is causing even more pain?

Only me. Only me. Only me.

Those thoughts quickly swept through my head, but I had no desire to go there at that moment, in the recovery room, so it was filed away. Unfortunately, the sling he put in place was too tight and after several months of great discomfort and the daily need to self-catheter, I had to go under the knife again to fix that problem. It required an overnight stay at the hospital, but when I arrived home the next day, I headed straight to the bathroom in horrible pain. I felt like something had torn.

Is it possible to tear the stitching?

Wasn't this supposed to help the pain?

Oh my, Lord. This is hell.

My husband called the urologist, and he instructed us to meet him at the hospital. In his examination he discovered that the nurses left the post-surgical packing inside of me and that was what caused the unidentified stabbing pain. He admitted he too should have checked this before my release. He removed a softball-sized packing from my insides, and I was too angry to react. My insides were burning up, not just in pain from the packing but in WTF level anger. I mean, I just didn't know how much more I could take. The cracked shell of me was fully shattering as I felt like a woman, a young woman who was marred in issues and pain—gross issues at that. How could anyone, especially my husband, find me the least bit attractive? I was losing my insides, I was riddled in pain, and I was catheterizing myself. And to think, I had a softball size packing left inside of me, as if I was not even human. My brokenness was beating me down good.

After the procedure, I still remained in intense pain for several weeks. No position (whether standing, sitting, or lying down) relieved, it so I was tested for nerve damage. You have to understand something, if there was a test, I was the one to have it. And with every test came the worrying as I waited on the results, panicking over what could happen if the results were positive. Nerve damage sounded pretty permanent.

I can't even sit! When will I be able to sit normally again?

Is this excruciating discomfort now my new norm?

How could I be neglected like this again?

Will I ever find relief?

How do I fix it?

What about my family?

Does this happen to everyone?

No. Only me.

My spinning mind would swirl every time until the results came in, and on top of that, I was worrying about my kids every move, on top of grieving my father still, on top of feeling like total crap, all while smiling and acting normal.

Eventually, my unidentified pain was diagnosed as a levator syndrome, also known as levator spasm, caused by using the bathroom while the packing was still inside me. It was a side effect of the softball. I tried hard not to take the pain killers, because that was basically all I could do to relieve the pain. I wanted to be a present, coherent, loving mom for the kids. The pain killers just numbed me out, and that's not how I wanted to go through life. So, I endured the pain instead while the kids were with me, and when I was alone or trying to go to sleep, I medicated.

A few months after the second surgery, the levator spasms slowed down and I went about life as normal again (whatever that meant). Still looming was the need to address the uterus, so I made an appointment with an OB/GYN. He said that the uterus was so severely prolapsed and the best option for my complete comfort would be a hysterectomy. So that was done next. Add that to the growing list of procedures.

Removing parts of me. Check.

NOT FEELING FAMILIAR WITH MYSELF, WONDERING IF LIFE IS WORTH LIVING

Between the time of the first and second bladder surgery, I was severely depressed. I didn't call it that at the time, because on the surface in front of people I was happy. I would make jokes about my messed up body, but pretty much laughed it off over dinner and cocktails with friends. Deep inside, deep in the core of my being, I felt unfit to live. I felt I was an enormous burden because I spent too much time in doctors' offices and hospitals. I just had so many issues at such a young age. My husband deserved a whole woman who was vibrant and healthy inside and out. My kids would be so much better off with a mom who could run and play without discomfort.

I had thoughts of taking my life.

I believed that my family would be better off without me as such a burden. I thought of how I would do it. I thought about being free from myself, and the guilt of being Jen. I believed that it would bring freedom my family needed as well. I really believed in my heart that my existence was causing more harm than good. I thought my wonderful husband and beautiful children deserved so much better. And, I thought if I died, I wouldn't be alone. I would be with Dad who understood me and accepted me as I was. Dad laughed at my craziness but also understood my pain. I pictured reuniting with him.

But then, I remembered what I was taught about suicide. I wouldn't be accepted in the pearly gates of Heaven. So I couldn't bring myself to do it. In my religious upbringing, it was made clear that if a person committed suicide, they would not go to Heaven because it was a sin. I struggled with that. I just couldn't handle the pain and the mental suffering, because even with all the surgeries, I had no relief in sight. I thought about what it would take to take my life. I calculated how much medication I would need. I planned and I tried to figure out the best timing. Each day, as I laid in bed and heard my family going about living their normal lives while I was miserable and feeling useless, feeling like a failure as a wife and mom, I thought and thought. And thought.

One day, covered in tears (and a lot of snot), I told Fred my thoughts. I will never forget the horror on his face. He asked me how I could think that would ever be a solution. "How could we live without you?" he asked. "What about the kids, Jen?"

He continued in a serious but gentle way, "I'm disappointed that you would think that is even an option. I love you so much. I can't raise them without you. We all need you. Don't you know that?"

I wondered, as he spoke, if I could articulate my desperation to be different for them all. How could I be a mom and wife when I was so broken? I knew what he was saying to me was his truth, but I thought he didn't fully see mine. "Fred, don't you see that there is a big struggle for me? I think of a life for them without a damaged mom, a mom that has energy. Shit, a mom who isn't always recouping from surgery! When will things ever change for me? I heal, then bam," I said loudly as I gestured with my hand, slamming it down on the comforter that was over my legs, "and I am right back to yet another problem. I'm damaged, tired, and I'm not even 40 years old yet! What kind of mother am I???!!!!"

"You're their mother, honey."

I promised Fred I would work on how I was feeling. We held each other for a while, but it didn't go unnoticed, that when he got up to leave me to rest, that he took the pain pills away from my end table next to my bedside.

That day was the hardest because I sat for hours trying to logic my way out the struggle inside. I had the nagging idea I might not be with my loved ones when I died, and that possibility was unsettling. Then I thought of the damage my committing suicide would do to the kids and my husband. I sat alone in silence as I thought, "Was being this crappy mom better than no mom?" I knew on a level that what I was thinking was fundamentally wrong, and I truly heard what my husband said. I knew the pain in his eyes and voice were real.

Then it came . . . the horrific realization that in my search for freedom from myself, I could hurt those very people I spent years protecting and loving with every fiber of my being! I couldn't be the one to leave. I couldn't do that to them.

Then I became horrified as I thought of the possibility that for one moment, one of those sweet souls could think I didn't want to be with them. Oh, the tears come just writing this! How damaged I was to think I could ever go through with that idea? How completely and utterly broken I was. Of course, me choosing to take my own life wouldn't help them. It would crush them.

I decided that there was no way I would take the chance that they would think my decision was in any way their fault. The love I felt for my family was stronger than the hatred I had for myself.

So, I put the idea of suicide away, and lived with this:

I am the wife of a great man.

I have wonderful, smart, and kind children.

I will show my love for them every day, in everything I do.

I will put myself on the back burner. I will hate myself in private.

Because really what else could I do but live with the guilt of wanting to be a different kind of mom?

ME AND MY BROKEN BODY BECAME MY SECRET STORY

At times, I was willing to forgo Heaven for some relief from my thoughts, but deep inside, I knew that my children would never be the same if I did that. I could not bring myself to put them through that tragedy, so I thought that if they had an "unhealthy" mom it was better than not having any mom at all. I felt ashamed. I thought of myself as the mom who always had a problem—no one could ever possibly understand what I was feeling or know the levels of my shame.

That became my story.

I listened to my thoughts about myself and believed what I heard. I saw everyone else having a great, healthy life, and I believed them to be better and happier people than I was. I saw my friends run miles and do just about everything, and they never had even one operation or physical problem to compare to my seemingly countless total. At that time, I knew nothing of the *A Course in Miracles*, energy, or the Universe, and how I related to it all. Our thoughts are magnets, and looking back I can clearly see I was basically willing in that broken body. "Bring to me this thing I do not want," because it was what I thought on endlessly day in and day out. (Oh, we'll get into all this in more detail later. Promise.)

I eventually got the thoughts of taking my life out of my mind. I decided to persevere, miserable as I was. I placed my attention on other things. Roughly a year after my last surgery, I began to experience a reoccurring sharp pain in my stomach. I knew I wasn't getting gluten cross-contamination, so I had no idea what it was. Apparently, my gallbladder wasn't functioning and needed to be removed. I prayed and prayed that this would be my last surgery.

Let's see. The list of surgeries to date include ectopic emergency surgery and tubal ligation, retinal surgery, cerclage, Morton's neuroma removal in both feet, bladder surgery, bladder surgery again (and the levator spasms that came with it), hysterectomy, and now my gallbladder! My body couldn't take any more.

Now my story, the one that I created about myself, was killing me. But the only one who got that peek into my thoughts was my husband. No one could ever tell what was going on in my mind. I was great at keeping it all hidden. I went to church and prayed, sometimes even begging God to make me better. I gave all the power I had to the thoughts of who I believed I was.

I filled each day with caring for my kids, and smiling and laughing with friends (often joking about my body, it became part of my schtick). But, inside, I wasn't laughing about my pain, I actually thought so little about myself. I was nothing but this failed body that was lacking in every way. I was a flawed body. I was heavy; not this fit in shape lady who had a problem-free body. I was deeply ashamed of what this body was doing, and I identified myself completely as a body. My story was a sad one, it was depressing, and I was stuck in it with no way out.

Happiness, love, and abundance were all around me, and yet I could never see it. I still felt I was lacking. Sometimes I would even believe I was being punished for something. Then I would quickly try to erase that thought because God would not punish me, right? Then I would read that "God never gives you more than you can handle". So, I translated that to mean "Buck up, buttercup!" or "What doesn't kill you makes you stronger!" I believed God was giving me this life and this was the life I was supposed to lead. But oh how badly I wanted to just push a button, yell "Uncle!", throw down the white towel of surrender, like "enough is enough"!

I would think of all the trials and hardships of the saints, and how they were in service to God despite what they faced. They went through such suffering and still remained optimistic and served God's will. They were showing God how strong they were and how their love never wavered in the face of pain and hardship. Yikes! Those were the role models I was up against. The pressure to live up to that ran deep.

I tried but I always fell short. I was not strong like the saints. In the face of pain, I was hurt, and I was angry, and I felt defeated by it all. I did attempt to think of my health problems as burdens that I was called to "bear" and by doing this, I would be showing God my strength and commitment. For goodness sake, look at how much Jesus had to suffer. The least I could do was live with all the pain, right?

But, with all these stories, encouraging words, and heroic examples of strength, I still couldn't seem to cut the mustard in the face of my pain and suffering. I had the hardest time living with it and having no complaints about them. I also had not mastered the art of true happiness, although I could fake it really well. The outside world saw loud, fun, and wacky New Yorker Jen, with the three fantastic kids and loving husband—I could act really well. Unfortunately, I couldn't seem to convince myself. Inside I was dying a slow, painful death through self-hatred and unworthiness.

I let all of the things that "happened" to me get to me, and so my story was a tale of woe. I had this very deep sadness within myself that remained hidden behind laughter and smiles. The way I saw the world was through my story. Seeing myself as I was back then, as a puppet to my thoughts, makes me want to reach back in time and hug the person who I believed I was and tell her to find a different story.

There was a sort of power that my mind, beliefs, and thoughts had on me-keeping my perception of myself as a *victim* of my story. I was not yet able to address it because I had no idea there was anything playing out in my life other than my misery. There wasn't any room in the story for the victim to be saved. Since I was unaware that there was a story being made and lived out, I couldn't very well address it, or identify who the leader (or writer) of it was, or figure out how to stop it from playing out. The secret continued to be just that, my secret story.

There was no way of knowing the journey I set in motion with that "body" based on the story I believed about it. I had never once conceived that there could be a different way of looking at myself and the life I was living. I never imagined that I could possibly have peace, joy, and love while I had a body so riddled with problems. Boy was I in for a surprise. Unfortunately, I still had a ways to go to the bottom before I would begin to see anything differently. You would have thought that a near-death experience, or the ectopic nightmare, or contemplating suicide would have done the trick and been my rock bottom, but apparently, I needed a bit more to shake me awake.

"Guilt holds us in chains, and a limited, chained-up being cannot soar. Believing you are more than what your thoughts have been telling you is a giant step to taking your life back. When you move out of your own way, the sky's the limit on the happiness you can uncover. A mind that thinks with the ego focuses on the body's suffering and dims the light inside that wants to shine. Getting out of a head full of limiting thoughts and stepping into life without them is truly living your best life. Knowing you are connected to all that IS, is like re-discovering yourself."
- From Meditations with Jesus and Jen

Trapped [trapt]

verb

> prevent (someone) from escaping from a place. Have (something, typically a part of the body) held tightly by something so that it cannot move or be freed.

> *I was trapped. There was no way out from this situation, thought, or experience. I have to live riddled with not only this body, this pain in the body, but also with this guilt and shame for feeling trapped in it.*

CHAPTER 8

Deli as a Diversion Tactic, Circle Time, and No Way Out

"A golden cage is still just a cage."
~ Anita Krizzan

"Jen! You always crack me up! I love this deli. I get to see the show and have a sandwich."

Yeah, I was pretty good at making other's laugh with my blunt and upbeat attitude, just saying whatever was at the top of my mind–that was the show. And that sandwich, that was because my husband and I opened a New York Style Deli in 2010, where the sandwiches were stacked high just like in the city I came from. When I had the idea to open a deli, my husband was hesitant but saw my enthusiasm and agreed. I thought it would be a great thing for our town and for me. I loved food and people, and anything to keep me away from myself being alone with myself was a good thing.

But, as the adage says, wherever you go, there you are—I couldn't escape myself.

So, there I was enjoying the success of our fun and delicious deli and even still, I continued to experience health issues. Overweight (for my small 5'1" frame), pre-menopausal, and unwell boss lady — that was who showed up to work each day.

I knew I needed to snap out of whatever funk that I was in. I didn't have a name for it, and I believed I was alone because I truly thought no one else was experiencing anything like me. If they had demons, they were keeping them well hidden. Looking back, I guess that makes sense because so was I. But, even with my new successful business, I still continued to believe it was my flawed "Jen" body at work again.

I felt like I was handling more than any person should have to. I knew I had all the "big" accomplishments under wraps: I had a husband, we had three healthy children, I was the owner of two successful businesses, we lived in a lovely home, I had friends, we belonged to a church, and I had good relationships with my siblings and my mom.

What is it that is wrong with me?

Why can't I be truly happy when I have so much?

Why can't I wake up pain free?

Where are the feelings of fulfillment?

What am I missing?

Why do I have to have this body?

How can I ever be truly happy with this flawed body?

Only me. Ugh.

Spin. Spin. Spin. I would go around and round with these questions and I never had a clear answer. I did, however, know that I was missing something big. I knew deep down inside that there had to be something more.

A huge chunk of my day was spent on keeping busy, being on my feet for 8-9 hours a day, working and laughing, meeting loads of new people. I did anything I could do to avoid the mirror so to speak. An unexpected benefit of opening the deli was having the opportunity to just observe people. I would notice how some people would walk in with a sort of *lightness*. I couldn't explain it fully, just that you know it when you see it in someone—they were floating through life, with an acceptance, a grace that was enviable. They didn't appear stressed out, and the ever-present smile had a serene energy about it. They were truly, deeply at peace where they were. I wanted me some of that!

ENTER ANGELS AGAIN
AND SO MUCH MORE

The deli opened up an opportunity for me to meet new people. A few of our customers were big into spirituality. Oh, yeah, I would chat with them and learn about energy, the Universe, and metaphysical ideas. I heard about chakras, energy of everything, and this energy-healing modality called Reiki. I listened to it all with an interest, but I still wasn't too sure about how these things could affect me and my life. But I sure did admired their enthusiasm and enjoyed the new information. I was also curious about how God fit into all of that.

The most I knew about energy was that you needed it for the oven to turn on and for a lamp to light up. Now, just imagine. Here I was feeling trapped in a body searching, seeking for some sort of peace, and God sent me some customers who wanted our signature sandwiches, and in addition to the eight bucks they paid for said sandwich, I found out about energy and so much more.

This newfound connection to deeply spiritual people triggered my interest in connecting with my angels again. Remember, they would come into my room and surround me while I was growing up?

Well, I had lost touch with them while the kids were young. Delving into this spiritual world, I purchased Angel Cards to see if I could communicate with them easily. I was drawn to them and was willing to learn about them, but really had no real idea what they were. I guess I thought it might also be something fun to do. I was open to guidance, and boy did I need it.

I was attempting to pray and meditate as often as I could each week. I had spiritual "energy healing sessions" with two of my friends, and I received Reiki. It was a very relaxing experience, but I still didn't quite understand it all. I didn't understand energy or energy healing or a lot of what they spoke about.

I was, however, doing really well with the Angel Cards, and I could hear and feel certain things, so I thought it would be fun to sign up for a mediumship workshop with a few friends. We spent the weekend doing a variety of exercises and practices with spirit. We had such a fun time, and we all received a certification of mediumship. The biggest benefit I received that weekend was simply confirmation and comfort. I felt very comfortable talking to the angels and doing Angel Card readings for myself and others, and I continued to receive confirmations from my father.

I also uncovered that I was not alone in the things that I heard or experienced. What a relief! I was learning to become more comfortable with the angels and with spirits talking to me, but I was not comfortable letting others know just yet. I lived in judgment of myself and what others would think of me.

I was a good Catholic girl, was this going against all I was taught?

Was it too "out there" for the small town I lived in?

Would people think I was off my rocker?

What would my family think of me talking to Dad?

I feared judgment, and this made me doubt some of what I heard and also prevented me from giving people the messages that I heard. I remained quiet and only did this communicating for myself, my husband, and a small close circle of ladies.

I learned in the workshop, and from certain things I read, that I needed to simply accept what came and not judge the message. I received the clearest messages when I was relaxed (not judging myself or having to do something "right") and did not fear the judgment of others. But I still limited myself to only certain people and a controlled environment, and primarily used them for myself and my loved ones. I had a triad of things on my mind when it came to speaking to spirit.

1) I had the fear of judgment from others;

2) I had a ton of judgment on myself for getting the wrong message, and if I should give the message at all; and

3) To top it all off, I had the lifelong habit of people pleasing so I wondered if speaking to spirit fit that story?

I was not willing to give a lot of time to practicing this because I held a firm belief that if that was what God wanted me to do, then it would be so. I shouldn't have to put so much work into it to make it happen.

WEIGHTY ISSUES AND A NEED TO CONTROL SOMETHING

Throughout the years, little by little, pound by pound, weight piled on my small frame. I didn't like it. In fact, I hid it by joking about my weight, but really, on the inside I hated how I looked in that heavier body. But I was really good when I decided to put my mind to something, so changes were underway for myself and my family. I took a good look at the ingredients of what we were eating.

Now mind you, this was not really "healthy" per say, but it definitely was an improvement. I started to feel better about myself, and it gave me something that I could control. My fears, my worries, and my pains were still present, and I felt I could not control them. But my weight, my food intake, here was something that I finally could keep in check.

As the weight dropped, I became very cognizant of every ounce on the scale. And if I seemed to indulge a little, that ounce would show up. I figured out if I ate a little less following the overindulgence, then it wouldn't affect me as much. It was a balancing act so to speak. Eat more, eat less, eat healthy. Eat more, eat less, eat healthy. All under my control, it felt natural and the number on the scale stayed pretty steady when I controlled my food intake that way.

Until it didn't.

The weight became a silent obsession when other parts of my life were out of control. I would over indulge at times, and so I would make myself sick afterward to get rid of the food. I did this when I felt haywire in other areas of my life. But, here's the biggest kicker, I had no clue that's what it was. I could mentally make excuses for my behavior.

Jen, you're not bulimic.

You don't have an eating disorder.

You got cross-contaminated.

You got sick because of all the food you just shoved in upset your stomach.

You can't have gluten. That's why you got sick.

Only me, only me. I can't even indulge without an issue.

But the funny thing was, it wasn't my stomach. It was ME trying to grasp control of just one area of my life when I felt most out of control. And it started out slowly. I would make myself sick after indulging only every now and then. Then it became a monthly occurrence. Soon, it would be every other week or so.

If this was an eating disorder, it would happen every time I ate.

That was what I believed. I believed it was my stomach revolting against the food I took in, and if I didn't get rid of the food I would be in even more pain. I just helped it out of my body a bit faster by getting sick. I just did what I thought my body was going to naturally do.

My mindset around weight was all turned around. Growing up, I would joke about my thighs but I was always small. My weight might have fluctuated a few pounds, but I didn't even care about the scale. I didn't even have one in my room. But this shifted after our son was born and our daughter called me fat. Well she didn't really. You see, I was leaning over the bathtub in my oversized night shirt one evening washing her and my oldest daughter's hair, and she had the biggest smile on her face as she began to clap excitedly. I watched, smiling wide too, as our beautiful two-year told me what was making her so happy.

"Mommy! Mommy! You are so fat and skubby! Right Mommy?!?!"

She found the right words. She was excited she had them and could describe me. She saw nothing wrong with fat or "skubby" (chubby). It's amazing how our minds can take an innocent moment such as this and use it as a beating stick to our self-esteem. I signed up for *Weight Watchers* the following day.

Well with *Weight Watchers* I succeeded in becoming a lifetime member, that is if I maintained the number on the scale. I was aware of every "point" I ate. This seemed perfect ~ as you know, I liked to maintain control. I noticed if I wasn't reigning in the "points" I ate,

I would feel like I did something wrong, and I needed to monitor closer if I wanted to maintain my status and my size. Well I lost that status as the years progressed. As life happened, with the stress of dad's passing and having multiple surgeries, the weight piled on once more. With diagnosed celiac disease, I found a new thing to control - not points, but gluten. And so this couldn't possibly be bulimia; in my mind, this was just an after affect of eating cross -contaminated food.

To the outside world, I was healthy. I just lost some needed pounds by eating differently. I couldn't believe I had an eating disorder. NO ONE KNEW how I felt about my body or what I did after I ate too much. I didn't want them to. It was my secret, because to me, it was no big deal. My need to control just one aspect of my life was greater than my need to tell anyone what I was doing. And so, my secret stayed.

"He will open up the way to happiness, and peace and trust will be His gifts; His answer to your words."
~ *A Course in Miracles*, Lesson 98 Page 175

CIRCLE TIME AND A COMPLETE CRACKING OF MY SHELL

As I mentioned, I had a newfound group of spiritual friends who I was exploring my spirituality with a bit. We would meet regularly for what we called our "Circle Time." But one of those meetings would change my life forever. I will never forget it.

The smell of incense greeted me at the door as my friend's soft spa music played in the background. It was just low enough because

I could still hear everyone's mixed conversations as I stepped farther into the space. I pulled my shirt off my stomach and stretched it down over my rear.

Is my ass covered?

Gosh, I hate when it shows.

Do I even really like leggings?

I know my body should never walk around in leggings without the full coverage provided by a big, long shirt.

No one else needs to see all of that.

I inhaled really deep and took a step closer to them as I let the breath out. I was there to absorb all the positive energy and learn something wonderful, maybe even magical, that I never knew before. Or maybe that would be the day I would unlearn what I thought was right and replace it with something cool one of those ladies had to share. I walked in both scared and hopeful, but either way, I was stoked to be there.

"HEY, girls!" I shouted. Hugs were shared, an "Oohh, that looks so cute!" and a "How are you doing? The kids? Fred??" were asked all at once. We bantered back and forth with our greetings like we did each week. I looked around for where I wanted to plant myself on what would be this particular life-shattering and altering day.

Sometimes I would sit on the floor cross-legged. I had always liked to sit that way since I was really small, but that day I felt like sitting on the chair with everyone else. We began to quiet down when it was roughly 30 minutes past our agreed upon meeting time and started to get to the meat of our meeting.

The meeting always began the same, by asking if there were any intentions anyone would like to state before we meditated. There were only a few on that day.

Do I want to ask for prayers today?

Sometimes I felt like I couldn't pinpoint just one thing, then other times I would be awake all night thinking of the things *I wanted*. On that day, I kept quiet.

We took a good 15 minutes in that peaceful state. Gosh, I always felt so good when I could get myself quiet. I remember the feeling well.

How come I can't feel like this all the time?

I am not thinking about me at all!

It's awesome.

My friend sitting to my right asked me, "How's the deli going? I absolutely love your chicken salad. I'm addicted! Did you know last week I couldn't get a seat. I was going to call you, but I knew you were so busy." I was surprised that she didn't call me. Of course, I would have helped her out, in the very least given her an order to go. The smile was huge on my face, and it made me so happy to think about how much everyone loved our food. I told her to please call next time and I would get her the order to go.

She said, "Thank you, but I wanted to watch the show, that's half the fun. And the way you greet everyone and know their orders. It sort of makes ya feel special, you know?" The smile on my face got bigger, if that was even possible. Pride filled my chest that we had created a place for people to come eat and enjoy themselves.

Our conversation quieted back down as another friend took the lead of the group on that day. We often would just do that organically, lead the group. If someone had something cool to share, they took over and then next week someone else would and so on. The memory of that day was sharp and clear. I remembered half listening to the leader discuss what we were going to do, but I was also thinking of the comments my friend just shared.

Why do I always want to sell that deli?

I loved it. It made me so happy to serve people, but at the same time, I wanted to be done with it even though we'd only just opened. I thought of the forget-me-nots when I was younger; *he loves me, he loves me not, he loves me, he loves me not.* When I would get to that last petal, and it was a "he loves me not," I was either bitterly disappointed or I picked another one until I got the result I wanted. Was my life a big ole forget-me-not?

Can I keep picking at things until I get the exact result I want, and what is the result I want?

Back to my group.

What is she saying?

Heart chakra.

Love center.

Self-love.

Oh man, not self-love.

This memory popped into my heart. Again, listening, but my mind wandered still.

I am sitting on my bed crying; he doesn't want me! All he wants is this other girl at school. I spoke that last sentence out loud to Mom. She wanted to know why I was so upset today. Well, there it was. I was dumped. Well no, I wasn't actually, we were broken up. I didn't really want to date him anymore, so I have no idea why I feel this way. Then he started to date someone else.

For a year, he would say "I love you" a hundred times a day (I counted once and he hit a hundred, hand to God), poems, phone calls at night, notes throughout the day. Sometimes it was all a bit too much, and now someone else has taken my place. Why the hell do I care? Shaking my head to make sense of it all, I look down at the pile of papers in my lap, pencil and pen drawings look back at me. He was an artist so they are all really good.

A tear hits the top picture. I am an athlete. I am a good student and I even take some honor classes. I have friends. He picked a girl a grade younger! My mom reaches for my hand and says, "Jen, I know it hurts, but you have to love yourself more. You know you can't truly love someone else until you do."

What does that have to do with anything?

Loving myself has nothing to do with this, Mom.

"So . . . when you all go home try and practice this." The leader was finishing and I was off in la-la land remembering something.

Oh man, what did I miss?

I should've sat on the ground. I could've sort of relaxed because this self-love topic was giving me this tingly feeling that I was not comfortable with. The leader continued, "Just look into the mirror and say 'I love you.' Simple as that, but really notice how it makes you feel. It might be hard at first, or maybe you will have a huge smile on your face. It is pretty neat to see how it affects us. Then you can meditate on how it made you feel."

It was all so new. I was learning about all these new topics: energy, meditation, chakras, spirit. I was learning so much with that group of ladies and it was really pretty spectacular. I had been told that spirituality was different than your religion, and I was starting to feel it just expanded on it so much.

I hit the grocery store on my way home. I ran by the middle school to drop off papers in the teachers' mail boxes. The PTSO has been my full-time, non-paid job since our move to Coastal Georgia over six years before, and I was sure it was one of the reasons I knew so many people in the town. My mind began to spin trying to occupy myself with anything to do other than what I was assigned in that class to do.

No Sam's Club run for me today; my husband said he would do it alone so that I could have the whole day for myself. For myself? Other than the "Circle" what else can I do? Haircut; nah, I am uninspired. I have it up in a hat and ponytail five days a week anyway while I work at the deli. At this rate it will be to my ass in no time.

I chuckled to myself, maybe it will cover me when I wear these leggings.

Is there anything else that needs to get done on my one day off a week? For me, nothing. For everyone else there is always tons, but I believe I have done everything.

There is that exercise of self-love my friend said to try.

What else might the kids need me to do today?

I called a friend to check on her. We chatted for a little bit on my drive home. I thought I could call my mom; no, it was a Monday and she was at mahjong. I texted my sister before "Circle" and she said she'd call me later that night.

What else, what else?

I got the supplies the kids needed for their various school projects that were coming up, and even grabbed extra snacks, too. We went grocery shopping yesterday. But there was nothing else I could distract myself with. Oh, how I tried.

I pulled into the driveway and looked up at the house. I remembered this almost as if in slow motion.

Man, I love this house; it's my dream home.

I smiled because the rose bush was in full bloom. I thought how much my husband loved it and how he just loved the outside. He planted those bushes and didn't tell me. He said he was waiting to see when I would notice them. I never did. Three months after he planted them, he asked, "Did you ever notice anything different in the front yard?"

I said, "No, why should I?" He should have known better: I never noticed things back then. I was spinning. Mind going in too many directions to notice rose bushes in front of my home. But, when it came to others, I noticed. I thought about being in a room full of my friends. I noticed everything! I picked up on the feelings of others and what they said. I noticed stuff at work, always.

I looked at the house, with my foot still on the brake and the garage door open, waiting for me to pull in, and I thought—*Why am I numb to so much in my life?*

How could I have not noticed those beautiful rose bushes?

Jeez, what else am I missing?

When I walked in the house, the dogs greeted me. I took care of them and then they ran off and began to play together. They didn't need my attention. I glanced at the stairs that led to our bedrooms and a bunch of mirrors; but alas, I decided to start making bread for the kids' lunch instead. 1 TBS of zanthum gum, ¼ cup oil, 3 eggs . . . I had the recipe memorized after seven years of making it several times a week.

If I push start now, they can have some for dinner.

Should I start dinner now?

It's only 1:30.

How come this day is taking so long?

Where are my beautiful distractions?

When will they all be home?

Fred was meeting with a friend, who was also our insurance guy, after his Sam's Club run, and he was going to get a haircut.

With nothing left to do, I finally walked up the stairs.

They are so beautiful, these stairs.

They mean so much to me.

Before the stairs were placed against the wall, we wrote a passage from the Bible in honor of my father who passed. He was a "stair man" like his father before him, like my brother, who built these stairs for us where he worked in New York, for our new home. Traditions, Dad, and family love. That was what I thought as I walked up the beautiful mahogany stairs.

I found myself in the master bathroom looking into my small makeup mirror, as opposed to the large ones that took up nearly half of the room.

Wow, these mirrors sure do catch everything from the waist up.

Looking back at me were my plain old brown eyes. They were filling up with tears and I hadn't even said a word. (My eyes have always slanted down in the corner, and I've often wondered where they came from), A tear trailed out of the corner tainted with my black mascara. I wiped at it quickly.

Why am I crying?

The tears wouldn't stop. I grabbed the beautiful stone counter top as I looked down at it. Mind distracting myself again.

How I love this counter, exactly at my height for easy teeth brushing.
My husband thinks of everything.
He never misses the details.

It had thick edging and tiny rose and cream colored stone tiles in an intricate pattern.

Stop, Jen, look back at the mirror.
I love this bathroom.
Stop looking at the stone counter, Jen.

I wanted a home with stone floors and no rugs and that was what we had. I turned back to that smaller mirror and glanced right above it to the large bathroom mirror that went all the way to the ceiling, the tears began to flow in earnest now. I was sobbing.

"I . . . I . . ." That was all I could get out. My chest hurt from the sobbing and I couldn't seem to catch my breath or even swallow.

I'd been here before; it was an ugly cry. I have never been a gentle, graceful crier like you might see in the movies. I was a real life, honest to God, turn your head away, it was gonna get messy, crier. It was messy.

Standing in front of the mirror gripping the counter, shaking, there was no looking away. Alone with myself. I had an incredible urge to go find someone, but everyone was busy.

I am stuck.

I looked forward to my people, but no one was there, there was nothing to distract me. I hung my head low until my chin was touching my chest. My shirt was getting wet, I used it to mop at my face.

So wet.

What I see, I don't like.

Who is this?

Does not feel like me.

Flashbacks. Flashbacks to a carefree Jen.

__8-year-old Jen__ ~ Looking down at my yellow shirt with a big rainbow, and my pink shorts, right before I climb on my bike. Today I am going to go find my friends on the block. Maybe we can go jump in the sound across the street. I wonder if James will be there? I wonder when I will have a chest? I want him to like me like a girlfriend. Maybe once I have a chest!

__12-year-old Jen__ ~ This weekend was the best! I went to see a Broadway play with a distant cousin and her mom, and I got this cool black t-shirt. West Side Story in white letters across my chest. The shirt is a bit snug over my chest because I have begun to grow boobs! My brother's friends are so cuttteee! I wonder if they will notice. Maybe when they get bigger, I don't look as good as the older girls yet.

I looked in the reflection of the mirror to the door that was behind me. It led to the toilet room. Shame washed over me. I thought of the times that I got sick in there and no one knew about it. Binging and purging and blaming it on my stomach. How long had it been? Five years? No, maybe seven? My excuses disgusted me.

I don't do it every day, sometimes weeks will go by and nothing.

You're fine, Jen.

You just ate too much.

But I get rid of the food when I think I've eaten too much.

It's your stomach, Jen.

No, it's not. It's time to get real.

I had this duality. Two voices inside my head, one telling me I was fine to continue going the path I was on, and the other feeling like she was about to explode in her own skin. No more faking it. No more smiling through the pain.

I make myself sick.

I can't get any bigger!

There is a reason you do it, Jen. Your stomach . . .

I am not bulimic.

People who do that aren't like me.

I have reasons for things.

Things happen to me!!

More flashbacks. Remembering, justifying, hurting, not wanting to face that part of me. That broken, ugly, messy part of me. Flashing back and holding back.

16-year-old Jen *- Why does this happen to me? Minutes after I walked away from the dinner table, my stomach began to hurt. I ran up the stairs to the kid's bathroom, and I have been in here ever since. It hurts and I can't stop going. I am rocking back and forth on the toilet. Oh man, my stomach is killing me. I am stuck in here and I have so much homework to do. This is absolutely excruciating.*

24-year-old Jen - *"You have retinal detachments. There are countless holes in the retinas in both your eyes. We need to act fast, like today, because I can't in good conscience, tell you that you won't lose your sight when you leave this office. Memories of the retinal surgeon flash.*

26-year-old Jen - *I am being rushed to the hospital. I know I am dying. How can this be? We went from being pregnant to me dying? This is so confusing and so not fair.*

38-year-old Jen ~ *"Your bladder is like those I usually see I in women I their late eighties." The urologist drones on, I tuned him out already. Is he F*$@ing serious?*

The memories like fireworks exploded in my mind. I continued to justify without fully facing that damn mirror. Circle Time never brought me to this place. All the fuck I had to do was say I loved myself, and all that was happening was hatred, disgust, venom toward the woman I couldn't even make eye contact with. And part of me, part of me still tried to stuff it down.

I have my reasons.

I am not like everyone else.

I don't need to go talk to someone about how I feel because shit happens to me.

What are they going to do to help with that!

Near-death car accident, bladder surgery, two pregnancies with bedrest, ER. visits, celiac disease, losing Dad: so much. I have to stop thinking of it all.

Getting sick is on me. I do that to myself because . . .

Just as another excuse was about to slip into my brain, I glanced back at myself in the mirror. And then finally, this thought . . .

The me I see is so not the me I want to be.

Shame filled my chest. I thought I calmed down, but I was starting up all over again as I thought of how much I loved my family.

They were the reason I held it together, but they weren't there in that moment—I was alone with myself.

I wailed out loud, "*Nooooo!*"

I fell to the ground, holding my head in my hands. And you know what I did. I still tried to hide.

At this point, I will have to shower and change.

No one can see me like this.

The kids will be home at 2:45.

The love and pride I felt for them was outweighed in that moment by the weight of the guilt and shame that was suffocating me. My hands dropped to the cold tile of the floor. I hadn't noticed how cold it was because I was cold all over. Like I had no more blood in my body. I was just a shell. Empty and raw. Only my eyes moved, and they hit that toilet room again and I cried. I cried until I emptied myself. Nothing was left. The suffocating feeling still did not stop. I was overwhelmed by it. I was trapped.

Mind racing again.

I have to pull it together.

I need to be whole, and I have no idea what that even means.

How can I feel like a shell and then have so much love in my life?

"AAAHHHHHHH!" I screamed again. "What is it, God! Why won't You help me, dammit!" Those words I said out loud, and loudly.

How could I feel both at the same time? Yet I did. If I focused on my family, I didn't have to think about me. The same old story played, "If only this . . ." "If I only could do this . . ." "If I was . . ."

Always looking for something.

All alone on my floor, on that particular day, I was not that feisty Italian deli owner, wife, and mom of three fabulous human beings. No, this was the me that I was. Broken me. And I needed to take her out of hiding, mend her wounds, and heal her. She deserved the same love I gave to others.

As I sat there drowning in my thoughts and feelings, I could only see darkness. There was no light at the end of that black hole I was at the bottom of.

God, I need Your help. I want to be happy! How can I be happy? Please, I have been asking You for so long. How do I stop being so unhappy with myself? I want to feel about myself the way I feel about everyone else.

Telling others I loved them was the easiest thing in the world. I looked forward to showing others how much I loved them, with a little note, or a special surprise. Each night was always a home cooked meal. I shopped often to make sure we always had everything that was needed or wanted, available at home. The notebook was always on the counter, and it was understood that when you needed something or you ran out of something, you wrote it there so Mom could get it for you. I didn't want anyone to be without what they needed. But more than the things, I liked to show them I cared by doing things for them.

It was so easy to tell others I loved them and to show them love, yet I couldn't do that for myself. Circle Time broke me.

I had been pushing myself down that black hole for over 15 years (and at that point), I was unsure if God would even be able to reach me down there or if I would ever be able to see myself as truly happy again. I might be too broken to be able to climb out.

Eventually I put myself back together and was presentable for the kids and my husband. When I began to start dinner, the kids were at the kitchen table doing their homework, and they were all rattling on. Boy was it loud as they excitedly talked about their days. That was what I needed. I asked them why they were so excitable today, and they all agreed that they stayed quiet at school, so as not to get in trouble, and they had to let it all out sometime. My oldest began to sing, while my son made corresponding beeping noises and the middle one broke out in a dance, and they all burst out laughing. I couldn't help but laugh too and shake my head, "You are all a bunch of wacky people!"

This was more like it. No more me—only them.

OPENING THE DOOR TO THE TRAPPED JEN AND LETTING FRED IN

After spending the evening with the kids and preparing them and myself for bed, I pulled my husband into our bedroom, then into our closet. He was confused why I had pulled him in there, and asked what was up. I started crying and told him that I was lost. I told him about earlier that day in our bathroom. I told him about what I did after I ate and my reasoning behind it all. The reasons made sense to me when they were just in my mind, but when I said them out loud, I felt like such a fool. I told him I actually felt that I hated myself a little bit and he hugged me. Big and strong. He hugged me as I cried, soothing me with his words of love and comfort. He said he would do anything I needed to help and support me. There in that closet, my husband told me that he hated how I felt so sad. He was baffled by how I saw myself, when he and the kids loved me with all their hearts.

Moving into our master bedroom after a while, we talked for a long time. I felt so much better and I agreed that I would make a real effort to not harm myself. I knew I needed more than that, but I didn't want to worry him further.

I've got this.

I can do this for them . . .

Oh yeah, and for me too.

After we finished our talk and went to bed, I stayed awake for the better part of the night mulling over this darkness I felt about myself.

19-year-old Jen - *. . . 99 sheep, 100 sheep. Do I count back down now? I am still awake. "Our Father . . . " Still awake. I look at the clock, now it's 2:00 a.m. It was just 12 a.m! Have I been awake this entire time? I need to sleep. I have classes tomorrow. Why won't my brain shut off? I run through the things I need to do. I even grab a piece of paper off my desk and jot some things down and out of my head. Yup, still awake. Now what? Ugh, more thoughts. Dad told me the last time I was awake like this to just keep in mind that at least my body is lying down and resting. I just don't know why I can't fall asleep. I wonder . . .*

As I laid there, I thought about all the wonderful things in my life and that always helped me, but they never seemed to be able to help me completely. Like here on my own, when I was alone with my thoughts became the running commentary that snuffed the light right out. I wanted to only feel good and happy, and I had absolutely no way of knowing how to make that happen other than keeping busier and busier so I could drown out the feelings. Yet as I laid there that night, I felt my heart beginning to race. I felt a little tingly, like I was nervous about all the things I was feeling and a lot overwhelmed.

The overwhelming feeling pushed me against the proverbial wall, and told me, "Jen, there is no way to escape me!" I felt desperate and a bit panicky all over again. That familiar hot and cold feeling washed over me, and I recalled when that feeling first began years before. That feeling mocked me right along with all the other thoughts. It was like I was being chased by a playground arch-nemesis that I'd tried really hard, for years and years, to ignore. My body just never seemed to give me a break, and thoughts of it were haunting my nights now too. It (my body) constantly poked me with a stick my whole life and didn't appear to be stopping. It was never going to end was it?

I began to pray to stop thinking about how I would never truly be peaceful.

Come Holy Spirit, fill my heart with Your holy gifts. Let my weakness be penetrated with Your strength this very day that I may fulfill my duties of my state in life conscientiously, that I may do what is right and just . . .

I turned my face into the pillow to stifle the sob and the sniffling. I couldn't wake my husband. I guess the panicking settled down because the next thing I knew it was morning, and time to start all over again. Ugh.

This is when I began the real journey of seeing ***all the parts of me***.

"Believe nothing you have learned from that thinking mind but all that you desire to be. There is your true 'form.' Peace, happiness, joy, joyfulness, joyous, bliss, love, eternity, contentment abundance, laughter . . . Wipe the slate clean of who you thought you were before. It serves you no longer. Just because it is all you knew, never made it right or correct. Fear has no place in truth. Fear arises when you have a belief system that makes no sense because it is NOT THE TRUTH."

~ Meditations from Jen and Jesus

BRIDGE

The Shift That Shifted Everything

"You're only one thought away from changing your life."
~ Wayne W. Dyer

My protective mechanism was to keep myself busy. My being busy would make the time alone with my thoughts less, and so I kept busy with the kids, my two businesses, volunteering at church as a teacher, and on the board of the PTSO. And while the busyness helped me to manage keeping any outward panic episodes to a minimum, I still felt shaky inside. It was like, an internal vibration, all of those feelings just in a bottle rocket inside of me waiting to burst. Yep, I knew something was going to happen, I just didn't know what.

And the "something" felt extreme. Either I would find a miracle or I would explode, and I would disappear completely under the weight of my feelings. I was just waiting for it. I mean, I thought I might have been having a nervous breakdown. Or I was going flat out crazy. I was not clear on the difference, but I thought it must have been both because I still felt out of control on the inside. One minute I was all right, and the next minute, I was panicky. The miracle sure seemed like a better option, but I was moving closer and closer to explosion mode.

It was a few weeks before Easter and I wanted to watch the movie, *The Passion*, with my family. Of course, they were not into it. I had already watched it once the previous week, but no one wanted to be sad again they said. I had a movie called *The Shift* that my friend lent to me earlier that week. She said it was great and the kids would like it, but that Fred and I would love it!

It was kind of a nonchalant moment putting the movie in. I mean, I was bummed we weren't watching *The Passion*, so I was just going to make the best of it with the alternative. I didn't know too much about it, other than what my friend said. The cover promised "finding life's meaning," but I couldn't imagine anything more meaningful than *The Passion*. I had no idea that the movie we chose as second fiddle actually held the key to the miracle I'd been waiting to unlock. Isn't that funny? Here I was just settling for an unknown movie, and God was smiling, knowing how He worked through the strangest of ways.

My friend was more than right. The kids liked it. Fred and I loved it. That might even be an understatement. When I watched *The Shift*, I sat there tingling and numb. Afterward, I felt kind of frozen. Like, what the heck just happened? I looked at Fred and I knew in that instant he felt something too. After a few moments of silence, when it was just the two of us, we talked about the movie. We shared what we felt was missing in both of our lives.

Connection.

Peace.

A deeper relationship with God.

I smiled and I cried my eyes out. It wasn't as if I didn't know those feelings. I have had a special connection with God and the angels since I can remember. Feelings of peace flooded back to me. I know those feelings, as far off as they seemed, I could remember them from somewhere in time when I felt that deep relationship with God.

Oh, how I wanted to feel again what Wayne Dyer spoke of. I

wanted to know that peaceful, consuming love and connection with God. Fred and I agreed—we both wanted to feel this way all of the time. The happy part, not necessarily the tears. But of course, I would take the tears if I ended up feeling this way constantly. I never wanted this feeling to end. It was as if all the parts of me just clicked into a "Oneness" with who I truly was. I felt more complete in that moment than I had in so long. I wasn't alone. I wasn't this broken body. God wasn't some distant being watching over me from afar. God was within me. My perception of life, of who I was, was actually just a misperception. And I could slip back into that "Oneness." I could be still in that peace-filled feeling of wholeness, I just needed to work on seeing it all differently—the movie said so! I knew this was where I was to begin.

I jumped up to grab tissues. We had none, so I grabbed a roll of toilet paper from the guest bath and ran back to the couch to continue talking to Fred. I knew this was nothing like my ugly cry, and I had to get back to that conversation because we were onto something.

Excitement bubbled inside of me. Ohhh, I kicked my knees up to my stomach in a goofy run as I made it back to the couch where I jumped, literally, back into the spot I'd vacated just 20 seconds before. I hadn't felt like that in I can't remember how long. I was running on all cylinders.

Is this what hope feels like?

It meant so much. I didn't even hide the tears in the shelter of our bedroom. I just sat right there on our family room couch, holding my husband's hand, and let it all hang out. Those kids could've come in at any minute, but surprisingly no one came through, and we had the time to discuss so much. The only other being to have interrupted with our talk (and tears) was our oldest dog, Bruno, who sat at my feet so confused. It looked like he was a little worried by my crying. Those were the tears of realization and oh, so much more. That sweet dog was probably having a nervous moment recalling the wailing from my bathroom all those days before when he was unable to check on me and my well-being—always my protector.

We talked more about how we didn't know how we got to where we were, feeling like something big was missing, even when we had always been faithful and did everything we thought we should be doing. Yet, as we sat there, we wholeheartedly agreed we wanted to feel as happy as that guy, Wayne Dyer, did on the screen. He just looked like he experienced rapture from the moment he placed his feet on the ground. He was in gratitude and looked at his life with a peaceful acceptance. I knew as sure as I was sitting there on that couch that I wanted to feel that feeling. I knew I was nowhere close to feeling how he felt, but *The Shift* was exactly what I needed to begin my own shift. When I set my mind to something, I could usually achieve it.

By God, I am going to experience this peace and live in this peace, I thought.

I knew that the man who wrote, directed, and starred in his own movie portrayed an image of a person who felt right in the world and in his own skin, and I knew I didn't. Not yet. But memories came flooding back to me. I remembered a time where I was *him*. I recalled, perhaps even before entering this world, a feeling of *Oneness*. And I remembered the angels, how they came to me as a little girl, and even after the ectopic, and in brief moments throughout my life—when the angels were near, I felt complete peace. And like a flash, that near-death experience (NDE) popped up again. I walked away from that accident knowing my Oneness even if I didn't have a word for it.

It was like a lightbulb that wasn't fully switched on, just made brighter. *The Shift* reminded me of who I truly AM, who we are all born to be. My NDE, my connection to the angels, even talking to spirits, were all integral parts of the Oneness that I craved. In *Oneness* we are all connected, and at peace, and in gratitude. Simply put, God created us all in the energy of love. Every being here on earth and all the divine. Nothing truly ever separates us; we just believe that it does. Believing that the body precludes our ability to connect to this Oneness was what actually stops it.

Whoa!

In the NDE I experienced a calm, in the presence of all that was. Like I was plopped smack in the middle of the Oneness that God created—there was a knowing that I could be fine right where I was. I was immersed in Oneness through that death experience. How could I have forgotten? But maybe that was what we were all to do with our precious time here. We were born of Oneness, and the journey through humanness and brokenness was essential to be brought back to Oneness. All those years feeling incomplete and now remembering who I am . . .

It must have been at least 3 hours that we sat there on that couch until one of the kids came in the room and asked when dinner was because they were "Starrrvved!" We looked at each other and burst out laughing. We forgot about dinner and feeding ourselves. We were just that excited! We looked at the clock, and sure enough, it was well past our normal dinner time. We were too involved with our new game plan, and we weren't going to stop this flow by making dinner, so we called in for Chinese food and faced the TV to watch that movie again.

"My conclusion about my origination is that I came from Spirit, and my true essence is that I am what I came from. I am a Divine piece of

God. I am first and always a spiritual being inextricably connected to my Source of being."

~ Wayne W. Dyer, quote from *The Shift: Taking Your Life from Ambition to Meaning*

PART THREE

My Oneness

Oneness [ˈwən(n)əs]

noun

identity or harmony with someone or something.

Oneness: connectivity to all that is.
The source of all creation, people, the earth, all living beings are all part of the Oneness of creation, God. And, in this Oneness, there is love. For that is what we all were created to be.

Unlearning [ˌənˈlərniNG]

verb

discard (something learned, especially a bad habit or false or outdated information) from one's memory.

Unlearning is breaking of habits and beliefs we have formed throughout our lives, uncovering the truths that support who we truly are, not what we believed we once were.

CHAPTER 9

Learning and Unlearning

*"Empty your cup so that it may be filled;
become devoid to gain totality."*
~ Bruce Lee

"Jen! You can't possibly be a princess with that rat's nest on your head!"

Oh yeah, that was my brother teasing me. I was five years old, and there was a snow storm outside so my brother was home from school. I was so excited because he let me pretend that I was a princess with magical powers, with long beautiful, shiny blonde hair of course. My hair was quite the opposite—brown, curly, and wild. It only hit right above my shoulder—not the hair of a magical being at all.

Every morning my brother would tease me and say that I looked like I had a rat's nest on my head. But no matter what he said to me or how much he teased me, I felt like I hit the jackpot that particular snow day. Playing with him was silly and fun.

I wrapped a blanket around my head, and I pretended to have long hair like the genie from the show, *I Dream of Genie*. I blinked my eyes, just like she did in the show, and pulled his left ear, and he turned left. I blinked my eyes, whispered in his ear to pick up the banana and give it to me . . . and he did! That was the best snow day in my entire life. We laughed and had fun. Oh, and his teasing was that of brotherly love, because if anyone else told me I had a rat's nest on my head, my brother would sock them in the jaw, I'm sure.

I was looking back at that time of my life, so simple and pure. And I wondered when and where things changed—when life became more about "getting through" the day instead of embracing it.

I had become a professional survivor.

Maybe even a little badass, because I went through a crap load of stuff and still lived a pretty good life. Watching *The Shift* lit a fire in me, but I had a lot to dig into, a lot to unlearn if I was going to really change my perception after decades of living in pain. I had a debilitating rough patch that lasted years, with so much private shame, hiding my emotions in closets and bathrooms.

Survival at all cost was the name of my game. After all, that was what I did most of my life and now was no different. Here I was a mother of three, a wife for nearly two decades, and for the first time I knew I needed to do more than just survive my hurt body and mind. Feeling buried underneath an unsurmountable amount of physical trauma, I desperately needed to be rid of these feelings about myself. I prayed and prayed for direction or a miracle that would simply wipe all of the hurt away and make me a strong human being with a strong, healthy body. I guess I still didn't accept all the parts of me, because all I really wanted was to be done with that huge part of me. I wanted to just forget her and shift into that peace Wayne Dyer spoke about—the peace he exemplified.

The thought of being happy all the time gave me such excitement that I would tremble, I could feel it coursing down my skin, exactly like I felt when I walked into Abe's candy store as a kid, anticipating the treasure that lay in front of me on his shelves bursting with every candy I could ever hope for. I would imagine being able to be happy with who I was all the time, and being able to "shine" when I was alone with my thoughts, not only when I was with others.

STARTING THE COURSE THAT PUT US ON THE RIGHT TRACK

Right after watching *The Shift*, I purchased two copies of *A Course In Miracles (ACIM)*, and Fred and I both started our journey, individually yet right alongside of one another. If you aren't familiar with *ACIM*, it is a self-study spiritual thought system, published by *The Foundation for Inner Peace*. Hello! Even the publisher spoke to my desire for peace! The authors are "scribes" as the entire text was given to Dr. Helen Schucman, dictated by an inner voice that she identified as Jesus. Dr. William Thetford helped her with the process of scribing that which was dictated to her. The whole backstory is rather fascinating.

The funny thing about *ACIM* was that I actually bought and sold it years before. When I started to read it, I was like *what the heck is this?* It felt so different than the things I was taught as a child about God. See, I always thought God was this big guy outside of me. Like He was literally watching down from Heaven, maybe even waving His finger at me like a father figure. And I knew about the Trinity, but that also felt like the Father, the Son, and the Holy Ghost were entities outside of me. And, yes we could pray to them, but the thought that Jesus was speaking to the scribers of *ACIM* was way too "out there" for my beliefs at the time. Jesus, talking to someone in modern times? Oh no, that was something from the Bible, surely not this century. I couldn't wrap my head around it all so I sold it at a garage sale for a buck.

But watching *The Shift* reminded me of *ACIM*. And I was open to just about anything to get that feeling of peace inside of me. I didn't even know that peace wasn't something I needed to "find", "get", or "achieve" at the time. I now know peace is a state-of-mind, a state-of being; we just need to unclutter all that clouds it, blocks it, essentially unlearn everything we've learned through human conditioning.

I figured a book published by the *Foundation for Inner Peace* surely must carry the promise of peace with it, so it was first on my list to dive into. Fred and I would often sit in our family room on our respective couches reading *ACIM*. We would read, discuss passages and concepts; we would even think of our lives and discuss how we could implement these new ideas. We noticed a definite theme of love and trust that made us both feel so comfortable—it gave us hope.

It just felt right and secure to see things differently than the way we had before. On the weekends we would often lose track of time as we sat there and had long in-depth conversations. Ideas would volley back and forth and we would often notice the massive improvements in our mental well-being that inherently spilled into the rest of our lives, when we would allow the ideas we uncovered in this thick blue book. Fred often woke before me and read, and in no time, I had my very own live-in mentor.

In time, I was able to be of service to him as well. It was obvious to us both that we could offer a different perspective when the other of us was in a jam. Every single time we saw something in our lives differently, and saw an improvement appear in our lives, we were sold. It was like our old thought patterns were poison and the way we were learning to address things was gold—if there was a measure then surely we would be considered billionaires.

When I began reading *A Course in Miracles*, it was a portal into looking at and examining my thoughts and my daily interactions in a whole different way. The first lesson is this:

*Nothing I see in this room
[on this street, from this window, in this place]
means anything.*

Then you are instructed to look around and say out loud that everything you see means nothing.

Nothing!

NOTHING!

The chairs mean nothing. The doors mean nothing. The TV means nothing. And even my body. I had to look at my hands and my feet, and whatever parts of my body I could see and say out loud, it means nothing.

Well, if my body meant nothing than what the heck had it put me through throughout my life? I was desperate and so I adhered to the lessons, and soon my whole perception of every aspect of life began to shift bigtime. And with this shift came difficult self-reflection. I must admit it was tough at times to look at my thoughts and behaviors. I was embarking on a new chapter of my life. I felt called to read this book.

The words somehow made sense to me, although at times, the ideas were hard to process. It was like my soul knew these words were truth, so it was comforted. My mind on the other hand had a bit to untangle. There was another way of seeing my life. I knew I loved Jesus, God, and the Holy Spirit. I had been going to church every week since birth, but this allowed me to get a clear understanding on my real relationship with the Trinity. I hadn't realized that what I had could be magnified. I began to see this incredible relationship with the Divine Creator.

Every word written gave me hope.

A Course in Miracles offered me a beautiful reminder of God's love. Throughout the text it is explained how we can find peace when we allow the Holy Spirit to guide our mind. It explains the ego and how it shows up in our lives and shows up as fear. And that we have a choice on who we allow our mind to listen to—when we choose the Holy Spirit, then we are aligned with God's love and can find peace.

The best way I could reconcile the idea that Jesus is the one who spoke *ACIM* was that I told myself, "Surely anything that could bring me closer to God and Jesus and the Holy Spirit can't be bad." *ACIM* isn't a religion, it doesn't take the place of one, but it was a tool that strengthened my faith even more.

Because I allowed myself to ignore the thing that blocked me before and just read it as if Jesus "could have possibly said this" I saw the similarities in all I knew of Him my entire life. The text and the lessons guided me back to love. Immense love of myself and God, and myself as being one with God, not separate but God within me. The lightbulb!

I hugged that thick blue book to my chest as a lifeline to knowing myself and God. I wasn't alone in the quiet any longer. In the stillness I heard hope. I felt it deep in my soul. When I was hearing the thoughts that pushed me into the blackness, I had a way out. Seeing the fear that I lived in for so long brought me even closer to the lifeline of the Holy Spirit and accepting His guidance. When I did, I was told about love, and peace, and hope. This blue book spilled out reminders of all the wonderful positive things I heard growing up about God. I heard my whole life, and knew fully, all about Jesus's messages of love, but I had been operating like it was all outside of me. The words I was reading and the feelings I was having led me to see that this is not the case.

I really wanted to get all these words in *ACIM* to sink deep into my awareness, and my life. But I had spent a lot of years thinking I was just a body, and God was not inside of me. I had been alone in this suffering and this damaged body. I was beginning to understand I had a lot of work ahead of me, but I knew it would be worth it.

To simply state, *A Course in Miracles* helped me along the way in all this learning, and what I call my "undoing" process. I was beginning to see, feel, and experience the something more I thought I was missing. The thing I knew I was missing still contained what I was quite familiar with—the Father, the Son, and the Holy Spirit, but deeper than ever before in my life. I began to practice relying on the Holy Spirit's guidance to unfold God's plan.

There had to be a "way out" of being me, the me that was miserable and in pain. I just knew it was out there and there it was. All this time always right there, God. Looking at myself, others, and God . . . well just about everything gave me a clear picture that every single thing started with me. My life literally became the practice field where I encountered daily reminders to center my thoughts to a God-mind not an ego-mind. After all, ego is "edging God out" so it certainly was worth the effort to look at it. I decided I was going to stop throwing up barricades to my own happiness. I knew I was heading toward something big if I gave it the effort. Also, I felt so much better when I did. After all what I was learning was: Who are you allowing to be the mind's teacher?

This is the way I was beginning to see this:

The ego is your mistress or secret lover. You spend a lot of time and energy with it and you ignore your one true love.

And our thoughts well: The human body is a thought bucket. It's full of thoughts to the brim and it overflows into your life.

Nothing is ever as bad as it seems. Meaning . . . nothing is ever as bad as your ego-mind will have you believe. Weed through all the thoughts it throws at you as roadblocks to finding your happiness. Get to the root of it all. You are love. You are perfect. Happiness IS yours. You are part of God. Period at the end of the sentence, done!

If you are attached to your story, and it doesn't work for you, you are unhappy. Then let's find you a new story.

The ego loves thoughts, it looks on pain as a vehicle to get you to move where it is more comfortable. And that is where you are less aligned with who you were meant to be—who you were designed and created to be.

Focus your attention and energy to it—you give it power.

If you accept and give it no more attention—it has no power.

It has no power over stealing your joy, your peace, and ultimately your life!

PERCEPTION AND PAIN AND PRESENT MOMENTS, OH MY

This period of learning and unlearning was mind blowing. I was moving toward the Oneness I craved, but my humanness and my brokenness was harder to shake than I thought it would be. I'm an "all in" kind of gal, so if I was really going to be in Oneness that other stuff had to go, or so I thought. And so I was sponging up all the learning I could, and in between my studies with *ACIM*, I would pick up books that were recommended to me. If it was aligned with seeing things differently, and maintained a connection to God as love, I was on it. I remember reading the *Power of Now*, by Eckhart Tolle. This book reinforced the importance of living in the moment, and once again this made sense to me. It's like all of these spiritual teachings had a home inside of me; they felt so very familiar because they are familiar to us.

I could see many correlations between this idea and that which I read in *ACIM*. I would practice being in the moment with the understanding that the ego is sort of like a bully. It used the past to keep me stuck. I was very familiar with how I allowed the ego to bring the past up front and center. When I thought about the things I did, or that happened to me (or the things I didn't do) in the past, I wasn't in the moment. Where everything happens. Where God is.

I remember once learning to never speak in "I should've" or "I could've" and I found it intriguing that by bringing the past to the present moment, I was in essence doing that exact thing. Oh, how often we all subconsciously do this.

The past is part of our history, but many times we make it our story. I was coming to understand we are meant to learn from it. The past gave us a lesson. But, to go back and torment yourself in what you could have or should have done is useless. You can't go back and change it. The only thing focusing on the past does, is ruin the present moment where you can be happy. Here, in this moment, we can make a choice to do things differently. Nothing is EVER a mistake. You wouldn't be where you are now if there were mistakes. Lightbulb again.

Being present was a great exercise in taming my wandering mind as it tried to use the future as a scare tactic. Attempting to steer me toward fear of the unknown: money, job, purpose, anything you could think of that wasn't happening in that very moment. Being in the present moment, I was finding out that I shut down a lot of the ego chatter. This practice was added to my daily awareness.

> *"Thoughts, thoughts . . . there is the root*
> *of all the problems you will ever face."*
> *~What I heard upon being woken up in the middle of the night*

The "knowing" is me, is who I AM. The "thinking things through" is the Ego.

The Mind: An inner guidance system that controls our thoughts and governs our body; it uses our thoughts to do so.

Ego has kept the body alive for lifetimes (using mechanisms like fight or flight—both are based in fear); it's just the human interactions of life.

Ego is that part of you that thinks, some of the things that come out of the ego have positive results; that is what it makes you believe.

My wonderful mentor and husband summarized it as this:

Body is the computer, and the mind is the program on which it runs.

Ego AND Spirit . . . they can both be the programmer. The programmer that writes the program that runs the computer!

It is your choice. Who do you want your program to be written by?

Mind is the fuel that runs the being.

My soul cannot sing when the thoughts are too loud. The soul, the spirit of me never changes and it is ever patient because it knows the truth of who I am. It does not fear. It only loves.

In learning these new yet familiar concepts, it is a total bummer to still have pain in the body, while trying to handle it and shift my mind about it. I had hoped at this point to not experience anything else. After all I was changing my mind, so I thought my body would follow, immediately.

Alas, I couldn't deny the ice pick-like pain in my head any longer causing me to drop a tray at work. All I could do was shut my eyes against the onslaught. There was no way to hide from it any longer. After over six months of this random pain, and a few bouts that put me out of commission for days, I went to the neurologist. He deducted that the occipital nerves on both sides of the head were being pinched from my compressed vertebrae in my neck, causing a shock like, stabbing pain. This in turn was giving me migraines, and causing nausea and upset stomach. Since the worst bout left me in bed for 4 days, unable to lift my head, or eat, I was up for a solution. First suggestion was a shot to the nerve, called nerve blocks. The second option was fusing the neck, a major surgery. I opted for the shots, which cut the incidences in half.

WHAT IS THIS THING CALLED THE LAW OF ATTRACTION?

Since this chapter is all about learning and unlearning, the undoing of my human conditioning so to speak (I'll discuss that more in a bit), the next tool that plopped into my lap was the *Law of Attraction*. You have to understand that while I was hearing of so many things, analyzing my thoughts and addressing my beliefs and cracking myself open on a regular basis, I was still Jen; the wife and mom of three kids, with a bawdy sense of humor who ran a deli and who still experienced pain. I was not off in a faraway land, hanging in a hammock overlooking a beautiful vista, reciting affirmations all day. I was not in a café in Paris reading and soaking up deep, philosophical thoughts discussing them over espresso and a scone. Oh, how I wish.

Nope!

I would read in between customers ordering a turkey on rye. I would do the practice while the dog was barking or my daughter was asking me to help find her favorite t-shirt. I would be cooking dinner and putting in a chapter between timer bells going off. During a lull, I would read. In the car I would often listen to *ACIM* on CD. I would wake up at the crack of dawn just to read. Everyone around me knew how important my learning and unlearning had become.

One day a friend lent me a CD by Esther Hicks called the *Law of Attraction*. She said I would like it. So, I gave it a try while logging in the hours I spent going back and forth to sporting events. Did I love it? Not necessarily. Did I think it was shown to me for a reason? Why yes, I did.

I always loved the phrase "no harm, no foul" and it made sense for me when it came to these CD's. Over the last few years, I had been noticing things were coming into my awareness, positive things, and they were aligned with the support of a loving God. They were helping me in my journey in healing, so it would further prove my gut instinct to trust in God's plan for me.

Esther Hicks was a woman who channeled a consciousness called "Abraham" that spoke of this universal law. Hold on now, I was right there with you, "What the F(*^?" But if you could see things as I was at the time, I knew deep within, that if this "thing" was not serving me, God would weed it out for me. So, I listened with an open mind, knowing I would get what I needed.

The *Law of Attraction* showed me that in remaining neutral, when I was in the turmoil from pain, I could attract neutrality. When I would think of myself in a positive light and remember the happiness in all that I did have (rather than what I did not), I would not only feel better, but I got more of that uplifting feeling.

Now, listen, if I learned one thing in my quest for peace, it is that there are so many resources and people and teachers to turn to, and within each teaching the lessons run deep. While the *Law of Attraction* had its place in my learning, I didn't do a deep dive into it or Esther Hicks. Heck, I didn't even watch the movie "*The Secret*". There are tons of books and people who could speak on this topic far better than I. But, while all of Esther Hicks teachings didn't feel applicable for me, what I can tell you is how learning about the *Law of Attraction* shined a light on my thoughts and the energy I was giving to my pain and suffering. It highlighted how I lived in a cycle of my own making where I was not escaping the pain and certainly not the suffering. I saw the pattern where I pulled myself deeper into suffering, the more I thought about it, lived it, and breathed it. I never came up for air.

I considered myself a bit of a "cafeteria style learner" with Esther Hicks and the *Law of Attraction*. I used the teachings specifically in relation to my health and money. It made sense that when you are always thinking you do not have money, for example, that you are energetically stating you do not believe money should be yours. OK, I can get that. Well then, I thought to myself, the same goes for my health. If I am constantly thinking I suck, that this body is rubbish and thoughts like that, in that context, the *Law of Attraction* made sense to me. It helped me better understand the phrase, "what you think about you bring about". Meaning, there is not room for the healthy positive thoughts when I am being buried under all the negative. I remained neutral and slowly was able to move into happy after some time.

Much like my daily studies with *A Course in Miracles*, each and every tool that came to me, was worked into my learning process, whether daily or only in specific situations. I was taking the doctorate program of life.

FITTING MY FAITH INTO MY TRUTH

"Angels descending, bring from above, echoes of mercy, whispers of love."
~ Fanny J. Crosby

My faith brought me great love of the Holy Trinity and angels and saints. I've had love and reverence in my heart for as long as I can recall.

Even though I was learning new and wonderful things about myself and others, uncovering truths of who I AM and who we all are, I was still holding myself prisoner of my thoughts through that stubborn old conditioning. I was doing anything and everything I could to tap deep into my most spiritual self. I felt like I understood the connection Esther Hicks had to Abraham. I connected with the Holy Spirit that way myself, and angels had been coming to me since I was a young girl, even through the ectopic pregnancy ushering me to the hospital. I was right where I was because of their presence in my life. At each stage of life so far, during the times I needed more than humanly possible, the angels were hard at work. So, it would seem like I took for granted that they were with me because that was their job so to speak.

When I was young, seeing their faces brought me comfort and a level of peace I needed while I endured the pain. I couldn't find a downside in having faith that God sent his angels to me. It was a surrender I came to easily because they were helping me to remain strong while my tiny body was overwhelmed with such agony. It all seemed pretty simple at the time; I needed the support and I was given it. Once it clicked that these faces weren't the creations of a mind gone loopy, I took in the love I received and wrapped myself in it like it was a warm blanket on a bitterly cold night. Surely, I couldn't have lost my mind, because I don't think I would have felt so loved if that were the case.

When I learned about Reiki, it intrigued me. But, I questioned it as well. Much like everything else coming to me, I eventually saw the reason it was in my orbit so to say. Reiki is a healing technique where the therapist channels healing energy into another through touch. This not only helps with healing but also restoring physical and emotional well-being. To me, Reiki was like I was given the opportunity to pray with a person. My upbringing had a hand in how I saw it just a bit differently. I saw that it showed up in my life to understand the connection to the Holy Spirit deeper. It was to show me I was there to hold a space for someone else while the Holy Spirit aided them toward their highest good. I was there to help, as a person that cares for them, to pray, and to add my energy to their process. It was between them and God. Things were becoming clearer and clearer.

Since learning about Reiki, I became interested in studying it and eventually I earned my certification as a Reiki master. My friends and I formed a small group that would get together each week and share our experiences and any new information; we called it Circle—you may recall I spoke of Circle earlier in the book. One thing I want to make clear, there was lots of overlap in my quest for peace, my Oneness, and my brokenness. My journey is not linear in that sense. And so yes, I became a Reiki Master even when battling my own inner demons so to speak. But, even still, even in my pain and brokenness, it was such a wonderful time of learning and enlightenment. It confirmed for me that I could hear angels and spirit if I simply allowed it.

One day, as I listened to my dear friend lead us through a meditation in Circle, I began to relax my body, but more importantly my mind. I had been having a lot of mind activity and it felt as though my ego tried to stir up fears and projections in the ongoing attempt to distract me from my holiness. But being so steeped in a human condition for so long, I seemed to buy into that mind. I was working on understanding that that particular thought and mind condition was false, but as I am working on it so much pops up for me.

So on that day, I silenced the mind and listened. I tried to see the chakras as I felt their color and energy. I relaxed deeper as I was breathing. I climbed the spiral stairs she was describing in her meditation. I felt as if I was floating. I finally entered the garden she was describing and once again I intended to see the swing she described. But at this point I heard my friend and her melodic voice soothing me.

In the deep quiet of this led meditation, I became encompassed by visions, scents, and words of love ~ I picked up a rose and smelled its fragrance, I swung carefree on a wooden swing, I noticed a box with my picture inside of it, and I heard the words, "You are loved, believe in that. Love yourself." I felt tears streaming down my cheeks and down my collar bones, yet I was unable to move. I knew that was my lesson and my angel, my own connection to my Divine support team.

I so badly wanted to forgive myself for what I created in this human body, this human existence; I wanted to release any guilt attached to it and simply love myself. Wow that is so easy to type and harder to do. But for me it was the key to it all. I swung a bit, feeling the love wash over me, knowing I was right where I needed to be. Then I had to go back down those stairs and begin. I knew I had to take the picture and look at it every day and understand that what I created can't be thwarted by the love that prevails. I have to believe that.

As I practiced what we learned in Circle and opened myself up to more than what I thought before, I was enjoying my experiences. One morning, while I was praying and meditating, something funny and a tad bit embarrassing happened. This experience would (again) validate for me that I was hearing my angels and that I was another step closer to seeing things differently.

If you grew up in a Catholic family like mine, or any branch of Christianity really, you probably have heard of the role angels play in the Bible and their importance, and you may have heard the more common names of the archangels. I remember being taught that archangels can come to any of us. We might not hear or see them, but they can be called into our lives and will assist us. I had recently found out the name of my guardian angel-it was Frank. This was a name that had popped into my life so much, I always wondered why.

"You may see me as huge, or imagine me as small, I am right by your side, and will hear when you call, I am loyal and true, you can trust me to care, I'm your Guardian Angel. I will always be there!"
~ Anonymous

My angels would come regularly again, just like when I was younger. I'm not sure if I just "tuned back in" to their existence, and my ability to be more present, but it was like they were saying, "Hey Jen, we are in your life and it is no longer a secret!"

I was feeling really good about being able to be quiet in meditation and hear if anything came to me, but I won't mislead you: there were (and still are) definitely times when it was simply peaceful quiet time where I heard nothing, while other times were full of answers. I had also been very blessed in speaking to spirits recently.

Now, this was hard to reconcile with my faith, but it was my truth, and I could not stifle it. I would hear from some family members (my dad, which wasn't a great surprise) and a few people I didn't know personally. The people I didn't know would come to me when they had a message I needed to share. Sometimes I would not know who or what the message was even about, so I would just jot it down. The proper receiver would always reveal themselves and I would always be amazed, but truly never surprised. It's kind of funny, people I didn't know would even interrupt some of my conversations if they really wanted to come through.

On that morning, I was listening to a deceased family member, and the conversation was long and detailed. I had been trying out a new meditation. It was a Tibetan chant, and it had parts that were loud and honestly sounded a little goofy to me. I got this overwhelming feeling that I wasn't the only one who didn't care for it; basically, I was being told to shut it off!

I silently asked who was asking me to do this. I heard the name was "Michael." I continued this internal dialog by asking, "*Michael? Who are you and is there something you want to say to me?*" I got back louder and with firm insistence, "MICHAEL." I felt no anger, just an insistence that I know his name. There was no further message to me. I would often times confirm the things I was hearing, because I was still doubting the accuracy and authenticity of what I heard. My go to source for confirmations was often Google.

Now here's where the embarrassing part comes in—I did Google search for the name "Michael" and the word "angel." Well, duh! It showed Archangel Michael immediately and in lists of plenty. Yep! Over 40 years as a Catholic Christian and I had to Google search "*Is there an angel named Michael?*" When people say they had a "brain fart," I know what they mean; this was the greatest example of one, and I felt like such a goober. I felt like I had just broken some secret cardinal rule of "Speaking with the Angels."

The next thought I had was, "*Why me? Why would the bigwig of the angel hierarchy talk to me?*" It took me a while to realize: *Why not me? Why not you?* God has angels for our protection, guidance, love, and to show us the light and strength and courage to live a happy and fruitful life with support. How else would they give us all their love and support unless they actually come to us and are heard?

The biggest key I uncovered that morning was to be still. If I am in need of solace or direction, I can get my answers from anyone in the Divine realm. You are allowed the same opportunity for assistance as anyone. Quiet, be still, and know that I am. God advises us to be still so that we can hear the message that we asked for, so that we can know His love. Try it out and see who comes to help you! It is quite miraculous and such a huge shift from trembling in fear to being encased by love.

The other thing I learned that morning was to not be surprised when I see how much love there is for me. Just be still and you will hear and feel that you are connected far beyond what you ever imagined.

I began paying intense attention to everything I was hearing. This whole other world of energy, love, and the promise of peace was happening right alongside of my world all this time. There was information about the mind, positive energy, perceptions, God, and the Universe, and this thing called the ego. Whenever I saw or heard the word "ego", I would flash back to my third year in college when I took the required psychology course where I learned of the id, the ego, and a bunch more information that I was not interested enough in to retain past the exams. The mention of it now, seems different then I recall.

"Jen, release the ego, stop edging God out." I had this thought regularly and every time I felt the ego release a bit more. It can have a tight grasp, you know. The ego is competitive and a bully and doesn't like to lose.

Ego is really just afraid. Fear is a distraction from God's love.

I fit my faith into the truth I was uncovering by reconciling it. I was trying to make sense of my "in and out" understanding in my relationship with God. I knew that if what I was reading or seeking or feeling or experiencing didn't distract me from the truth of God's all-encompassing love, then I knew all was well. The second it distracted me from that, or I let the ego thoughts convince of something other than the truth, then it was game over.

Anything that aides in changing my perception of a situation to a more loving state of mind, then I know that my happiness is right around the corner, and that is what I am always open to. Allowing the Holy Spirit to guide me and the universal knowing to lead me where I need to go.

It is a process of uncovering and healing. These tools that God has shown me to both learn and unlearn are not out of alignment with my faith, but rather integral in bringing me to it, and bringing me the peace I so desperately desire.

DUALITY AS IT UNFOLDS

My big blue book *A Course in Miracles* and all the other teachings I was being shown, not only represented a change in perception of everything, it showed me the mind that is split—dual mind. It truly resonated with me because that was how I felt for the second half of my life, split. Feeling my energy decrease and my shoulders slump when I thought about everything that kept happening to me and this body left me feeling dejected at every turn, especially when I compared myself to everyone around me. Then came these fabulous moments of clarity and love that left me breathless.

How was this possible?

No wonder why I felt unhinged at times. That made a ton of sense when I would look at how I felt about myself. But being aware of this dual mind was like listening to the orchestra play an overview of a musical as theater guests walk in. You get a hint of what the show is about, and then you must dive in to really understand the story. It truly was and still is a journey of perception: how I saw myself, others, the world. Each interaction, every response I had to stimuli, I began to notice from a different perspective, because after all I was just learning I had this ego at work that I had apparently been listening to. I did this work throughout every day, like it was my life's work.

It was years of learning and unlearning, and attempts to be non-resistant of the ego thoughts. I gave the ego thoughts a lot of attention throughout my life, looking at them under a microscope as if my very life depended on it.

"I have a right to feel the way I felt about myself. I was a victim of all that has happened to me." Each time I fell to the bottom, it made sense to me. Even my fall to rock bottom was justified in my mind. Battling against my ego, gave me a run for my money let me tell you. In the beginning there were some rough patches, and they got easier in time.

Initially, I thought I was losing it and needed to take a few days off from noticing it because it felt like I was getting worse instead of better. Isn't that the way healing just is? Go through the muck to pour the light into it. I wanted so badly for myself to be peaceful, and have no intruding thoughts, so getting the opposite at times was frustrating. *Why can't you stop it and make it all better?* Yelling and pleading inside myself, *What are you missing, Jen?*

As I dubbed in my teenage years, I had this *humanness* and it was getting in my way. It was there banging at the door, saying, "Don't forget me. I know you want to heal, and see things differently, but you can't without me!" Trying desperately to leave it behind and be this spiritually enlightened being who was unaffected by the body was my goal. After all, wasn't it the body that had been giving me problems all along? I would ignore it and forge ahead, I decided. I would leave all thought of it behind.

I am unattached to the body.

I believed I was a good person and that I had a fun personality, but it became harder and harder to reconcile that this person was the same one with this very flawed physical body with all these burdens. There had to be a way out from underneath what was my life. I wished I had magical powers to make these parts of me disappear.

Here's the thing, we all have been affected by what is termed "human conditioning." We all have certain learned behaviors and have had familial and societal expectations placed on us. It isn't until we uncover what doesn't serve us that we recognize this human conditioning. Only then, can we learn to undo the effect which they may have on us.

We have a sort of program running in the background of our life based on what we were taught as children. In our families or upbringing, we are experiencing generations in effect. Our parents only knew what they were taught by their parents and they pass these beliefs, thoughts, and traditions down to us. Or, possibly religion or church dictated these things. When we enter school, where much of the same happened, we had the added expectations that were placed on us: teachers, school, church, sports, society is all at play in our human conditioning.

Some examples of influence may be:

"Good children sit still and listen."

"You need good grades if you are going to achieve anything in life."

"Better to be seen than heard."

"You better _____if you are going to get ahead."

"Money is the key to true happiness."

"Money is the root of all evil."

There is an exhaustible number of factors that add to our human conditioning. And it is a pretty individual thing because we were all raised a certain way, but we also perceive things differently than each other. Human conditioning can support us in our lives or have the power to pull us down.

If a child is loud and not listening and is then excluded from fun, he learns that his behavior has the consequence of no fun or exclusion. It is all based individually on that individual's perception. We get a look at how we might be driven, by our perception of things and our conditioning, to achieve this.

You might have never considered this conditioning before. You might have never thought you had some of the aforementioned pressures, but you did. We all did. There is no one to blame about this, it is just part of being human. It is part of our human condition.

Do you know the story of the Russian scientist, Ivan Pavlov and his famous dog? He demonstrated that showing the dog food and ringing a bell, that eventually, only the sound of the bell alone would elicit the same response as presenting the food and bell together. This is known as classic conditioning or Pavlovian conditioning. It is the conditioning learned through association.

There was another scientist, John Watson, who proposed that the process of classical conditioning (based on Pavlov's observations) was able to explain all aspects of human psychology. Everything from speech to emotional responses was simply patterns of stimulus and response. Watson completely denied the existence of the mind or consciousness. He believed that "all individual differences in behavior were due to different experiences of learning."

I add this interesting information in, not to get into the psychology too deeply, but to show there is a way to see how conditioning is present in our lives, then undo its hold on our minds and ultimately on our happiness.

Watson's proposition denies our spiritual nature. I believe that we are affected by our spiritual existence as well as that of the whole of the universe. Watson made his deductions based only on the physical world, but there is so much more to who we are. As we are in the human experience, we are also a spiritual being with a deep desire to return to the love we are born of, to be peaceful and happy.

Through our human conditioning we hear, perceive, or believe what we need to have this peace. There is an apparent disharmony— something just feels off. Something is missing. There are so many examples through our time, in society, and even in ourselves that we have societal patterns of unhappiness and searching. It is seen in all people. No one is immune to this. What is it that all these people have in common? The human condition and our spiritual essence!

Love has proven to be quite an impactful component in our life experience. Since love is what we were all created in, when my mind is seated in the awareness of God's love, I know I have everything I need. I have the strength of God. His voice is the one I want guiding my thoughts. You can see now, as I came to see, that having a mind that is sustained in God's love is the same as knowing all is well. You can no longer see life the way you used to. Hell, why would you want to? It is so hard to stay in the same darkness that used to consume all of your thoughts—once you begin to see the light of God.

As you may recall, I heard a hundred times that we enter Heaven without illnesses, but apparently this did not sway me. The only way I stopped having this fear was when I finally understood who I truly was while here on earth—in this earthly illusion! I had no clue I was a child of God, that I was light, and I was love. I was everything God had promised I was, for eternity, not the limited person I thought I was. I believed my ego thoughts over the reality of who I truly was, and that continued on for over 40 years. Coming to understand that human conditioning is just that, and not who we are born to be, we become undone in the best of ways.

I began to realize that you can't have light and darkness at the same time. I began to see that you can't also have fear and love occupying your mind at the same time. So many points that changed my perception. Love doesn't require you to sacrifice and it sure doesn't require you to change what makes you . . . YOU!

I CAN DO IT! OH, YES I CAN! BUT SOMETIMES, I STILL CAN'T . . .

Amidst this tremendous amount of self-reflection and learning, my husband and I treated ourselves to the *I Can Do It!* conference in Atlanta. We were drawn to it because Dr. Wayne Dyer was speaking, and I could also take an Angel Card seminar. This spoke to me since I was rekindling the special relationship I had with the angels. Being in a state of deep reflection strengthened my yearning to connect with the angels any way I could. *Through cards? I'll take it!*

Plus, a ticket to the conference meant we were able to listen to at least ten different motivational and spiritual speakers. We had never done anything like this for ourselves, and it was fabulous and a very rewarding experience that we both needed. Inspiration 360 degrees around us and soaking right into our pours. These were my people. This was my home. I felt inspired, connected, and open to any and every possibility.

You may recall me sharing about my father leaving us "pennies from Heaven." These signs always pointed to writing a book and sharing his message on a broader scale. I would always think, *Me, an author? Who am I to do such a thing?* That, "who am I" business is rough. We all feel unworthy to some degree when we are not plugged into our power. Well, after this powerful weekend, I knew that I needed to publish the children's book about Dad's pennies from heaven. *Heaven Cent* was a subject very close to my heart, and I felt that it needed to be shared. I knew that it needed the right artwork, a light, care-free style and playful, almost childlike artwork. So, I decided I would do it myself.

My biggest motivation for this decision was that I just wanted to get it done. I did not want to place any more blocks or excuses in my own way. I thought that if this book could help at least one person deal with the loss of a loved one or feel something in common with our story, then the investment (and my not so professional artwork) was worth it. I was inspired to complete it all by myself, and within months of attending *I Can Do It!,* I did it. I published that book! I was an author! I was actually very proud of the book and even my attempts at illustrating, because the end result was exactly as I had anticipated.

I would meet the most lovely and extraordinary people whether it was at work, a special event, or even at a party. Oh, how I loved signing the book and writing some personalized message for people after hearing their stories. So much comfort and confirmation was shared in each of these conversations. I recognized that people were searching for someone to validate their signs from heaven, but were nervous to tell others for fear of being judged. When someone would ask for advice, I felt honored that they did and that they wanted to hear a part of my story as well. It was such a moving experience for me to have people share that I had a stack of books at my deli and would speak with people and sign copies.

Now, as you may have gathered by now, I am an entrepreneur at heart. We still had our family business, the deli. I still had a jewelry line, and I was an author. After this conference, my husband and I felt guided to another inspirational concept—putting our various entrepreneurial dreams under "one roof" so to speak. We thought it could be an inspirational company, and the name *Do Life Inspired* came into our hearts. It felt so right. *Do Life Inspired* would be the avenue we would use for products, ideas, or books in the future.

Creating the logo and theme of the company was fun but took a bit of time. Along with establishing this corporation, we trademarked our idea, logo, and merchandise. We honestly felt this sort of pull toward establishing this company, and we just couldn't explain why. We followed the signs that were presented to us, and we just did it. We had very little extra money at this time to invest in this company, but yet here we were doing it with, what my husband and I both agreed, was an overwhelming calm.

Sometimes you do things and they don't really have a "purpose" in the present moment, but eventually the purpose comes to fruition and what you did earlier from a space of the unknown was necessary to make that happen. We had no idea why we were creating this new company when we already had enough to worry about and deal with. But, nearly 8 years later, it all made sense and *Do Life Inspired* is the brand that brings forth joy, peace, and love into the world. We are selling items and spreading the positive messages of love that we faithfully followed so long ago.

My husband read the merchandise tag just recently: *We are dedicated to encouraging people to find their passion, overcome their fears, and to "Do Life Inspired."* He was so amazed at how perfect the words were. He said, "That sure is good! Funny, I don't even remember writing that. Maybe that was because it was divinely inspired."

But see, in this period of learning and unlearning, tapping into my Oneness, and soaking up all the information I can for changing my life, inspiring others to change theirs, I moved ahead with great strides, and yet I was still caught in the trap of 10 steps forward and 5 steps back.

I remember at one point, I had just finished signing a few copies of *Heaven Cent* and had placed them in a bag to take with me to the deli the next day. I thought, as I did this, about how proud I was that I wrote that book for myself, my dad, my family, and all the people I don't know but who needed it. When I was done, I headed upstairs to our bedroom to meditate away from the busy afternoon hubbub of three kids and three dogs. All I needed was 20 minutes.

My son's old Sponge Bob CD player was sitting on the floor against the wall so no one would trip over it, and sitting beside it was the new CD I bought, *I AM Wishes Fulfilled Meditation* by Dr. Wayne Dyer. I was so looking forward to hearing it because I read that he and another man did a lot of research, and found the sounds that associated with the name of God, I AM like in the Old Testament. They produced a meditation using tuning forks from the specific numbers assigned to the letters of I AM. It sounded so cool!

In my standard post-work "home uniform" of pj bottoms and a t-shirt, I crouched down and plopped the CD in the old machine, and then got myself comfortable on my yoga mat on the cold stone floor, which actually was oddly comfortable. I pressed play and listened. I breathed in and out and let the thoughts glide in and out.

I will not pay attention to them.

I listen to the introduction as I relax my shoulders and work my way down my body.

I will let all thoughts glide on by.

I pray, I AM that I AM, over and over on a loop as instructed.

I'm not focusing on anything more, non-resistant to the thought battering at the walls of my peace.

In time, I sensed a lightness that I really loved and often times wished I could live all day, every day, in that same feeling.

Love and lightness, I exhaled wondering why I couldn't always feel like this.

Why would I ever have doubts at all?

Why can't you always help yourself, and be completely happy and at peace, like you felt a second ago? I heard that thought that creept in at my most sacred moments.

Ignore it, Jen.

Why are you interrupting my peace ego? Why are you still a thing?

I sensed I was getting uptight and that was SO not the point of doing this meditation.

Find it, Jen, get it back.

Deep breaths. Ignoring the tears that were falling down my face, I shook off any and all thoughts from my mind.

Oh, how I wish I was stronger to be rid of them all.

Quiet, Jen. Quiet.

I was eventually able to arrive at quiet, a little perplexed by the number of tears that I disregarded moments before. How long had they been there? It was like a wave building and building, until the point when it hits the shore and you think, wow that was a powerful one. That was what I experienced, there on my bedroom floor. I felt the love overpowering me in the stillness. It was a love that was unconditional and powerful in its genuine nature.

It knows me, and I know it.

In the stillness that I had not paid attention to for more years than I could count, I began to sob, half with gratitude and half with apologies. I was whispering aloud, through the sobs, a low almost choked rumble, too hoarse to hear clearly.

I have missed You. I am sorry. You have been with me this whole time, and I missed you. Oh, Holy Spirit, You have never stopped guiding me, I just can't hear you all the time over Me! Yes, I can feel Your love. Thank You, God, for not abandoning me.

This warm feeling wrapped me up in a cocoon, I sat in it and cried for the sorrow of missing the love I felt at that exact moment. But, also the ego-mind kicked in, and I reverted back to questions. I reverted to wondering why I couldn't just be still all the time and why I made myself hurt so much. But, for the first time, the "revert back" hurt me a little less. I wanted that beautiful state above all else, to be part of me like I couldn't explain.

When I am wrapped in this warm love that I feel when I am quiet, all feels right.

These arms of love hold me together. It was there on that floor, face wet with tears of joy and sorrow, that I wondered how I could be both the person who had pain and the person who could bask in God's love.

Much more to unlearn still.

"Forgive your misperceptions of who you thought you were
and step into the light of who you ARE."
~From Meditations with Jesus and Jen

INTERLUDE

A Deli for Sale and a Huge Lesson Learned

"Happiness depends on how you accept, understand,
and surrender to situations."
~ Mata Amritanandamayi

I loved the deli but my husband really did not. The desire to sell it was huge. He craved the freedom he had in his past businesses, which allowed him to be outside—not stuck inside a building. It soon became strikingly obvious to me that I was not the type of business owner to relinquish control easily. I was who everyone wanted to talk to, and I was the one who ran the kitchen. Doing both fed right into my need to be distracted, have multiple "pokers in the fire," and to have a finger on the pulse of everything that went on in the deli.

Between the daily practices with *A Course in Miracles* and other prayers, it improved my listening skills as an employer who worked closely with her employees. In time, I eventually relinquished some duties and even took a day off when absolutely necessary.

Despite these great improvements, it didn't look like I would get a complete personality change in delegating all my duties, so eventually I willingly agreed to selling our business. We went on each day with the hope of selling, having it all neatly planned out in our heads, only to be disappointed when it did not happen. Oh, people would come and look, or call and ask questions. But over and over, no viable offers.

Nothing.

Nada.

Zero.

Ugh.

We were sadly resigned to the fate of where we were. And it was frustrating. I finally was ready to give up control and no one wanted to take the wheel from me. I couldn't understand it. And I thought about it a lot. I thought about all the mistakes we made, and I thought about all the things we did right with the deli.

The deli provided me with the human contact I loved. I loved seeing everyone in town and creating new friendships. I enjoyed being known as the lady with the great deli. It was like being at the deli provided me with the ability to see all the people I knew, but normally wouldn't get to see on a weekly basis. The deli was the meeting place for so many and I loved to provide good food for people. I sent love too as it was being made.

With all those positive things the deli brought to my life, I was still unhappy and felt there was a place I needed to go. I was constantly trying to figure out what, how, when, and where I was supposed to be other than here at this deli. I thought I needed a different career, needed to make more money, or maybe go back to school. There was this ongoing feeling that I had somewhere else to be and I was missing it! I just didn't know what I needed to be doing or where I needed to go, but I kept *thinking* that it was not here. I felt like this was something I had to figure out. And this unhappiness went on for YEARS. YEARS, I say.

I had hit a point and was ready to crack. I was tight as a knot but fragile like glass. There was no forest through the trees, there was no way out. And on this one particular day it all bubbled up to the surface—I was DONE. I remember it so clearly. I was getting ready to go to the deli. I pulled my black t-shirt with our deli logo over my head, and I ruined my ponytail. Frustrated, I took my hair all the way out of the scrunchie and re-did it.

Man, my hair has grown to the middle of my back, and it's getting gray, again. I could have sworn it was just three weeks ago that I did my roots, I thought to myself.

I tightened my ponytail back up and scooped the end of the tail back into the scrunchie forming a bun of sorts. Gotta love the benefits of wearing a hat for work, I pushed off thoughts of coloring my hair. A sudden feeling of dread took hold of me before I took another step and I sank onto the end of our bed. I felt like I was living the movie *Groundhog Day*, every day the same.

Is this my purpose in life???

Those thoughts invaded my brain, once again pondering if I was truly happy. Wondering if there was something more for me. I knew that feeling too well—it had been my battle for years—as a wave of panic set in. I had felt that way countless times. I swore I must have missed something really big in life. The opportunity for complete happiness had skipped right over me, I just knew it. I was stuck in that freaking deli when it slid by. I had so many desires to do different things, but I was obligated to my business.

Thoughts like this popped up in my head like thought bubbles in a comic book:

Will happiness ever come?

Is total peace really possible?

Will something else show up for me later? Will I be free when it does?

Is this what I am supposed to amount to? Feeding people and knowing their sandwich orders by heart.

To be honest, I actually did love that last part. A smile formed on my face as I thought of Frank who ordered his sandwich the week before and forgot to tell the gal at the register to hold the tomatoes. I yelled from the kitchen, "Frank, no tomatoes, right?"

He ran to the cut out in the wall that lead to the kitchen, "Oh man, Jen, I forgot to tell her! Thanks!"

"Hey, Frank I can't go following you around to make sure you eat right!" We both laughed as he jogged back to his seat.

I both loved and hated that job. I loved knowing the entire town and what made them happy, but I hated that I believed I was trapped and I was missing something else. The praise people gave was awesome because I did feel immense pride in our product. I thought about the day before, at the grocery store when I saw a man and his wife, *Lady Liberty, no onions.* I knew the sandwich he got weekly, but I couldn't recall his name. He said hello to me, and as he walked away, I heard him tell his wife that we had the best sandwiches in town. Pride. Hard work made the days go by, because most of the day was hours of full out hard work. I would call it my "gym membership."

I had to get out the door, yet I felt myself getting really deep into these thoughts. They plagued me, like a sickness that crept up whenever I hadn't warded against it. I knew there was more than this job waiting for me. Frustration bubbled up to meet me. Thoughts of Fred—he kept reminding me we work for very little money. Can't I be more? He wanted freedom, outside, and an outcome far different than the deli provided. We felt stuck because there were so many wants, and we hadn't been able to sell the deli yet. I had to find my purpose.

I closed my eyes from the onslaught of thoughts and panic that I would never ever have a meaningful purpose and job. Then I remember thinking maybe God wanted us to stay put or else we would have sold it. I just needed to deal with it. I felt my shoulders slump on that last thought.

Voted "Best Sandwich" four years in a row and it still didn't feel like enough. My thoughts jumped to the catering that we had that day and how we did the best when I led the kitchen.

"Who will be the next 'Jen' if we buy your deli?" This comment flashed in my mind, and it had been the general opinion, in some way or another, with anyone who looked into purchasing our business.

Now let me reiterate: we were trying to sell the deli for years, and for years we were right back where we started. This was not a fly by night thought. We literally felt trapped. We both wanted out. We both wanted more. But we were met with lousy offers and worries that the deli couldn't run without me. ME! I was the stumbling block to my freedom from the deli because I made it so. Even after all the time I spent learning and unlearning, I had such a tight grip in certain things. *"Who will be the life blood and pulse of this place when you are not here? Will it be the same?"* These comments led me to believe that being good or just being me had actually hurt us in selling the business.

Only you, Jen!

Relinquishing control was difficult for a long time, but the girls that worked with us were given so many more responsibilities and were doing great, I just knew the customers better, I would reason.

Have I helped to create something that I could never sell because I made myself indispensable? If my shoulders got any lower, I would have fallen off the edge of the bed.

Ugh.

Who will take the place of 'Jen'?

Really people, can't you see that we need to move on?

Confusion in how to deal with this job and wanting happiness settled right on top of my shoulders. That must be what was pushing them down. Again in my head, ME ME ME. I had to figure a different way to sell it or find a way to replace myself, so I could find the thing in life that would make me happy.

I grabbed my lukewarm coffee that had been sitting there cooling as I deliberated over a million distracting thoughts that morning, and I headed downstairs to the family room. Standing in the family room, I put my hands up in the air, and I plopped ungracefully down with a thud onto the couch. My body felt heavier with all those feelings about the deli. That was what it meant to have the weight of the world on your shoulders, that crap was heavy. I opened my thick blue book to my lesson for the day. I could not leave for work without *ACIM*.

It was like I heard the choir of angels, 100 trumpets, a big band, and a ticker tape parade, because right there in paper I had some direction:

God gives me only happiness.
He has given my function to me.
Therefore my function must be happiness.
— ACIM (lesson 66, pg. 110-112)

Two tons began to lift off my shoulders, a pound at a time, as the seconds clicked by, sitting there with these words. I closed my eyes and I felt what God was telling me deep in my core. Is my spine straighter right now? I felt taller somehow and yet I was still sitting there, in the same position. Understanding settled in my mind, it could be as simple as this; I have a choice in my own happiness because that is all God wants for me. After all, Jesus was saying that happiness is my only function and that is what God wants and wills for me.

I knew I heard before that happiness was an inside job, but now I understood its real meaning when I read these words in my trusty blue book again. I knew I had the answer to my obsessive need to sell the deli and all of the feelings and fears that those thoughts elicited. My function here on earth (job, career, or simply just being) was happiness, despite what it was that I was doing. I had a choice to be happy or not. I smiled and spoke out loud, "I want to do this. I can do this!" I was simply a thought away from happiness.

I walked in the doors of the deli that day and straight into my husband's closet, which was his office, and told him things were changing for me, starting today. I girded my loins, took a cleansing breath and began. I kissed him and said hello, then I asked him to let me finish before he said anything. I went on to tell him that I did not want to speak of any more plans to sell or how "miserable" it was or wanting to be somewhere else. I expressed how I wanted to accept where I was instead. I told him of today's lesson and what I felt. I desired my happiness to be placed in God having me right where I was in this moment, and I no longer wanted it determined by the sale of the deli. I exhaled the breath I had been holding for my entire speech and waited for what I was sure was going to be his rebuttal.

He said, "Okay, I'm in. I can do that. I want to be happy too."

I'm sure my eyes bugged out in disbelief. "I am not sure if you mean that or not, but I am doing this because above all else I want to be happy!" He said he was committed. Beginning that day, there was tons more smiles and laughing, and lots more tips for the girls. We had a week of great sales and success and we actually did it all with joy. On the third day of our happiness journey, I said to Fred, "I am glad we chose a deli rather than one of Mike Rowes' dirty jobs to find our happiness in this lifetime!" Perception is half the battle.

It was exactly one week after that first morning of acceptance and understanding happiness was God's will for us, that a nice man walked into our deli and asked me if I was the owner. I said I was and he said, "I want to buy your deli."

It turned out that he had seen a free ad I had placed so many months before—I'd forgotten it was even there. He spoke with my husband, and wanted to close within the week. We told him there were a few things that needed to get finalized before that could happen. We settled all the details and sold our deli two weeks from our decision to accept happiness in where we were in life.

You are always right where you are supposed to be . . . how often I fought that. I could see the truth in that way after the "thing" was over. But when I was in it, I hated the lesson with a deep passion. The deli experience was something we needed to do, that is why we were guided to open it. Having that deli employed so many cool people that we got to meet and know well. We met people in our town that we might never have met if it wasn't for the deli. I was able to help people and provide them with health advice and gluten-free diet lifestyle tips. Friendships we carved. Two of our kids even gained work experience.

I learned how to best manage people and how to begin to observe judgment. I began to see the patterns of thought that *ACIM* and so many other motivational and spiritual teachers were talking about. I personally learned so many countless and valuable skills. I also learned that I loved to serve people that went beyond my own family. This deli was actually a gift I had not realized because I was too busy placing another "plan" right on top of it. The gift of happiness was always there, I was too distracted by my thoughts to see it.

Would I be able to see my life in this body as what was supposed to happen as well? I must surrender that too.

"Wipe the slate clean of who you thought you were before. It serves you no longer. Just because it is all you knew, never made it right or correct. Fear has no place in truth. Fear arises when you have a belief system that makes no sense; because it is NOT THE TRUTH."
~ *From Meditations with Jesus and Jen*

Surrender [səˈrendər]

verb

to give (oneself) over to something

The acknowledgement that you have a duality in the mind and you have now placed your trust and guidance to the wisdom of the Holy Spirit. You relinquish control of thoughts that you are being led by the ego and into darkness, and allowed another teacher to guide you in your thoughts, actions, and in your life.

CHAPTER 10

Undoing Attachment to the Body and The Practice of Surrendering

"I have been driven many times upon my knees by the overwhelming conviction that I had no where else to go."
~ Abraham Lincoln

"Jen, seems like the arthritis is worse after the surgery, and it wasn't the screw protruding from your foot, but rather your bone."

Oh sure, that makes a ton of sense. I had surgery to fix a bone in my foot, then another surgery to remove a screw that seemed to be coming out of my foot from the first surgery, only to find out that ain't no screw and the fix didn't fix a damn thing, but made it worse. No more "poor Jen!" or "only me!" Now it was more like show me what I need to see!

Here I was deep in *A Course in Miracles*, handing over my thoughts and changing my perception, being open to Divine guidance, shifting perceptions left and right, finally selling the deli, learning and unlearning, and trying so hard to view this body as a gift just as I was viewing everything else as one. Yet, my body kept presenting me with all kinds of pains and issues. This had been my entire life and although I had done so much better dealing with pain in the body, I was quite done with it.

Let me explain. My foot, which I was ignoring, had become progressively worse, and my daily walks were becoming a challenge. My bone had moved and grown outward, causing this strain. I was told I needed surgery. Since walking and wearing shoes had become a chore, I agreed to have a surgery. I had previously decided that I was not going to give any emotion or judgment to ailments and that included this foot thing. So in the past, even the thought of surgery made my stomach turn and my head spin. At this point, my view was shifting and I went into the surgery in "neutral."

Well, my foot healed but the surgery felt like it created a bone that now protruded from underneath. The doctor thought it could have possibly been the screw coming out, so he suggested I have it removed. I went under again to do just that, but it wasn't the screw. Hmmm. The doctor took X-rays and examined me a month later. He then explained that the X-rays showed the arthritis was worse than it was before the operation. He was so surprised. He also added, "Since we removed the screw and you are still uncomfortable, we have to understand that bone movement and protrusion can sometimes happen. To alleviate the feeling of the bump under the foot, you can wear inserts, and if that doesn't work, then surgery. But I would hate to do that because it is not a great surgery." He said that my left foot seemed to have the same problem.

My first thought was, "Hell no! No more surgery!" Yet, deep within me, I knew I would be fine. So different from the Jen of just a short while ago. While my humanness thinks this kind of sucks, deep in my knowing, it was okay. You see I just had a huge run with my back, a cyst on my spine that needed spinal back fusion (which I put off for seven months in an attempt to ignore the body).

After fighting what was the last time, I decided I must remain neutral to this new thing, every part of it, hard as that was. Pain, general unwell health, yet unattached to the body. I am free! Arthritis, occipital nerve, shots, back, foot—I got the idea I was _not_ a body! But, here's the thing, I started to ignore my body, ignore symptoms, and that created a little bit of trouble for me.

Where I would run to the doctors before all the time, I began to do the opposite and ignore my body in an attempt to push home the teaching "I am not a body". My "neutral" got a little carried away! I hadn't really gotten the idea yet that I was BOTH a body and a spirit while I was here. And this was just the hardest thing for me to reconcile and fully understand. Several steps forward and one step back. It was like the childhood game I used to play growing up, Red Light Green Light, 1, 2, 3 . . .

I get the green light, move ahead.

RED LIGHT, JEN, you have to stop.

Dammit, the 8-year-old me shouts, I was winning!

That is all it seems to take this 47-year-old Jen to crush her happy go lucky thoughts. Pain. The body. RED LIGHT, JEN!

I was healing my body and my mind, but the judging didn't stop completely. I continued to judge myself as less of a person. "*Well, of course you are!*" my mind would scream. I had given the mind, that was hard at work distracting me from freeing myself, yet another physical struggle. It was just another thing to add to the story of "Jen"—where she was the victim of the body once more and where she showed up to the world as less. At times even I couldn't believe all of the things that I had gone through.

SPIRALING FORWARD INTO FORGIVENESS

As far as I had come, I could still feel myself slipping into a spiral of self-pity once more. It felt as if I would unlearn and learn, and yet still needed to address the same things again. I was able to distract myself with my studies. I had earned many other certificates of study and even a health coaching certification. Yet the most beneficial study I was receiving was that of learning I was <u>not only a body</u>. What I came to understand clearer in years to come, was that I was more than just a body. This was one of the biggest and most challenging lessons I would have to understand in all of *A Course in Miracles*. It truly seemed to be the lesson of this lifetime as Jen.

These things only happen to you, Jen.

I never liked to hear that, and I couldn't deny the truth in those words. Lesson 201 in *ACIM* states, "I am not a body. I am free. For I am still as God created me." I would say this over and over to myself—like a mantra. I was created to be more. I soon learned that no matter how much you repeat something, and no matter how many times someone else has told you, it sticks only when you believe it to be completely true. And I thought *I* needed to work out the truth of it for myself. I was always putting such a burden on myself.

But my husband would say to me that I didn't need to work on it, that all I had to do was surrender it all to the Holy Spirit. He would remind me that *ACIM* stated that all I needed to do was provide a little willingness to the Holy Spirit, and the Holy Spirit would take care of all that I need. Men! They have this uncanny gift of simplifying things, but I wasn't having it that day.

I remembered saying, "That all sounds easy, but you have no idea what I go through, what I have been through! There is always so much pain!" I still could not see what it was that would set me free of this life of pain. It all just felt like only words.

Unfortunately, as many concepts in my studies were well received and at times liberating, there was many that I fought and even cried over. I felt like such a failure because I would still have ailments in this body. I figured if I was truly following all that I'd read, shouldn't I have felt great and pain-free or at the very least, find peace in my mind about where I was? I would take in all of this beautiful work, so many books of inspiration, *ACIM*, and still find myself lacking because of my body.

I would read and then think to myself, *Jesus is telling me that I have the power to move mountains, but I can't even stop this body from going through one pain and problem after the next! What am I doing wrong? Complete and utter failure.*

I identified all of this chatter now as the ego and it was playing a reel in my mind:

You are less.

Your body is rubbish.

You aren't like anyone else.

Look at all those people who are pain-free!

Look at all the things you are missing out on.

See all that you should be doing?

Look at everyone you know exercising and running marathons.

No matter what you read, you are still in pain.

When will you learn this is JUST who you will be in this lifetime?

Then my favorite: *You can't even fix this! You are lacking once again!*

How could I compete with these thoughts which I believed were cold, hard facts? I couldn't fix this or anything else. I tried hard to *think* my way toward fixing this body. I tried and tried to meditate on what I needed to do to escape who I believed I was. When I was feeling down and doubtful, I would wonder why this was continuing to happen to me? I was trying really hard to absorb it all and getting pissed at myself when I didn't see anything change for me.

I want you to understand and not sugar coat anything, it took work to undo the attachment to the body. You've heard the term "overnight success." Most people who have an overnight success usually have been working for years, struggling and striving, yet all of the sudden one day it clicks and they seem like an overnight success. Well, that was like my healing. It didn't happen overnight, although to some who didn't see the inner workings of this shift, it seemed like it did.

For the next couple of years, I went through a sort of seesaw effect: for a block of time I would understand who and what I truly was, and then a large block of time, I believed I was nothing but a flawed body. The times on the downward swing were quite a hit. It was during these times that I saw the guilt I placed on myself. I would allow my mind to wander. I could see where I led myself, but it was too hard to escape those thoughts.

I would go back over the words I read where Jesus would speak of forgiveness. It was a difficult concept to embrace when I didn't fully understand the role of forgiveness. My immediate thought of forgiveness was to forgive those who had "trespassed against me." I mean that sounded right—that was what I'd learned at church. It had been ingrained in me since I was a young child—forgiveness was a nice thing to do to those nasty people who did bad things. Thinking that others have "trespassed against me" implies that others have wronged you in a certain way and need your forgiveness. And that was the real meaning of forgiveness—to give a sort of "pardon" and release of any resentment. Not quite so.

Forgiveness begins within. It begins with ME. What? What did I do so wrong that needed forgiveness? I didn't rob a bank or commit any of the big No-Nos of the 10 Commandments. That forgiveness stuff was huge, but really was another part of our human conditioning we needed to release. I was learning that I had to forgive myself. I had to forgive my perception of everything. I had to forgive what I believed others were or were not doing to me. I had to forgive what I believed I had done to myself. I had to forgive all the limiting and self-deprecating thoughts I held about myself. I had to forgive what I thought I needed to be in this body and as this person named Jen. I had to give _myself_ a pardon!

I added forgiveness to my daily practice.

I had to set aside the guidelines that I had put in place for my "healing."

I never left God, He is in me and I am in Him. My biggest lesson or challenge; to understand that I am spirit, at one with God, while experiencing humanity.

I began to see I was waxing and waning between acceptance and beating myself up. And I saw how everything in my body had a "connect the dots" sort of effect. In the years following the spinal back fusion, I addressed the nerve pain in my head, that often times resulted in migraine headaches almost daily. The more uptight, stressed, and the more I listened to my ego, the worse my pain was, therefore more migraines. The Botox shots began about the same time as I had foot surgery. I couldn't go on the recommended walks I was told would help with my spinal back fusion and the tightness that resulted. The back being hurt for so long resulted in the bone in my foot growing outward. I got that surgery solely because I was going with the neutral position as I said earlier. I was not going to judge if something needed to get done.

Botox in the head, fine.

Migraine, need to take a pill, fine.

Foot surgery to be able to walk, that is fine too.

It just seemed futile to judge myself for doing what I needed to do to be non-resistant to it all. I began to not care if I took a migraine pill, or if I had the shots, or if I had to incur more bills. For nearly two decades I lamented over the financial burden I placed on our household because of my health. No matter how many tears and heartfelt conversations I had with my husband, with him pleading with me to stop thinking that way, that we were a team, I felt the guilt on my shoulders and on my heart. I didn't want that burden on myself anymore. I forgave it.

I saw that as I forgave it, things stopped happening and things came to me. I had been removing myself from identifying with any ailments or pain in my body—that seemed like the best option. Now, I was truly learning to undo attachment to the body and practice surrendering.

THE ATTACKER AND THE TEACHER

From what I have learned of the ego, it will fight back when it feels threatened. If you fight it, it fights harder. I went through this when I first began studying *ACIM*. I would have thoughts that were like a run-away train (attack thoughts), which I attributed to the ego-mind. I saw a pattern with the ego thought system: attack when feeling attacked. I learned to be observant, see the thoughts, and then let them slip by without attention, emotion, or anxiety—to be peaceful. I saw that this was what I needed to do with my body.

I observed that when I was happy, the ego would feel jeopardized again and would attempt to sway me. I practiced remaining neutral.

The ego-mind needed you to feel as if you were body and limited. But as long as we are alive, and have a body, the ego has a home, so I might as well learn to live in harmony with it. Whether I listen to the ego or to the Holy Spirit was completely dependent on what I allowed.

Who would be my teacher?

As I mentioned, looking back, a lot of the old pains I had been ignoring started to demand attention. After selling the deli, and all 3 of my children were out of the house (yeah, hard to believe I know), I had nothing to distract me or occupy my thoughts. So, in my doubt I let in the wrong teacher lead the class that I called my life. The ironic thing was that I strove to have quiet time to be closer to God, but instead I gave my quiet mind (and therefore my thoughts) over to the ego. The ego was reigning supreme once again and I was allowing it. It was such a process, I had released a lot, and yet I had not fully surrendered. I still had my blocks to complete freedom from pain. I had come so far.

What else is there and why does this seem so hard?

But try as I might to be unattached to being a body, I was inviting in an inner dialogue reminding me I was the person who had things happening TO her. I still had many moments of giving what was happening in my body lots of thoughts and emotions. As long as I believed in separation and believed I was a body, I would be just that, a body. Could I treat my body and its need without being attached to the need or the actual treatment itself? The thing which I thought about, and gave my energy to, was the thing which I would bring forward. I tried to remove any emotion toward my yucky feelings and just experience them without any expectation of an outcome.

I realized all things held wisdom at some level and that even included pain. When I began to experience dizziness, nausea, and insomnia I didn't panic or go into self-doubt, this time I remained neutral while staying put. While I understood the human body was experiencing some thing, I had a further desire to uncover the reason behind it. I didn't rush off to the doctors immediately. Instead I listened to what I needed to see rather than the old patterns of reacting to pain and discomfort. With weeks of insomnia and vertigo it provided me with the opportunity to uncover a little more about myself.

It turned out the body needed treatment for the stage of aging I was entering (women insert menopause here), I also uncovered something deeper about myself. In the stillness and quiet of home and those bodily symptoms, I found myself to be pondering my life's purpose and the belief that I didn't have one. I slowly continued to surrender to these things as they were unveiled to me.

FACING THE TRUTH WITH MYSELF

It became clear that my desire to have a purpose was co-mingling with sadness from having an empty nest. I really liked the job of "mom." Many people tried to tell me I would have a hard time once all my children were out of the house, and my identity would change, but I would rarely give what they said any credit. Sure, I cried when my kids left, and I missed them horribly, but I was so excited and happy for them. How could I be sad when I was so happy as well?

About a year later, I realized it. I felt like I lost the job I loved and valued: being a mom. Now what was I supposed to do? What was my purpose? I was being forced to face the truth with myself, detach the ties of my worth to the things that I did, such as being a mom. I began to understand that it was a season of life and my role of mom, while still a viable job, was being re-structured a bit. What I needed to do was not react to the "ego attack thoughts" that found the opening in my empty nest.

I feel it is important to mention that "ego attack thoughts" do not have guidelines or limitations. Ego is an equal opportunity attacker. As I was getting acquainted with my new role as mom of grown-up kiddos, I looked at surrendering in a new way, one that didn't have anything to do with my physical form, but yet did affect the physical form. I began to see that surrender needed to be embraced in all facets of my life, not just a select few like my body or career. When I allowed life to play out—like allowing my adult children to make decisions on their own or not being tied to any outcome—and saw what new thing turned up each day, then I was surrendering it all to the Holy Spirit. Even though my humanness reared its ugly head as the empty nest was staring down at me, I saw that I definitely could have a life full of happiness and peace.

I had a tremendous gift of knowing that all that I loved was taken care of because my biggest lesson needed to be well and truly learned—a year in solitude. But, I'll explain all about that later. While I was worlds better than I once was, I was still attempting to conquer my attachment to the body, but I still didn't see who I truly was. I had guidelines and special exemptions to what that meant. Like: I needed to know how I was supposed to show up in this world as Jen now! Meanwhile, it only means ONE thing: You are the Son of God, created in Love. (Period.)

Oh, I spent years in search of the missing piece—as well as my missing peace. I had a desperate need to free myself from pain in the body and to realize I was spirit. It was just that in doing so, I sort of forgot that I was still in the human experience too. As crazy as it may seem, I couldn't get rid of my humanness, I had to co-exist with it. It was a part of me and I had to see that I could still have peace while being a body too. I had been going about it by trying to discredit that I was here and experiencing the life in human form. And while I am human, the body will have experiences. The only difference was, now I knew I was oh so much more. A subtle reminder that I was spirit first and foremost.

I do not have to let the humanity (or the ego-mind) of myself control all that I am in thought and misguidance.

I do not have to allow anything that happens to this body to mean I am less.

I do not need to believe I am less.

Where I once gave the power away, now I did not. I once allowed the belittling thoughts in to rule my mind and body. Now I knew I was perfect. Both human and spirit while going through this life; therefore, I couldn't ignore one or the other.

Both could be acknowledged and accepted, but I must remember that there was only one that was eternally connected to the source of who I am, always. While I enjoyed my humanity and all my experiences, and I received comfort and love from remembering the source of all that I am, I could not forget that I am both as "Jen." It was an understanding of all that I am that had the power to free me from it all.

A SEER AND A KEY

As I was in the process of surrendering, challenged still a bit with vertigo and insomnia, even while understanding the source of it, I had a conversation with a wonderful gentleman, who my husband came to know a few weeks earlier. One might call this humble man a "seer."

He did not charge for his time or assistance. He accepted his insight and his gift and would share it freely. During our conversation, he provided me with the reminder I needed at that time, which was to change my mind back to the way it was before I began "noticing" the symptoms.

On this day, I was at home, and we were speaking on the phone. He asked me to get a key, any key at all, and instructed me to place it on a chain or a string and wear it every day. He said he would tell me when I could stop wearing it. He then told me that I had forgotten and needed to be reminded that I already had the key to the Kingdom of God.

<u>I have all that I need with me, always.</u>

He said I was never alone, but that I had forgotten this. He agreed that I knew this once very strongly. He told me that I had a bit more to go before I knew that I was well, but I would stop being dizzy and not experience nausea. Then he said, "This will be immediate."

He asked if I could do this for myself. Another truth I had to face. Another part of me not fully surrendered. I could not see in front of me because my eyes were so full of tears. I missed my peace. I missed knowing that all was well with me and with my soul. I missed knowing that there was nothing to fear. I knew in this moment that I had simply forgotten, once again, who I was. It was just a thought away. A shift in perception was all I needed. I said yes to this kind man on the telephone who asked nothing of me other than to remember that the Kingdom of God is with me.

I wore that key around my neck for a long while as a constant reminder.

And with that knowing, I was non-resistant to any physical problem arising. I chose to see that I was perfect. I made a choice not to bring the past forward and relive it. I remembered that key around my neck was the reminder of my relationship with God and all the gifts that came along with that. I chose to accept where I was now without resistance. I chose to get out of my own way and see heaven on earth.

This is a daily practice still.

This very morning of writing this section of the book I heard, upon waking, "Wake up in gratitude as a Son of God, not a victim." Can it get any clearer than that?

HUMAN CONDITIONING AND THE EGO CLOUDING CONSCIOUSNESS

In all of this time, I am remembering how to live in conscious awareness, fully in the present moment, consumed by the all loving Holy Spirit. By the way, this is not unique to me or to anyone. This is not reserved for gurus high on a mountain or seekers living among the woods. This is accessible to us all, even those of us living in suburbia or in the city or by the water, those of us surrounded by honking horns or rushing around with to-do lists ten miles long. We all can tap into the memory of our Oneness and shift back into it. We are all born in this pure state of consciousness. Yet, as we experience human conditioning, being conscious seems so distant from reality.

Hmm. Being conscious. *What does this mean to be conscious?*

Years ago I was told a wonderful statement of truth from the spirit of a passed loved one. He told me to share this with my husband. It was, "Stop thinking, start allowing. Therein lies your peace."

What he was instructing us to do was to "allow" our minds, and our lives, to be directed by God: By allowing the Holy Spirit to guide the way. When we are able to be led by a force that has no desire

285

other than our complete happiness, then we can say that we are fully conscious. Consciousness is being present. Living in the moment of where we are in each second connecting to the Oneness with God. We are utilizing the part of ourselves that wants for us to be happy. It is when we are truly happy that this beautiful light flows out of us for the world to share in. Yeah, the source of our creation wants this for us and for all. So cool!

When I heard those words so many years before I had yet to learn about the subconscious mind's workings from programmed beliefs. But it was at a time that was right smack dab in the middle of all the work and studying I was doing with *ACIM* and countless other teachers so I could uncover peace for myself, that the statement that was shared from beyond the veil, made so much sense to me and to my husband from the perspective of God (love) vs. ego (fear).

No matter what I later learned about the conscious or subconscious mind, I still embraced and saw quite clearly the ego-mind and its agenda toward our happiness. The ego can be found in both conscious and subconscious because the ego is part of the human condition. Oh boy.

ACIM had directed my thoughts and understanding to see a much more loving God, world, and self. It was through understanding what was referred to as duality that made everything so clear.

"A Course in Miracles distinguishes two worlds: God and the ego, knowledge and perception, truth and illusion. Strictly speaking, every aspect of the post- separation world of perception reflects the ego. However, the Course further subdivides the world of perception into wrong-minded and right-mindedness. Within this framework the Course almost always uses the word "ego" to denote wrong-mindedness, while the right-mindedness is the domain of the

Holy Spirit, Who teaches forgiveness
as the correction for the ego."
~ *Theory* (adapted from the Glossary-Index for *A Course in Miracles,*
Fourth Edition) by Kenneth Wapnick, PhD

So, it would go that we would think of the ego along with the body, because as long as we believe we are limited and only a body, the ego reigns supreme over our thoughts. We allow that to be so.

"You regard yourself as necessarily conflicted as long as you are here, or
as long as you believe you are here. The ego is nothing more than a part
of your belief about yourself."
~ *ACIM* pg. 67, chapter 4

Basically, as long as you are disillusioned by who you truly are, it still cannot touch the fact you are a Son of God and an eternal, spiritual being. What the illusion does do, though, is keeps you in state where you believe you can be hurt by so many countless things. This is what it means to be in a dream of your own making which can seem more like a nightmare, I know. It means we are lost in this ongoing fear where we are never enough and things can harm us, when in reality, we are not. What you can do according to *ACIM* is learn to associate misery with the ego and joy with the spirit.

"When the ego is in charge, the body's existence is one of sickness,
suffering, and death, which witness to the seeming reality of the body as
opposed to spirit, which can never suffer pain, or die."
~ *Theory (*adapted from the Glossary-Index for *A Course in Miracles,*
Fourth Edition) by Kenneth Wapnick, PhD

It is in thinking, that we never fully appreciate the moment we are in. It is in our consciousness we can actually live in the state of happiness and fulfillment. It is in the obsessive thinking, where we believe we are "planning" things for the future or thinking how we could've changed things from the past, that we have handed over our peace. We have left the space where we can be guided by the Holy Spirit and stepped into the land of the ego.

The ego's desire is to distract the mind that is conscious and to pull it out of the land of peace and take control. We, in turn, hand over the wheel so to say, to the subconscious mind or live from a position of fear. It plays these old programs that we aren't even aware of, and more than likely were learned from someone else or an experience. This is how the subconscious mind works. It is fantastic at being on autopilot. That part of us that loves to keep us lost in these thoughts. I can now see that this is also the space where my humanness has gotten in the way, by way of subconscious beliefs.

There is no thinking in the subconscious mind—it is. So, when we are thinking we are bringing things up in our conscious mind and then, without our knowing, we are being led by subconscious programs of the subconscious mind and the ego.

When we are thinking (jump into the future or past) we are using the conscious mind but it is actually the subconscious mind doing the work. Woah! Lightbulbs bright!

Our conscious mind can address the details of the day ahead, and the subconscious mind can drive the car based on learned patterns and behaviors. They work together as a great pair.

The path to learning about the role of the subconscious mind was given to me after a year of prayer and surrender (you will read all about that year in the next chapter). I prayed for God to show me yet another way that people could examine their thoughts and beliefs, to be a good bridge of understanding from all that I learned to truly be of service people. I prayed for a way that wasn't necessarily spiritual in nature, but something they could sink their teeth into and ultimately lead them to examine the ego. While I stand completely in knowing what helped me could (and has) helped countless others, I was thinking as a person in service to others, there could be an easier tool and if there was indeed something out there, the Holy Spirit would orchestrate it.

I prayed and I waited.

In divine orchestration, I learned of a process called PSYCH-K® that facilitated change at the subconscious level where 95% of our conscious mind operates. While I could take a person through my spiritual process, and I stand behind it 100%, this approach, more scientific in nature, changed people's subconscious limiting beliefs in a quicker way. Sure, they wouldn't go as deep, but it was quick - perfect for our humanness.

The evening I knew I should study PSYCH-K® further; I had just finished writing a few pages in preparation for this very book you're reading, and I loved the words I typed "You are a Spiritual Being having a Human Experience". Just moments after I stopped writing, I received an email from a group of friends about a scientist speaking in Atlanta. Now I received an email from my friends about this guy twice before and I deleted both of them without a thought. His teachings were absolutely not something I would ever be interested in listening to, ever. But here's the kicker, this was their third email, and on this night, after a year of praying for a bridge from my spirituality to reach people still in their humanness, I clicked and saw the same words I had just typed moments before "You are a Spiritual Being having a Human Experience". Prayers answered and PSYCH-K® here

I come! In walks the concept of subconscious beliefs and the exact moment it was needed and not a second earlier.

SURRENDERING IS AN ONGOING PRACTICE

After the sale of the deli and surgery, I asked for guidance for where I was to work next. I felt myself trying to figure things out again. See, there's that tango again. Me trying. Boy is it hard to break that conditioning. Shedding the painful truth about my eating disorder and my need to control, I soon began to embrace good eating habits. I guess you could say I was embracing wellness on the level of both the mind and body. I adopted good healthy practices for myself and of course my family, since I was the chief cook and bottle washer. I did extensive research on anti-inflammatory foods and diets and studies many different eating modalities and picked and chose what worked best for myself and my family. I learned about herbs, and tissue salts, I even found out I loved Kombucha! I was so interested in wellness and nutrition and they had become very important to me, so the next thing I did was research schools to get certified!

I dove right in and had so many certificates and certifications under my belt. I was a health coach and Reiki master and had so many expectations for myself, but it seemed as though my plans were not unfolding. So, I prayed and expressed that I would fully surrender, as *ACIM* and my husband had shown me. It had worked for me in the past with the deli. I wanted the relief of not having to figure it all out. I wanted to feel that freedom.

I had read Michael Singer's book, *The Surrender Experiment* and I wanted to know the feeling of being guided to do as God instructed like the author experienced. In meditation and prayer, I stated that whatever came into my life next was where I was meant to be for the greater good of all. I surrendered my decisions to God. I sat there until I felt it deep within. I mean, at this point I was thinking *why not*? We have been led to where we need to go each and every time, despite the thoughts and ego poking that we once listened to over God's voice. There was still so much in my life I was seeking, maybe this was a better way of deciding where to go work next.

The day after this decree, I got a call from a friend who said there was a job at the high school. I noticed the more I practiced forgiveness and placed no judgment on how I was feeling, I began to see a difference in how I felt. The more I practiced, allowing the Holy Spirit guidance over the ego, I was able to do more. I surrendered and got the job with the high school, which in turn provided our family with health insurance, and me with time off. All those worries about money for decades and I had it all covered now.

And, the surrenders continued. When I left the job and moved, we thought we might be without insurance for 2 months before our new insurance picked up, somehow, we were still on that school plan. I received an email that it would be stopping April 30th and our new insurance began May 1st. We had no idea how, but I knew it was in the surrender that it happened. In my 14 years of volunteering for the school system, this was my first paid position, so I was ecstatic when a check 2x's my normal paycheck came in the mail one month after I left, it was the rest of my contracted salary. It was a gift for sure. Money was not my focus or fear any longer. I was seeing that come true in our life because it just showed up.

Eventually, I stopped getting nerve blocks with a low dose muscle relaxer at night that helped with nerve problems. In the years that followed, months would go by with only 1, sometimes zero migraines. The feet that needed surgery were the same ones I use now to get me through hikes of up to 8 miles and up rock formations in Sedona. The neck that I had been told needed fusion several times over the course of the last 20 years has not had any work done on it. It would be a lie to say that my feet don't ache at all, or that this body doesn't experience aches or even hurt after a hike, but I don't give it any attention. Once I put a stop to thinking about wanting to be different or caring that I didn't have the body I thought I should have, all the stress began to melt away. I just continued to eat a healthy, low inflammatory diet, and gave less attention to the body, which in turn gave it less power over my peace. That is how I handle any and all parts of my body and my life.

Over the years, Michaels Singer's book showed me how peaceful trusting in surrender to the spirit of our creator can be, and I realized that "surrender" isn't a one and done deal. We don't "surrender" and then arrive to the Holy Grail of Oneness. Like we shout from the rooftops, "I SURRENDER!!" and the seas part and the skies open up and it's over! You've won the surrender game! And you are received by lights beaming down and cheers from the heavens!

Nope.

Sorry, honey, but that just isn't how surrender works. Makes for a good movie script, though. In life, we have to practice continual surrendering, with awareness of when our humanness is holding a tight grasp, we surrender that hold and let it go. As evidenced by my first big surrender with the sale of the deli, I still had times where I just didn't surrender until it hurt so bad that I did. And that awareness of the difference in how it felt to hang on with a tight grip versus the peace that came with true surrender, I had made a practice of it in my own life. The calmest times of my life were when I allowed myself to be led. And I can see the fruits of continual surrender looking back. Whenever I surrendered to my true self and this Divine guidance, (without resistance and judgment), everything worked out. Often times things worked out better than I had hoped for.

Reflecting on times of struggle, and the endless "waiting" for some particular thing to work out the way I had organized or planned, was very painful and emotionally brutal for me. I never considered anyone else's life path when I was lamenting over what I wanted. I also never considered the multitude of other things that could work out in my favor while I was stuck thinking about only my one plan. I had to concede that during certain times I thought I was waiting and waiting for something to happen, only to clearly see now that the situation needed to be right for all parties involved; not just for myself or my family (ie: selling a house or a business . . . heck, even a particular job!).

When I finally saw that torturing myself could end, I saw no earthly reason to do this to myself ever again. It was that concept of once you see something differently, it is very hard to go back to seeing it the old way. The lightbulb clicked on brighter than ever; it will always be for my highest good, when I allow the Holy Spirit to guide me! And it is at these times, I noticed, I was the happiest I had been in a long time. The necessary requirement for this guidance was surrendering to it. Being in a state of allowing, so that you can see what needs to or wants to come to you.

"Going with the flow" requires surrender. It is living in a state of allowing and being aware when we are holding on too tight and must surrender. It is flowing with the stream, not swimming against it. Oftentimes a situation did not turn out exactly as I had planned, but a positive result occurred (none the less), a result which held so many more positives than I had ever imagined.

My favorite example of this was our move to Atlanta. Several years back when we still lived on the coast of Georgia, there was a horrible snow storm in Atlanta and many people were stranded overnight in their vehicles. I remember telling my husband I would "never live in Atlanta" when I could live where I was. There were other times in discussing population and traffic that I made this sweeping declaration once more.

Well, fast forward to my husband starting a new business after we sold the deli, and his business expanded. In typical Fred-fashion (post *ACIM* Fred I should say), he made a desired list of nine points for his business and for us personally. The way my husband handled this list of desires was with complete surrender. He prayed about these desires, he visualized them, and he had a good idea of what it would feel like when they were obtained. He also accepted that he didn't know when and how they would come about, so he surrendered them to God. He didn't think of them, and he trusted that if they were to come to him (to us), they would. He set himself up to allowing without the painful struggle.

We would often remind each other of the example we once heard: It's like when you place an order at the restaurant; you don't go into the kitchen and keep asking if it is ready yet. Or "Did you make it the way I wanted?" No. You trusted the order and you wait (hopefully patiently) while you enjoy the restaurant and your company until your food comes out to you.

I know at this point you may have already guessed that his list of desires for his business did eventually come to him. It took almost two years. Also, he listed a desire to be in the northern part of Georgia. Yup, that is where I am typing this book, North Georgia. Remember my sweeping declaration of no Atlanta? Well, I moved to where I swore, in my "planning," that I would never live.

My time here has been a continued journey of growth and expansion to the likes of which I could have never imagined. I have met people and had opportunities that I didn't even dream of when I made that limiting belief statement. We do not live in the city but we aren't too far to enjoy all it has to offer. We have so many things at our fingertips, food, the mountains, an international airport, and our children. I went with the flow of my husband's business and personal desires and what happened was miraculous and rewarding in countless ways.

I remind myself when I see that I'm trying to plan or control an outcome: Is it fair to say that there is a better result to this situation than the one I have planned? Possible. Is it also fair to assume that the solution can turn out better for more people than just me? Also, very possible. *Then, Jen, surrender!*

In this world of perception, I also placed a timeline to all of my desired outcomes. A timeline that didn't serve me because all it did was allow the ego to swoop in and tell me what I wasn't receiving when I wanted it. I noticed that each time, and in every situation, myself and my family were always provided for. At times worry or concern might have consumed me, but as soon as I let it all go and trusted in God to provide what I needed, it was given and often it was better than expected. Once this idea was firmly and completely learned, we allowed and did not worry and stress over the details of how the situation would be resolved. There was only our ultimate and peaceful surrender.

I have viewed many past situations as horrible financial setbacks, but with time, effort, and surrender I am now able to see these past situations and events with a different set of eyes. I cannot think of my idea or plan the same way ever again. Why? Because I cannot possibly "top" all the possibilities available to me by the Universe! I now rely greatly on what is presented to me. This is not to say that I don't lay preliminary work down—of course I do. I am still human after all!

For example, when we were looking for a house, we contacted real estate agents to aid in the search of where we thought we wanted to live and the type of house. But then, we let it go. My husband and I didn't go to a place of stress, worrying how fast this would happen, how it was going to happen and if we could find something we liked that was in our desired price range.

We both make an effort to not attach emotionally to the imagined outcomes. Instead, I place a child-like excitement in seeing what comes to us.

Life has been so rewarding and adventurous since my husband and I have been on the same page with allowing what is to flow to us. We have proof in our lives that when we surrender and allow, we are peaceful and very pleased with what comes our way. It is when we push and plan (and push even harder), that we experience strain and emotional upheaval. It is like we are not aligned with our true selves and what is to come to us naturally if we allow it. We are getting in the way of this energetic flow that is designed to come to us. I prefer to live my life, in all areas, through surrendering to what is in my highest good. I placed my order—it will come to me when it is time!

A few months ago, my husband, myself, and our eldest daughter went on a hike, which led to beautiful waterfalls. Once we arrived in front of these falls, it was peaceful and majestic to simply stand there in the beauty of it all. I heard these words as clear as a bell, "All you need, you already have." There is a difference between needs and wants and desires. This peaceful reminder was for both my daughter and myself.

We seem to always have what we need, and our desires are coming. There is absolutely nothing wrong with having desires. But

I have found that when the desires are taking hold and making me have a belief that I am lacking in any way, I need to re-evaluate and see what mind I am thinking with. We can surrender peacefully to the knowledge that everything will come to us, and believe it to be so and rest in that.

To think that we can change our thought processes and human conditioning in the blink of an eye would seem miraculous. It may happen for some, but for most it's work. In my work with *ACIM*, I addressed countless limited beliefs and ideas I held about my relationship with God, myself, and others. I experienced a process of undoing which led me to the state of allowing. In this state I know I am taken care of and a world of opportunity is open to me.

"Surrender completely and all thoughts evaporate. Nothing has any hold on your happiness. It is yours."
~ From Meditations with Jesus and Jen

Spirit ['spirit]

noun

the nonphysical part of a person which is the seat of emotions
and character; the soul.

*Spirit is the true essence of who we are individually, and it
connects to the whole of everything that is. Spirit is eternal and
never changing because it is created perfect and part of God.*

CHAPTER 11

In Sync with Spirit and My Year in Solitude

"We are not victims of aging, sickness, and death. These are part of scenery, not the seer, who is immune to any form of change. This seer is the spirit, the expression of eternal being."
~ *Deepak Chopra*

"Jen, you are not going to believe this."

Yeah, he was right. I almost didn't believe it. This conversation took place almost 20 years ago after Fred received a frantic phone call from his mother. She saw something on the news that caused her great concern. Now normally my mother-in-law's worries can be a little over the top. But this time, her worry was 1000% warranted. So what didn't I believe? Let me start from the beginning.

Earlier that night we were heading home from New York City. I had taken the train into the city for an acting class straight from work. Oh yeah, forgot to mention, I had fun with that back in the day. Anyhow, my husband, who worked at the World Trade Center, took a cab to Midtown where my class was, so that we could catch a train together back home. We would have been on time for my husband's usual train if we hadn't decided to grab a slice of pizza from a tiny restaurant inside Penn Station.

That night, for some reason, we decided to stop for pizza. There was this one pizza place that had a salad with vinegar dressing plopped right on top of the pizza, and it was my favorite. Oh boy, I can still remember the taste of that pizza. Delicious and one of the things I miss about New York. We hadn't had a slice in a while, so since I loved that particular pizza, we thought it was worth the delay to grab a bite on this particular night.

Once our bellies were satisfied, we headed toward the terminal to take the next train to our town. It was on a different track than the normal one we took each week and different than the one Fred takes home each night. Once we were on the train, and moving along toward Long Island, we saw a train that was stopped on a parallel track.

Nothing could have prepared us for the scene that we slowly rolled by. Inside, the train was lit up, and we could see there were a lot of people, and there was blood splattered all over the windows. That was the very track and the exact train we would normally be on. I froze. Did you read what I wrote? THAT WAS OUR TRAIN. I am shaking thinking back about it even after all these years. We would have been on it had we not missed it 30 minutes before. We were so confused and frightened at what we were seeing. What the heck had happened?

When we arrived home, we climbed the long flight of stairs to our second-floor apartment and we heard our house phone ringing inside. We hurried in and my husband ran to grab the phone before the answering machine picked up. That's right, this was a while ago and we had an answering machine. He began talking right away and was reassuring someone that yes, we were fine.

He said, "Yes, Jen is here with me too." He paused to listen intently to what the person on the phone was saying. I heard him exclaim in disbelief, and again now even quieter, reassuring this person, who he mouthed to me was his mom, that we were both fine. He told her we did see something, and that we were a little shaken up because we had no idea what we were looking at, but we were safe.

After the call we noticed several messages beeping on the answering machine as well. Keep in mind: This was 1993, these were not the times of immediate information download or cell phones.

He hung up the phone and turned to me. His face a bit ashen for his normally tanned complexion, "Jen, you are not going to believe this. My mom was totally freaking out. She wanted to make sure we were both all right, as you heard. Remember that weird scene we saw when we passed the train on the track on my regular route home? Apparently, a gunman shot someone on the train a little bit ago. On that train!"

We were both stunned. We knew it was a miracle that we were not on his normal train that night. We stood there with fear in our eyes thinking about this unreal story. Words cannot do justice to the feeling of gratitude and relief we both felt, as we clung to each other in a strong hug. We thanked God and our angels and whoever would listen, that we were not on that train. Choosing to grab a slice of pizza because we couldn't wait to eat until we were back home saved us from being on the train we normally took back home. We later learned that a gunman opened fire on that train full of commuters. Six people lost their lives and many people were injured on that horrific and fateful night. We were in complete and utter shock—feeling fear, sadness, and once more an enormous amount of gratitude.

Here's the kicker. Normally we stick to a budget, so we can do fun things on the weekends and that means not eating meals out during the week. Yet that night, we chose to break our budget and grab a slice of pizza over running for the train. Normally we make good time, and scurry to the track and catch the train, on the routine track. Making the normal train saves a few minutes during the commute. We would have made our normal train if we didn't choose that pizza.

It wasn't until many years later that we truly understood the spiritual aspect at work, in saving our lives, simply through choosing to grab a slice of pizza. We did not realize at the time that we actually had listened to the Holy Spirit telling us to do something other than take our routine trip home that night. That night we obviously went along with the Divine guidance, without realizing it was at work. We were led, we unknowingly listened, and that is why we survived that night.

When we later realized the magnitude of listening to the Divine guidance and the Holy Spirit in our lives, it became hard not to listen, especially with proof like that. But being human, as we are, we seem to slip into forgetfulness and listen to the ego-mind, forgetting the miraculous things that can occur when we remain open and just go with that inner guidance system. Being in sync with spirit means listening to the Divine direction, even when you have no idea that is what you are doing.

SPIRIT TAPS UNTIL I ALLOW MYSELF IN

Throughout my life, I experienced a "tapping" sensation. I ignored it really, for the better part of 4 decades. Flat out didn't give the taps any mind. For one reason or another, I disregarded these gentle nudges that were being presented to me. If I did pay attention, it was not at the level that I could really understand what I was experiencing—it was only on a superficial level.

Looking back on those experiences, I never got very deep into spirituality or the truth of who I was and what was happening enough to transcend my thoughts, obviously. I even went as far as to think through the things that occurred to me and around me as things that were really neat or cool or a gift for that moment. I knew everything came from the one source I believed I knew so well: God. But I did not see these nudges as something that I as Jen needed to address deeper.

For a while, this back and forth kind of irritated me. I felt up and down in my faith, connected then disconnected. When I finally started to understand that I was the block to my own experiences, I began to pay a bit more attention. Basically, it became obvious that in order to have the peace I had been searching for, I needed to quiet the mind to learn what was being presented to me time and time again.

The near-death experiences . . . tap. The angels . . . tap. The car ride to the hospital . . . tap. The pizza . . . tap. The dreams I had that would come true the next day . . . tap. Spirit . . . tap!

At one point in time, much later in my life, I felt I needed to know who was delivering the messages to me. If I was quiet and heard something wonderful, who was it? An angel? If so, which one? A spirit? If so, then who? Jesus? The Holy Spirit? A guide? This was me just finding another way to erect a blockade to the real message. Was it that I was lacking because I couldn't "hear" who was delivering the message? I thought, *Shouldn't I be able to know exactly who it is?*

The tapping on my shoulder was happening but my mind found a way to dismiss it and create a separation from the message, hence separating me from my Oneness, and to who I truly am.

Because of my studies with *A Course in Miracles*, I was able, eventually, to step back and see that this was the ego-mind I was catering to. I knew this to be true because when I fretted over the messenger, I would lose sight of the message. When I thought about myself not being worthy of hearing something, I was again listening to a part of my mind that did not want me to listen to the other teacher, the Holy Spirit. I was taking a message of love and trying to make it into something of lack, fear, and ego-based thoughts instead.

For almost my entire lifetime I ignored the signs. Then, when I began to question in earnest, the source of the message, I uncovered the lesson of Oneness. And get this, the source was no longer important . . . and I, like anyone else, was worthy to hear a message, hear words of guidance, and see signs based on the common love we all share.

I didn't want any distractions from the point of the message any longer, so I listened rather than thought. At times I would experience a clear understanding of who was giving the needed message, but at other times it was not as clear. So, I would just carry on. I learned that all the value was in the message, and it is all ultimately from God when it is about love and Oneness (and it is from ego when it is not rooted in love). As I began to see the value in the message, it was then that I saw that it is for the highest good of everyone. Since I learned the difference between a life led in the mind of ego vs. God, I knew these loving and motivating message were from Source.

For most of my life, I perceived God as outside of me. And in my relationship with the Father, the Son, and the Holy Spirit, I was merely the spectator. Like, the big guy has bigger fish to fry than dealing with Jen. God, and the Trinity, they were there for me sure, but I did not think I was one with them. I see now that I had a limited understanding of God.

And Jesus . . . well, Jesus was this amazing man, who is the Son of God. I watched him from afar, perhaps drawing close at times in prayer, holding him in the deepest, most loving regard, but never feeling at one with him. Who was I to be worthy of that? That was reserved for the bigtime angels and saints and biblical figures. Not Fun Jen from New York! Not this gal doubled over in pain on my bathroom floor bawling! Not the mom who couldn't even lift up her daughters to play with them because her insides were mush! Nope, I didn't have that kind of clout.

But through this time of learning and unlearning, undoing attachment and surrendering, and being so in sync with spirit, I finally understood I was invited to the party and the party was actually right inside of me all along. I honestly understood the magnitude of what I could be part of, infinite peace, joy, abundance, if I allowed it. The endless well of love was there for me when I would simply shift my mind.

LOVE COVERS ALL

"Don't let words divide us when they are holding the same meaning."
~ From Meditations with Jesus and Jen

I had a deep knowing to write this book for many, many years. It started as a tap, and then a whisper, and then it pretty much knocked me out. It was like my eyes were being opened to all those around me who were in pain, suffering, speaking limitation into their worlds. I began to notice everywhere I turned that people were fed up with not feeling good. And oh, how I understood what I was seeing. I wanted to run up to each and every person and give them a hug, but that would be weird. I wanted them to know they were not alone, and I understood, and they had a way out that didn't include somebody outside of themselves to "fix" them. I wanted them to know they were not broken! But, instead, I might have just smiled, or lent a hand, or gave a listening ear.

To be honest, there was still a part of me even after my big shift that had a fear of being judged. I mean, even I thought this stuff was unreal and hard to believe when I first heard about it. Talking about Jesus was scary enough in some instances, now I'd be running up to strangers telling them their whole life is a dream of their own making. Oh yeah, sounds nuts and I was afraid I might say the wrong thing and turn them off to possibilities for peace, and that was the last thing I wanted to do.

We can all get caught up in words, and I realized that's just another form of ego trapping. Okay, this is going to get a little deep, maybe a little "woo woo" to some, but please hear me out. Words will have meaning for people specific to how they learned it, and do not hold all the meaning for what they are naming. Once you can get beyond the word or name for this "thing" and its conditioned meaning it holds for you, there is so much that can open up for you.

For example, I was once discussing a topic with someone and I said "God." They told me that the word "God" did not resonate with them. It was a big learning moment for me. I asked what they called the source of their creation and their answer was "Universe." I respected this lesson so much because neither of us lost the meaning of our conversation and what we gathered from it because of the different name we called the same thing.

There are so many names for God that resonate deeply with people. I have heard these various names for the meaning of the same thing, such as: God, love, source, chi, higher self, gaia, all that is,

Holy Spirit, I Am, Allah, King of Kings, Yahweh, Creator, Jehovah, life force, and Universe. Accepting a friend's ideas, even though they called God a different word, doesn't threaten your religious beliefs. It is helping us all connect to one another. Society is beginning to understand that not every word or new idea is a threat to what they hold to be valuable or true. There are so many opportunities for people to take a look at their own understandings about who they are and learn new understandings. They are freeing themselves from being blocked by words or different concepts. How exciting! We are building a new world!

No two of us are exactly the same because of so many factors, also known as our "personal self", as the book the *Impersonal Life* by Joseph Benner states. It is our individuality, our personalities, that make us uniquely who we are. But, what I love so much about the book is in its title *"The Impersonal Life"*. While acknowledging our uniqueness, the "impersonal self" runs through each of us, and that is what makes us at the core all the same! Yep, what we all share in common my friends, is the "impersonal self". This common thread, this wonderful thing, that runs through each of us, is God. It is Love and it unites us. And we are each blessed to allow our personal self, our personalities, to shine the "impersonal self" into the world.

There is a statement in the *ACIM* teacher's manual, which is lovely; it says, "Words are but symbols for symbols. They are twice removed from reality" (M-21. 1:9-10). We are becoming a society that is learning to be tolerant of words and get to the core of a shared concept. We are bridging gaps and learning to understand the Oneness that we all share with the universe.

You can see how this had once divided us as a species and still has the power to hold onto us with these limiting beliefs if we allow it. You can also see in our world how when we set words, titles, and symbols aside, the world is a loving place and less judgment is placed on our brothers and sisters. We can reach out once again to the common thread that we each have, the spirit of who we essentially are.

We drop our human conditioning and reach out for the vibration of love that is thrumming through us. What a liberating feeling to love rather than create a wall based on judgment, conditioning, and words. And love comes in so many forms, in the physical world and beyond. Yep, you betcha, it's all waiting for us to open our hearts to receiving it.

WHAT THE WHAT?! I CAN TALK TO SPIRIT

After my dad died, there was a huge hole in my heart. He sent us messages in the form of pennies, sure. But I missed him dearly. I'll never forget the first time I actually heard him speak after he passed. I was rocking in a chair on the front porch of our home, the sun very bright, I was peaceful. I didn't feel like getting up to grab sunglasses. I had just a little snippet of time, while the kids were playing, before I needed to start Sunday dinner. So instead I closed my eyes against the glare and soaked up the warmth. I was in a relaxed state.

I should note that this was before my "shift" began, I was desperately missing my father. The weather was perfect in the 60's. The Yankee in me still marveled at that since it was November. Mom was staying with us now. She sold everything, I mean everything, and came to live with us until she knew her next step in her new life. One thing was for sure, she knew she wanted to live near us.

Serene, and warm, I was thinking about Dad. Then I heard, in my mind's ear, "Thank you." It sounded like my dad. And it felt like him. I knew, without a doubt, it was Dad. He continued on saying that he loved mom so much and he always will. He was so grateful to me and Fred. He loved the kids and he was happy.

What the what!? Riveted there in the rocking chair, with my eyes still closed, I just listened. I was quiet and I was peaceful and I just listened. I had tears leaking out the corners of my eyes in a slow roll, but I had a smile on my face.

Ohh, Dad, how I miss you.

My face began to scrunch up. I felt more tears falling, but I knew I needed to stop it before I got on a roll and fell into an ugly cry. I didn't want to miss a thing. So, I just composed myself as best as I could, and I sat there for probably 20 minutes. Waiting patiently, and quietly, and I would silently ask a question here and there, and I would hear an answer!! It was wild, yet felt so right.

Finally, when I didn't hear anything more, I ran inside the house to where Mom and Fred were watching TV. "I just talked to Dad! I mean really talked to him, I swear." I began to explain all that I heard. They were so amazed and there wasn't a dry eye between us. The joy and warmth we shared that day in knowing that Dad was with us, was priceless. We held onto the belief that he was among us, with great hope, and now we knew! It was certainly real. And, that is how Dad would come to me throughout the years.

He came in the form of signs, like the pennies, or songs, like "Calling All Angels" by Train, and in words, he would speak with me. Yes, we held conversations like this. And at first, as real as it felt, part of me thought it was just wishful thinking. I would have these kinds of conversations, I'd feel so good and my heart so full, but my head would have me questioning myself. As I mentioned, this was before I was really tapping into my Oneness, but certainly a huge motivator for me to do so.

I was skeptical of my signs and messages and even dreams where I spoke to Dad right after his passing. I went to a medium out of a dire need to hear from him—for some reason I thought that would be more "official," more legit. I mean, it made sense. If my back was out of whack, I would go to a chiropractor for an adjustment, I wouldn't adjust myself. People go to the professionals all the time for all sorts of things. My grief and need to connect with my dad was so debilitating, that calling on a professional certainly felt in order.

At the time, it was imperative to my mental state. Like I needed it to survive the grief of losing him. So, I did what anyone would do, I went to someone who knew how to talk to spirit, because I thought I really had no idea how to do that. My mom and I went together to talk to a medium, and I went by myself twice.

"You speak to your father since he is passed. You are a medium as well," the woman stated as a matter-of-fact.

"No, I am not!" I answered quite emphatically.

How can I be something that I never studied, and if I could do that, what am I doing sitting here giving you money for? These thoughts were bubbling up in my mind, just glad they didn't spill out of my mouth.

I came to this woman without reservation, and as she spoke to me about Dad, she hit it all spot on. When she got to the part of me talking to Dad, I was doubtful of her words at first, they seemed kind of generic. Until she said, "You dream of him, and most of the time, you are on a cell phone."

We talked on the cell phone when he was alive, every day, sometimes multiple times a day. It boggles the mind how much money we spent for those phone calls, from New York to Georgia, and from Georgia to New York, at a time when you paid by the minute! There was no way of researching me, as I never gave the psychic my last name, and on top of that, Dad was from New York.

Yes, I did have dreams of Dad and me on the cell phone. Yes, I guess this was another way of him communicating with me, my dreams. Little did I know that communicating with him would change and grow from there.

Dad's passing brought me closer and closer to spirit, and ultimately led me to the desire for peace as I saw in the movie, *The Shift*. Looking back, I am so glad my friend listened to the divine tap to give me that DVD, and perhaps my dad, who saw me struggling from the other side of the veil, even played a role in that tapping.

But, here's something amazing about the connection I had with my father. Almost ten years after the passing of my dad, I was in my office meditating. By this point, I had been working on myself, working to find peace, and just flat out trying to be happy with myself. I was studying a great deal. Getting certificates of study, in various areas, while all the while reading daily from *A Course in Miracles*. I even took a course on mediumship a few years before.

Yet, on this particular day, I was feeling low. I had a lot on my mind, and I wanted to talk to my dad. He had come through so many times, but for some reason, crickets this time. I couldn't hear him. For days, I had been trying to communicate with him like I had so many times before. As I sat on my office floor, a white candle glowing next to me, and a pen and paper to my right, I heard nothing once more.

"What the heck, Dad?" I said out loud, starting to get upset. The tears began and I thought:

Why have you abandoned me in my time of need. I need to talk to you, Dad! I want answers and guidance. I need you to help me!!

Then, clear as day, I heard him . . .

"Jennifer—"

311

Uh oh, I am in trouble, I never get called Jennifer unless I am in trouble.

"I cannot come to you when you need me like this. I know it is hard for you. You must understand that you are there, and you have to do this journey. I can't do it for you. I can't give you the answers. You cannot rely on me, but you must rely on yourself. The answers you need are there for you, but they cannot come from me. When you no longer look to me for the answers for living, then I will come to you." He was stern but loving in his tone that came through on my heart.

I sat there and wept. There was a part of me that was pissed, but the greater part of me got it. How could I desperately seek the answers from Dad, when he was peaceful on another part of his journey, and I was still here being human?

<u>In desperation, I was debilitating my connection.</u>

After that day, I didn't talk to my dad for probably a year. I had a lot to work out with myself and a lot that needed to be understood. And only I could do that for myself. I finally understood that Dad could help me with anything I needed, but my state of mind was imperative. When I was desperate, I closed myself off to the natural flow and order of things. I closed myself off to the blessings and the Oneness and was out of sync with spirit, out of sync with my highest self. I needed to understand me, who I truly was, and embrace my true nature. Dad couldn't do that for me.

And as I was becoming fully in my Oneness, I began to feel more connected to Dad than ever. I remember sitting in my office listening to meditation music, trying not to cry on the anniversary of the loss of my dad, as memories flooded me. So many thoughts of the joyous times and the laughter and the parties. I began to think that even in eternity when I am with him, I would not experience what I did when he was in physical form. Then I quickly realize how very wrong I was.

I heard him say, "Stop, Jen! Live in the now." He continued to say that he was there in each smile of our son. In each time our middle daughter made us laugh and in each beautifully written word our oldest daughter wrote.

In that exact moment of joy, it was the same joy and feeling of love that I had when I would laugh with him or make a joke with him or when we were cooking together, and I realize that it didn't matter—in the physical or not in the physical form—it was the love and the joy we shared! That feeling! It was like no other feeling—and he was there the entire time!

I could see that while I may crave the hug or my dad in physicality, I could still experience the love and joy we shared. I began to see that it was the same vibration and uplifting giddiness and feelings of love I thought I was missing when he wasn't here any longer. I still had the ability to feel it! And this lesson clung to my heart—when I allowed the presence of my Dad to be felt, then the very same feelings of happiness I had in my life with him were achieved.

The understanding of this is one of the hardest things of all, because we have conditioned ourselves to understand that this human world is one we must see with our physical eyes. But, there is so much beyond what we see in this physical world, and when we shift into allowing that, we become fully in sync with spirit, and experience bliss at a level beyond compare. All the years I searched, I think I was really looking for some quick fix, something outside of me to give me peace, I was on a fruitless pursuit, because I was looking everywhere but where peace could be found—right inside of me! Really, the whole time it was always inside.

I caught glimpses of it when I would communicate with my

angels as a child, my near-death experiences, the tappings, moments of connection with Dad, but I didn't realize the key to moving that bliss from moments to the constant was simply in my stillness, my presence, and my willingness. And the truth is, nothing we do here is important other than the love we share with others. All others!! Not our select few, all. I am not demeaning the accomplishments of life, but we can all see that anything we have done or created, when it is not done in love, it is lacking greatly.

I have learned this the hard way and the easiest way. Hard because of the loss of someone I loved too early, and easiest because of so much love that enveloped me.

I received this message from my dad that validated all that I knew in my being, "Because this is one of the last bridges to the Kingdom. The attachment severed from form and embracing the formless. The spirit. The etheric and eternal [body] connection to all that is. If you can sit in that and know you are loved without the form, this is vision."

Woah. Dad really went there with that one. The physical is infused with Spirit. It is one. But even without the form, Spirit is there. Spirit is part of that same energy that is in everything and yet it is in us individually as well. (I know "Spirit" may be one of those trigger words my friend, just hang in with me here and try to see how I began to see it.) To say it simply, we are everything. The spirit that is within us, that makes us who we are, and connected to God while in the body will return to God and all that is, when we die. Most of us have heard that in our lifetimes and we can understand it that far. But the everything part includes the birds, the trees, those loved ones who have passed, people on the street, the ocean and so on . . . all that is.

I've heard of many other words like the Sonship, Christ

Consciousness (that Jesus Christ showed us with His life and His death) and the like, but I am trying to explain how this process came to me . . . and although I have shifted my perception on many things, it was certainly a process of learning new terms and understanding different than what I knew before.

Here, I'll continue and clarify further. That which makes us who we are can still be felt and heard (even seen by some) the essence of their loved ones because of this LIKE energy. People touch trees or walk around outside, or feel drawn to the ocean, that is energy. So, like this energy, so too our spirit is in kind.

When we shift our minds and open to this great Oneness God has provided us with, we can follow His Divine guidance and feel so many things shift into happy accord. Look at the beautiful sunrise, and the smile on a baby's face and feel that giddy feeling, experience love. It's not in the flashy things, the designer bags or fancy electronics, but in the connections that move us deep within. This spirit of each of us, and the energy connection of all that is, brings an elation in knowing who we truly are! You are actually an integral part of the Oneness.

I had come so far and yet I knew I still had yet to believe who I truly was. Throughout my life, I would get a deep shiver when someone mentioned "eternity", like an automatic reaction. I still would feel guilt when I thought of myself as the "Son of God". When I heard "You are the Son of God", my mind would scream, "NO YOU ARE NOT!" This is the opposite of what my human conditioning taught me throughout my life, and my human conditioning ran very deep!

I now understood thoughts and the ego, perception, acceptance, surrender, the Holy Spirit's relationship, and even my relationship with my Creator. I always had a firm hold on who Jesus was in my life, so there was that. I was feeling good in my skin and making great strides, but these words my father spoke really hit a chord in my greatest shift yet. Having spent nearly 40 years consumed with the belief that I was a body, I was finally seeing something more. This last moment released me from something that I was holding on to since I was eight, when fear began about the body.

I have a very vivid memory of my First Holy Communion which actually became a traumatic memory for me. At the celebration party after church, amidst tons of family members gathered at our home on Long Island to honor this huge day in my Catholic upbringing, I stumbled upon something very disturbing: Eternity.

Here I was, eight years old, cloistered away in the hall bathroom of my family home sitting on the cold toilet bowl lid crying. Someone must have told my mother I was crying, because she came rushing into the bathroom with me. She asked me why I was in the bathroom crying when the entire family is having a great time. From her tone, I could tell she was a little mad with me. Me being in the bathroom crying was creating a problem.

I told her that I was very scared. I explained to her that at mass, the priest spoke about eternity and he said that we will live forever with God in Heaven. I told her I thought that this was the most frightening thing I could ever imagine. I did not want to live forever, even if it was with God in Heaven, and I couldn't wrap my brain around such a long everlasting thing! My mother did not understand my dilemma at all. She tried to make me see the beauty of being with God forever. Then she decided to simply tell me to not think on it. She told me to give this problem to God, and he would give it back to me at a time when I could understand it. I appreciated this advice (because, let's face, it all I wanted to do was stop thinking about something that scared the s*&$ out of me!), and I went back to being a kid. Unfortunately, it was not as easy as just giving it over to God. This was not something I would easily forget.

So, yeah, starting at eight years old, I began thinking that a human being going up to heaven meant the body and all its trappings would arrive in the pearly gates. As the years continued, I became more and more attached to this flawed body. And this was going to be my eternity? Hell yeah I was scared. Who the heck would want that for eternity? I couldn't even fathom the spiritual being that I was; there was just no proof of it I guess.

As the concept of "eternity" reared its ugly head, time and again, I was faced with a gut retching fear deep in the pit of my stomach, each and every time. Thinking about eternity or even hearing someone else talk about it, felt overwhelming and would often bring me to tears. I tried to talk about it with my parents or with my husband, but they just couldn't see where the fear of living with God forever would come from. Everyone tried to dispel it with their ideas of blissful heavenly scenes. I couldn't conjure up the same feelings as them. They simply could not relate to my fears, and I had no clear way of articulating them either. I had this discussion with friends as well, and each person would tell me their take on eternity, and they would conclude what a wonderful place to be, forever with God.

To me, eternity meant having to face this crippling fear of something lasting forever- without end. It was not until I began this journey of undoing the little limited self, I believed myself to be and seeing myself as I truly am, that it all started to click into place for me. And through my father's words, I got the answer I had been searching for since I was that eight-year old girl who locked herself in the bathroom. I found the peace I had been missing since the day I received my First Holy Communion.

WE CAN ALL BE IN SYNC WITH SPIRIT

If you can't tell by now, I am just a regular person. Like you, I found out that all I needed was already inside of me.

The fabric of everything is within reach for all of us.

I am no different than you because I have come to see this. I have ins and outs just like the rest of humanity. I think that is part of the human process. We sort of forget at times what we know is best for our state of mind and happiness. We fall asleep a little. We are all "works in progress." Working through our humanness to see all that we can receive from life, not all that will limit us.

You can access all that you need at any time. You can help yourself to be peaceful. You can help yourself to connect with the essence of what you were created in. You can connect to loved ones who have left the earth. You can connect to that most peaceful part of yourself. Your most peaceful soul, your God mind. The part of you that you were conditioned to believe is outside of you or were taught to believe was difficult to access.

You think that you need someone else to talk to your passed love one, when in fact you can do that for yourself. You just believe that you can't. Somewhere along the path of life, we learned that when someone dies, they are not connected to us on earth any longer. You were conditioned to believe that this is not something a regular person can do. I am here to tell you we all can do this! Quiet the mind's chatter telling you all the things that you cannot do, and listen to what it is telling you—the things you are ABLE to do.

God created everything. He created all that is and all that we are. He told us that we never die, but the body does die away and leaves this earth. Jesus walked this earth to tell us this and make us believe. Yet we still do not get it?

We have believed a conditioning that told us we are without the ability to find peace, without the ability to feel all that is, and when someone dies, we are completely without them. We listened too much to the part of us that tells us we are lacking. When a person passes away, they are no longer in the physical where we can touch their hand, this is true. We want that so very badly when they have left, and coming to terms with that loss is a great challenge. This is where signs come in to soothe our mending hearts. It is hard to wrap our minds around the fact that they are with us when we do not have the physical evidence of it. The signs they are giving to us to help in healing. There is countless way that we are given signs for our healing. We have simply been conditioned that they are not ours, but they are. A bird, a sound, a memory, a penny, the list goes on and on.

I am of the belief that if God created everything in perfect and Divine order, surely He would create the ability for us to be comforted during the hardest things, like losing a loved one or our bodies experiencing pain or the countless other things we can encounter in our human existence. Signs are messages always available to us. They can come to us when we are down on our knees, when we are feeling happy with the things of this world or when we are feeling totally lost and confused, when we lose a job, a home, a friend, or when a loved one crosses over. It is recognizing them as such that make the difference. You are entitled to a sign or message of comfort just like everyone else!

They can show up for big life decisions or small, like where to go for dinner. God brings you Divine direction when he re-routes you due to a road closing, only to find out later that the 10 minute detour saved your life; or when your alarm doesn't go off and you are running late to work, only to find out that a 3-car pile up happened when you would normally be on that very road; or when you get lost on your way home and see a beautiful store for rent that would be just perfect for the business you've been dreaming of. I try to remind people as often as I can to pay attention to their signs because I see how uplifting it can be when they do. They feel so connected and acknowledged. What a lovely feeling.

There is great comfort in knowing that God, not ruling from afar but rather guiding right from within, is the great I AM that lives within YOU my friend.

MY YEAR IN SOLITUDE

The Oneness I felt connected to was clearing a path to healing and understanding like I never knew. Remember I mentioned I was questioning my true purpose and the biggest lesson I had yet to learn? This came from my year in solitude. I had time, I had the space and opportunity to listen. This time in quiet and solitude. We moved into a temporary home for one year—my kids were gone, we were not near any friends or family, I had been spinning, and aside from Fred I was alone. So, yeah, vertigo, moving to a new area, and having ZERO distractions had me "staying put" as I said earlier. This gave me a year of love and it blew the doors off of this Oneness I was learning about. During this year, I spoke to Spirit easily, and heard the voice of Jesus and the Holy Spirit often throughout my waking hours, in meditation mostly, and occasionally I was woken by a beautiful uplifting and inspirational thought to ponder.

Let me explain. Here I am questioning my purpose, away from all that I am familiar with and virtually alone. (Although I can hear my husband in my ear, gee thanks!) But truly this is my experience after our big move. Everyone in my family had their jobs whether it be schooling or actual work. I was in a rental house in a place that was new, without knowing a soul. What started off having all the elements of the webster dictionary definition of "isolation" turned into the greatest gift I could've imagined. I would say this year in solitude became my year of love, knowing, and Oneness.

It began one summer morning. I sat in the space I created for prayer and meditation. In the stillness of that morning, I heard my dad come to speak to me. As tears of joy filled my eyes at hearing him after so long, I breathed in all that I heard, and he was quite persistent in telling me to sit, just as I was doing this morning, each day in quiet prayer. "Try not to miss a day," he said. He told me that I needed this. So began the year in solitude. Every day for that year I sat, just as Dad instructed. This was the year that it all clicked and my shift totally aligned.

For years I worked at seeing myself and the world differently, as I chronicled here in this book. The journey toward my self-realization was long sought after. Mainly, I sought happiness and peace. All that time I was actually in hell. Not the hell made of fire and ash you see depicted in movies. Nope. Hell was not some hot and desolate place that I would end up if I failed God. It was the state of mind I lived in for so much of my life and had spent countless years suffering in.

Hell was a place where I believed my thoughts and learned beliefs, and where I believed God was outside of me. It was where I did not fully realize the love that was waiting for me to claim. But during this year in solitude, I was alone while this tremendous love, that never left me, was waiting for me to remember that it was there! It was buried in the deep recesses of my mind. I needed to remember who I was in order to leave the hell of my own making.

I slowly removed this programming and this guilt and uncovered love. The love that I found enhanced all that I ever knew and made me see things I never thought of before. Then I found out that I would never be able to see anything the old way again.

I learned not to judge myself. I learned not to judge others. We are all simply doing the best we can with the tools we have (a great friend of mine coined this wonderful statement). So, as I chipped away at the human construct, I built around myself and, in my mind, I realized anything is possible if it is God's will.

Yep, I did as my dad told me and in doing so, I heard so many beautiful words of love, guidance, and inspiration from what I could only describe as God's Divine team. I would hear Jesus, and then the Holy Spirit, and often times I had no idea who to say that I heard. What I did know was that they knew of my love and devotion to God. They wanted me to know of the Oneness that I believed I already knew. Some of those words are at the end of each chapter of this book and more are in the epilogue.

This year in "solitude" answered so many questions I still pondered and even those which I thought I had the answers for. It provided guidance to removing the barriers I still had in place between myself and God. This year I sat in love. I sat with the kindest words of confirmation of what I was created in and for. I was not separate, ever. I was part of all that God created and I was given this gift for me, as well as for others, to see the beauty of Oneness. This year shed a bright light on who I AM as Jen, as a spiritual being and how I am to serve.

I no longer mind walking in a grocery store and not knowing a name because in fact I know everyone. They are all part of me, and I am part of them. I am never alone. So much energy spent all those years searching! This is the uphill battle for happiness that many of us experience as we search for happiness and peace outside of ourselves. It all stems from not knowing who we truly are and were created to be. In the search for it we look to people, places, and things to fill this <u>missing peace</u>. The chaos feels real and the anxiety can be high when in this search. When you can begin to see that all you need is within you, happiness is yours for the taking. Those outside things just become icing on the already phenomenal cake.

In my life I've come to realize this: while we continually search for happiness in the things of this world—that shiny new car or the job of PTA president, that new puppy that you think may fill the hole in your heart, or that bottle of wine to numb the day—peace, joy, and happiness can be found right inside of ourselves!

My journey from humanness through brokenness and ultimately to Oneness is absolutely, positively not unique to me or some prize I won for being me—it is a gift given freely to us all. And if that seems hard, just hand over the wheel to the Holy Spirit—it's a hell of a lot easier!

"Have faith in Me and not the little self that convinced you that you are weak and have human flaws. You are light and have Love's strengths. This is where you need the surrender, in knowing who and what you are. If you feel doubt, then surrender to Me and trust in Me alone."
- From Meditations with Jesus and Jen

EPILOGUE

Remembering Your Oneness

This book was my story, the story of "Jen." Who was I before I became Jen? I was expansion. I was part of everything. I was with the cosmos. Imagine stretching your arms out as wide as you can, and the width of it is forever. That's what I was part of. It is what we are all a part of.

I chose to compress myself, to limit myself into this body, where I gradually forgot who I truly was, part of everything. Throughout my life I craved a peace, I craved love. And it was in this space of wanting that deep down I was simply trying to recall what it was like before I shrank into human form—to have that pulse of energy, of Oneness and of love coursing through my being.

I wasn't separate as my human conditioning led me to be.

It's all part of God. We are all part of God. But in order to experience this journey as a human being, you gotta shove yourself in to that body, make yourself small.

Really, do we have to play small? Do we have to be small? Oh man, I can think of a million examples of where I played small.

If we can only just remember that we come from everything! Instead we come into this human form and believe we're nothing as fantastic as all that. We have beliefs about ourselves and many of them are disempowering thoughts, some even self-loathing thoughts. No matter who you are or what spiritual journey you are taking yourself on, you have a mind as well. And that same mind slips into its humanity and believes itself to be small, in one area or another.

Does everyone think about their disempowering thoughts or do they sometimes just flow in and out of our awareness, throughout the day, grabbing our attention every once in a while? Meanwhile these very thoughts are wreaking havoc to our view of ourselves and just about everything. Do we believe it's:

the other person;

our job;

that we didn't have an education;

that we didn't have enough education;

that we are limited because of where we lived;

that we are limited because of money;

we are limited because we have a disability;

we were limited because we are heavy;

we were limited because we are skinny;

we were limited because we have a certain hair color;

we were limited because we didn't know any better;

we were limited because we didn't have certain opportunities . . .

The list goes on.

. . . there are honestly a countless number of limiting beliefs that could be running our lives at this very moment. They can pose one excuse after another to why we can never be fully at peace.

What I'm suggesting is that we believe we are limited. As I sit in quiet, with eyes closed, I can feel what it was like before I had limiting thoughts of myself. Before I was me. It was like I was everything! And that is everything. The thing is we don't just recall that with the snap of a finger. But we can when you are intentional about it.

If you close your eyes and you go to that place of Oneness and quiet where you can get what you need to see . . . you will feel what it feels like. You can see what you need to see. You have a holiness inside of you. You are Holy, and anything that is holy cannot be flawed, you just believe that you are. You believe your thoughts. You believe you're limited. But in fact, God is IN YOU! You are not limited. You are not the things you think you are. You are part of God. God created you in His magnificence. In His glory, and in His endless peaceful love. That's what you are!

That is just a tiny sample of what I began to experience in my year of solitude, of quiet, and of love.

And, at the core of all is forgiveness. Through forgiveness, you are led to remember who you truly are, quietly yet powerfully, and begin to erase the "perceived" importance these things once held.

Forgiveness is an inward job.

Of course we can use forgiveness with others for things we believe they have done to us. Or believe that they have "trespassed" against us. But the healing that comes with forgiveness is forgiving the human things that we did that might have hurt us. Forgiving the thoughts. Forgiving actions. But even deeper still, even possibly considered "heavy" in thought or concept, is forgiving the human journey.

Forgiving the separation from God, when we chose to experience this human journey or condition, with all of our human trials and tribulations. If we had this human life and had absolutely nothing wrong while in it; no trauma, no drama, no altercations, no pain, no sadness, no loneliness, no fear; no ego thoughts of any kind but instead only joy, happiness and bliss, then of course there's nothing to forgive.

As we are here journeying this world, we actually forgot that we are part of God. On some level we forget that He created us with all of His beautiful attributes and blessings. He created all of our goodness and in likeness, like Him, we are created in love. We forgot this.

Because we chose this human experience, we hold a certain level of guilt from the separation from God, home, heaven to this world of trials and experiences. There is the need for forgiveness because we chose to be without him. Or so we think, deep down in our soul, we chose to experience this human condition, and we feel alone because of it.

But God never left US. God is not a punishing God. He is with us while we journey this earth in our human experience, knowing, with love, comfort, and assurance that we will return to Him. God never left us, we just forgot this fact as we get bogged down with all of the things that have the ability to "trap" us in our thoughts. A big part of healing was accepting that this is the journey I am here experiencing as Jen, but I am NOT separate from God!

One of the many things that helped me to heal my body and my mind and forge an even closer relationship to God, our Father, and embrace His unending love, was forgiveness and understanding who we truly are; remembering that we are divinely created in love.

THINGS TO REMEMBER

Here are some important things to remember:

- A change in perception can change everything.
- God is part of you and You are part of Him.
- Taking a look at thoughts gives you the opportunity to see who is driving the car.
- Recognizing the spirit of who you are can give you a true understanding of the magnificent being you were created to be.
- You are not just a body; you are spirit too.
- You are a spiritual being having a human experience.
- Human conditioning affects your thoughts (self, others, the world, situations).
- Thoughts affect the world you see.
- You see the world from the lens of your thoughts and perceptions.
- If you are quiet, and still your thoughts, you will allow guidance to come from the Holy Spirit (not the ego).
- Ego is Edging God Out.
- No matter how wonderful people say that you are, it doesn't hold any true meaning if you don't believe it yourself.
- Recognizing the spirit of who you are can give you a true understanding of the magnificent being you were created to be.
- You can change subconscious limiting beliefs to empowering beliefs.
- You have all the power to live the life you desire.

STATEMENTS TO AFFIRM

Here are a few of my big "a-ha" moments that can serve as affirmations for you, too, since we are in fact the same after all. I am You and You are Me, and we are part of the Oneness of God. Here goes:

- I am not this limited person stuck in this flawed body riddled with problems. I recognize that I am so much more than just this body and in fact, I am everything positive in life because of who I was created to be.

- I have a choice in everything! What I see, how I feel, whether I am happy or joyful, how everything affects me. The ball is always in my court.

- All my happiness comes from within and I will experience life from that perspective.

- I see the world from the lens of how I see myself, and my thoughts.

- The mind has one teacher: God or ego. How I see it is, you can't have light and darkness at the same time, so it's the same with the mind. You are using one thought system at a time. One that empowers you or one that weakens you.

- God has been inside of me the whole time, not outside. Knowing that, I know I am never alone.

- I had the choice all along who I let guide my thoughts. I never knew of the ego or the Holy Spirit's role in it all. Once I understood it, there was no going back to the old tortured life I once led.

YOUR DAILY PRACTICE

Here are some things that may help you create a daily practice of your own, as this was instructed for me to do directly from the year in solitude:

1) Begin each day in meditation and prayer. Set a timer early, before your normal rising, and sit in prayer, whether by music or silence, and connect to me, to All that is, before you lend your mind to the influences of this world which have begun to take precedence over my [being].

2) Set an intention for the day, even if it is the same every day until your demise in this form, or whether it has special act of your humanness, set it with love and positivity. For example:

   "Today I will filter all I say and do through love and thoughtfulness."

   "Today I will live in God."

   "Today I will surrender my mind to the Holy Spirit's guidance."

3) Find yourself through your day at any point of wander, and repeat your intention. As a reminder that you are not of the right mind. Choose again to see peace.

This practice will allow Me, Us, to bring to you the things that you desire and we can use for others. You see we want the same things; peace, joy, happiness, and a return of all of God's creations to the understanding of who they really are, so that as they journey this lifetime away from "home," they can do so with happiness and helping others to do the same.

WISDOM FROM MY YEAR IN SOLITUDE: MEDITATIONS WITH JESUS AND JEN

On the following pages, I've included some of the life affirming wisdoms I heard. I would sit in meditation, and these words would speak straight to my heart. I've learned that the messages we all receive can sometimes be for us, or sometimes they are for another. Often there was back and forth banter where I could ask questions and receive an answer, other times I was there to listen solely. The things I was in need of this year in solitude were given to me and for all. I have written them down and share as I believe God directs me to do.

And it's funny, because they often hit me during meditation but they ultimately come when they want to arrive. There are times when I am woken in the middle of the night, waking me straight out of bed. I've learned to keep a notepad bedside. Sometimes they just pop up throughout the day. I can be in the midst of a conversation with someone, ordering a coffee at the drive-thru, or going on a walk with my dog, and BOOM, Jesus speaks!

It is so wild, and yet so right!

Often the words are just what I needed, and sometimes I speak them aloud to another, even midway through said coffee order, and as it turns out, it is just what the barista needed to hear too! I'm not gonna lie, I've seen tears flow not just from myself but from complete strangers when I share these random words from Spirit. Man, I love God so much! You can't make this S!@#$ up, it is THAT good.

No one can take away your true inheritance.

———+———

Forgive your misperceptions of who you thought you were and step into the light of who you ARE.

———+———

Wipe the slate clean of who you thought you were before. It serves you no longer. Just because it is all you knew, never made it right or correct. Fear has no place in truth. Fear arises when you have a belief system that makes no sense; because it is NOT THE TRUTH.

———+———

Surrender completely and all thoughts evaporate. Nothing has any hold on your happiness. It is yours.

———+———

Complete surrender is done with faith—not fear. Fear of losing control in an uncontrolled chaotic environment means nothing is ever right! I have told you that these projections of this chaotic world are the dream, not the serenity surrender will provide. The peaceful surrender is the only truth you will witness. I AM not a dream. I AM everything

———+———

Surrender all decisions and guidance to me. The one who knows best for your highest good on earth as my instrument of expression. Faith is not questioning that which you know is done for the highest good of all.

———+———

I am leading you to a place of necessary complete surrender.

———+———

You are the essence of being. From which you are given light from your creator

———+———

You do not seem to doubt the world you see. You do not really question what is shown you through the body's eyes. Nor do you ask why you believe it, even though you learned a long while ago that your senses do deceive.

———+———

You can't stop what you already are. Once you understand what love is, then you can use forgiveness. It becomes easy to forgive when you realize nothing, no one, or no event can take away the light of the love that you are.

———+———

Trust in Him to empty yourself into Him. All the thoughts that have been your life long companions, lay them aside, walk over them, and step into your new world. Once you begin to see yourself within this new awareness, you will be reborn. Into the new skin—shining in the light of who you were always meant to be. The burden you have been carrying is the imagined self who was covering up all that you ARE.

———+———

When you uncover the truth, you have broken the chains that bind you to an unhappy life. You can live again: You are free. Free from limiting thoughts and beliefs.

———+———

Who I AM is love! I just had a belief that I was something else. I equated who I was to this human body; a thing that showed me nothing but problems and trouble.

———+———

The God that created you is a God of inclusion not exclusion. No one is excluded from His love.

———+———

No one person has the monopoly on God's love. He is an equal opportunity source of creation and source of love. We can all share in the greatness that we were created to be. If you see that someone who understands God and His love, so much so it looks like they are just in it, DO NOT for once single second think that there is not enough for you too. We are not talking about lack here! God's love is infinite and abundance at its finest! The great thing to know about God's love is that it never excludes or judges; no matter where you are from, who you are and even what you believe you have done, God's love is always there—flowing without end. There is enough of God and His Love to go around! Likewise, the universe has infinite abundance; if one person is successful and has great abundance, there is enough in the universe for you to be just as successful.

———+———

Thoughts, thoughts, there is the root of all the problems you will ever face.

———+———

Pull the plug on the dark light that covers your eyes. Covers your life. Covers your awareness. Covers up Me.
I am only present in the light.
I have told you before, if a thought or feeling brings up anger or fear and makes you feel unwell in the mind, then it is not from Me.

I am not there in that thought or the results of it. I don't believe them to be true, so they are not Me.

Go to the place of solace. Seek for indifference, the neutral. I am there. There you will find peace. And it replaces the chatter of misdirection.

————————

Live this life non-resistant so that you can be the tool of love, the instrument that can be used for others healing. To show light into the world for others who do not know the difference.

————————

As each person uncovers their true Self, that part of them that dwells only with God, their believed Father, Creator of All that is, then they will know the truth. Then they will know Peace.

————————

For I will use your fear, and guilt, and lead you to forgiveness if you allow me. It's here where I can show that you are not alone. Where we were all creations of the one greatness. You are not singularly special. You are all special because of your creation. Your Father, our Father, is All that is, and it would stand to reason from this, you are special.

————————

Lay aside all thoughts of plans. It's in the planning I am not. Do what Inspires you to have great joy. Do not compare to what others are doing.

————————

The master of deception needs many tricks to have your mind. The truth needs only one—love. Breaking down the barriers you have constructed; you against the truth of your full potential. You feel inferior that is why thoughts revisit you. I have imbued you with all that I am, you need not search any further than within.

————+————

All peace is yours.

ACKNOWLEDGMENTS

To Fred, my champion and biggest supporter. We have laughed and we have cried and we have surrendered and we did it all—together—with God. Thank you for the family we created and the three gifts we have in our children. Thank you for always seeing all the parts of me: the love, the light, and the mess—and loving me still.

To my dad in heaven. Thank you for supporting me always, even though you're no longer here in form. I know what love is because of what you and mom taught me through your unending love and support.

To my mom. Thank you seems so small. You have always been there for me and my family. Without your dedication as a grandmother, we wouldn't have the children we have. You have been both mother and father to me since losing dad, and you did a fabulous job. I am so proud of the strength you have displayed. You've taught me that I, too, can do anything I set my mind to.

To my children: Alexandra, Corinna, and Nicholas. You are more than we could have asked for. Go out into this world. Sparkle your own unique light. Do life inspired.

To Alexandra Shimalla. Thank you for editing everything written in my life. Thank you for your unending support in all things Mom.

To my siblings. Thanks for the hysterical memories. We had a great childhood, and I look forward to creating more memories.

To Jenn Tuma-Young. Thank you for molding this book to be something I am immensely proud of and for helping me express my heart. You are a love.

To all the friends who have come into my life. From grade school to the present, there have been too many to chronicle here, but you know who you are. I treasure each one of you for what we shared and for the laughs. No matter time, or distance, each and every one of you have made an imprint on my heart that will never be erased.

To all my entire family, near and far: Thank you for making a valuable impact in the story of my life. You all have a role in the love that I have in my life.

To my sister: Life forged us as sisters but we formed our bond as friends! Thank you for always listening and helping to organize me. I can always count on you to tell it to me straight.

To Cheryl Buchan. You have been my best friend for so long I don't know a Jen without a Cheryl in her life, and I couldn't be happier about that. Thank you for the memories and for the time when you were actually my memory- the details escape me and you helped a ton.

ABOUT THE AUTHOR

Jen Fiore Shimalla, co-founder of Do Life Inspired, is a spiritual mindset teacher and coach, energy worker, author, and artist. Jen specializes in helping people who are suffering from pain, anxiety, or fear by teaching them how to overcome their limiting beliefs, observe their thoughts, discover the magnificence that they were created to be, and to live the joy-filled life they deserve.

Jen is also the author of a children's book, Heaven Cent. She has extensive training in health and wellness, the mind-body connection, and healing. Her research and teachings focus on shifting perception; energy healing; removing blocks in the subconscious mind; intuitive modalities and practices; and how our minds can affect our health, relationships and life in general.

Jen worked in the service industry for three decades and has been a business owner for over 20 years. A passionate, serial entrepreneur, Jen knows business and brings the perfect blend of divinely connected inspiration and down-to-earth sass to everything she touches. Along the way, she founded a jewelry company, opened a restaurant, and now has a website Do Life Inspired that offers a line of inspirational t-shirts, hats, stickers, and other items. In addition to running her online store, Jen has a coaching practice. At the heart of all of her work is connection with people, helping them realize who they were created to be.

Jen is certified in health coaching by the Dr. Sears Wellness

Institute and holds a bachelor's degree in marketing from Hofstra University. Jen is also a Psych-K® facilitator and Reiki Master and holds certificates in herbal studies, Biochemic tissue salts Level 3, and mediumship.

Jen loves to crack herself up (and hopefully others) whenever she can. She expresses herself 100% as she whips up her family's gluten-free recipes on her YouTube channel, Glutenfree and Me. She enjoys painting, hiking, meeting new people, and reading. In the evenings, you can find Jen catching up on her Netflix binge-watching with her husband. Jen loves to remind others that spirituality can be fun and life can be full of amazing surprises if you will allow them to unfold for you.

www.dolifeinspired.com

www.jenfiore.com